THE
CHARTERED INSTITUTE OF
PURCHASING AND SUPPLY

Graduate Diploma

Professional Stage Study Guide

Commercial Relationships

Written by Peter Stannack

MIDDLESEX
UNIVERSITY
PRESS

First edition 2002
Second edition 2003

Published by:

The Chartered Institute of Purchasing and Supply
Easton House, Easton on the Hill
Stamford, Lincs, PE9 3NZ, UK

Tel: +44 (0) 1780 756 777
Fax: +44 (0) 1780 751 610
Email: info@cips.org
Web: www.cips.org

Edited, designed and typeset by
Middlesex University Press
www.mdx.ac.uk/mupress

on behalf of

The Chartered Institute of Purchasing and Supply

ISBN 1-86124-115-1

Disclaimer

While every effort has been made to ensure that references to websites are correct at time of going to press, the World Wide Web is a constantly changing environment, and CIPS cannot accept any responsibility for any changes to addresses.

Printed by: Copytech (UK) Ltd, Graphic House, First Drove, Fengate, Peterborough PE1 5BJ.   www.copytechdigital.com

Commercial Relationships

Contents	Subject	Page

Preface

From its former position as a cost centre within the organisation, purchasing and supply management (P&SM) is now recognised as a value-adding profession, able to make a significant contribution to the bottom line.

To maximise this contribution is one of the key roles of the professionally qualified buyer and so the importance of professional qualifications applies to all working within P&SM – from junior buyer right up to director level. In today's fast-moving commercial and technological environment, purchasing professionals need to keep up to speed with the latest developments, and they must be able to make correct and informed decisions.

There are many areas where developments are taking place with particular rapidity – eCommerce is one. Procurement specialists possessing professional qualifications will be well placed to grasp the opportunities and recognise the threats arising from such issues. Notwithstanding recent developments, traditional aspects of purchasing are still vital; what professional buyer can survive in today's competitive environment without knowledge of, for example, negotiation techniques and contract law and procedure?

As well as covering these established areas, these new editions of the CIPS Study Guides provide in-depth analysis of the latest thinking in all aspects of P&SM and related areas, and as such are a vital resource for those aiming for professional qualifications in procurement.

Using the Study Guide

These guides have been carefully designed to equip the purchasing and supply professional with the knowledge and resources required to undertake the examinations of the CIPS Graduate Diploma. As it is the only guide written or approved by the CIPS Chief Examiner for the subject, you can be assured that it offers the best possible preparation for the examinations.

- Tutors. If you are teaching this subject, you can be assured that, with the active involvement of the Chief Examiner for each subject, these are the authoritative guides on which to base schemes of work.
- Part-time students. The layout of the guide is such that busy professional people, studying in their spare time, can dip in and out of the material with ease.
- Distance and flexible learning students. This guide will complement any materials supplied to you by your provider.
- Home study. If you have chosen to study on your own at home, you will find this guide invaluable: its features have been carefully chosen to help you gain knowledge, relate it to your workplace and test your progress.

An Action Planner is provided, designed to be kept on your desk or displayed on your wall to help keep track of your progress. Inevitably, demands of work often mean that you need to break off before completing a section, checking the self-assessment questions, or following up all the references. This action planner allows you to keep track of what you *have* done, and note any elements which remain *outstanding*.

Section features

- **Overall design**. The material within the guide mirrors the examination syllabus, which is reproduced on page xiii and xiv. Each section of the guide corresponds to a section of the syllabus; the different elements of the syllabus are covered in separate subsections of the guide.

- **Learning objectives**. At the beginning of each complete section there is a set of clear learning objectives which reflect the content of that particular section.

- **Activities**. Each section includes a range of activities, designed to consolidate learning and reinforce knowledge gained by applying it to your organisation. You are strongly recommended to carry out the activities provided, as these provide invaluable opportunities to relate the theory to the practice.

- **'Stop and think'**. Throughout the material, you will be asked to pause and consider a point which has been made, to reflect on how it applies to you and your organisation – or just to gather your thoughts prior to moving on to the next topic. These elements require nothing more than a pencil and paper on which to jot ideas, and you are strongly advised to take time out for them.

- **Section summaries.** There is a short paragraph at the end of each section which reviews what has been learned in that section.

- **Self-assessment questions (SAQs)**. Each subsection contains SAQs which are designed to test you on knowledge gained. The responses to these can be found at the end of each section.

- **Examination questions.** Each Chief Examiner has prepared examination question or questions on the topic for a particular section, and these are included at the end of most sections. Indicative answers are provided in a separate section at the end of the guide.

- **Reading**. The study guides are written to be self-contained; however, reference is made to recommended or supplementary textbooks or journals at appropriate points where the author feels that more in-depth coverage of a topic might be of value, or of interest, to some students.

Note that the Professional Stage of the Graduate Diploma is at the same standard as a degree-level programme. It is therefore strongly recommended that you read as widely as possible. This will help consolidate information, provide other perspectives on topics (from which arguments can be constructed) and ensure that you are up to date with current practice, initiatives and, where appropriate, legislation.

- **Internet.** The use of the Internet is recommended. A variety of website addresses are given in the text, which have several purposes – they are usually kept completely up to date; they allow the user to see information in the context of specific companies or organisations; they are excellent and readily accessible sources of reference material. You are strongly advised to visit the sites mentioned, and to explore the Internet for similar sites.

How to study

Being organised and well planned is the key to success in your studies.

You have chosen to undertake a degree-level qualification and you must be prepared to set aside time each week to study and read. CIPS recommend a minimum of 90 hours' student-centred learning per unit. For a typical student studying over an academic year, this amounts to three hours or so per subject per week, in addition to the recommended 45 hours of direct tuition per unit.

If you are receiving tuition, do follow the course and complete any assignments. This way you can monitor your own progress, and get advice from the tutor on areas you find more difficult. If you are studying on your own, complete the activities – many of them build in some form of consultation with your own senior managers or other colleagues, ensuring that you get meaningful and relevant feedback.

To produce a satisfactory answer in the examination you must have good knowledge and be able to demonstrate your understanding of the subject. This can only be gained from reading – books, journal articles, quality newspapers, conference papers and the Internet are all good sources of information.

Use the Action Planner provided with this guide and monitor your own progress towards completing the syllabus. Plan your revision and devise a timetable to ensure you cover all the required topics in your revision programme.

The material is presented in readable 'chunks' of information, and substantial use is made of bullet points to focus the attention on the core issues. Research has shown that this form of presentation of material has a higher recall rate than material presented simply as paragraphs of text.

There is a wide margin on each page – use this to make notes as you work through the text. Use a series of highlighter pens, and mark the text as required – use, for example, red for key points; green for points which you may wish to follow up; yellow for points which you feel may apply differently to your sector or organisation. Make marginal notes of details of relevant Internet sites, or articles.

Clearly, no single text can be manageable *and* fully authoritative with regard to all areas of the United Kingdom, let alone all areas of the world. Different sectors – such as public, manufacturing, retail, financial – are all likely to have subtly different requirements regarding the theory and practice of purchasing and supply, as are different social and racial characteristics. Negotiating styles, or the management of people, for example, will need to be considered differently depending on your location and the people with whom you are working. You should use this guide, therefore, as a springboard. Consider all issues raised in the context of *your* surroundings; as indicated earlier, many of the activities are worded to require you to check your response with work colleagues. By constantly considering your own work practices, and relating your study to the work carried out in your organisation, you should achieve a sound appreciation of the issues. Your studies are not intended to be dry and theoretical – by relating your study to your daily work, and/or to that of organisations known to you, you will be better able to make sense of the issues, and this, in turn, will ensure that your knowledge is more firmly embedded.

The examination

Practise on past examination questions – available free to registered student members from the CIPS website – under timed examination conditions. As the examination approaches, knowing you are well prepared should help steady your nerves. However, the CIPS bookshop staff will be happy to supply you with the titles of some very good guides to assist you further. CIPS examiners report a number of common mistakes when marking students' answers. You may find the following pages will help to avoid making the same errors.

Examination format

All the Professional Stage Graduate Diploma examinations follow the same format:
- **Section A** (Question 1) This is a case study and is compulsory, and will require you to undertake a number of tasks. It carries a maximum of 50 marks.
- **Section B** (Questions 2-6) You are required to choose two questions from five. Each question carries 25 marks, and may be subdivided. Where a question is subdivided, each part will carry equal marks unless otherwise stated.

Answer the question asked – not the question you would have liked! This seems very obvious, and yet many candidates simply do not answer the questions posed. It is understandable, in the heat of the exam, that you may drift – so keep looking back at the question to see if you are still on track and have answered fully what is required.

Avoid overkill
Avoid the tendency to list every technique, philosophy, or approach in the subject or area as a solution to a problem posed. This is particularly relevant in section A (the case study) where the candidate is usually invited to suggest approaches to improve the condition of an organisation depicted in the case. Keep answers appropriate. Frequently, candidates offer solutions which are out of all proportion to the problem posed. For example, if the question is to do with a small, low-tech company, then a solution involving extremely high-technology computing with large new departments is unlikely to be an appropriate solution.

Sector
Unless a question specifies otherwise, your answers should refer to examples in all relevant sectors: private or public, manufacturing or service. Obviously, if the question is a case study involving a specific type of organisation, then it is appropriate to refer only to that specific type of organisation.

Style
The question will make clear if the examination answers should be written as a business report or as an essay. Be careful to write in the appropriate style. Essays should contain a clear introduction, a logically ordered, well-structured series of paragraphs which argue a case, and a concluding paragraph. See the following pages for more detailed information on the suggested format for essays, memos, letters and reports.

Structure
It is important that a sensible order of events is indicated in an examination response; this is particularly true in section A, the case study. It is worthwhile writing down as many ideas as you can think of, in brief phrases, sorting out the order of the ideas, writing up your exam response and then crossing out your phrases, before passing on.

Time management
Whether you decide to tackle section A or section B first, do allocate your time proportionately to the marks for each section and question. Thus, you should devote about half of the three-hour exam to section A and about 45 minutes to each of the questions in section B.

Legibility
If your writing is difficult to read, there are a number of things you can do to improve it – double-spacing your answers may help; the fact that the exam script can be read is very important. If your answers are unreadable, then no marks can be given. In addition, try to make the page user-friendly, using paragraphs, subheadings and correct punctuation.

Essays, letters, memos and reports

Many examination questions require you to write either an essay, or to approximate to a 'real' business situation by requiring you to write a letter, memo or report. The following pages indicate recommended approaches for presenting your material in each scenario.

The essay

If you are asked to write an essay, you should spend a few minutes planning your answer; this will give your answer a logical structure and help you to avoid repetition. Then structure your essay in the following way:

Essay structure
Every essay should have:

- ◆ **An introduction**

- ◆ **A main body**

- ◆ **A conclusion.**

◆ **The introduction**
   This should be brief and to the point. It should:
   - state very clearly how you intend to answer the question and indicate what points or arguments you will be making
   - show that you understand any technical terms that are in the question by defining them.
   Do not go into detail at this stage. Keep background information to a minimum.
   The key purpose of the introduction is to give the essay *focus*.

◆ **The main body**
   The main body is where you produce arguments together with supporting evidence for those arguments. It will comprise a number of paragraphs – each of which should argue or explain a particular aspect of the essay question that you have briefly mentioned in the introduction. Every one of the main ideas that you mentioned in the introduction should become a paragraph. For example, you may use three paragraphs to discuss the advantages of certain procedures and another three paragraphs to discuss the disadvantages. The paragraphs should be linked; good linking words include: *however, nevertheless, on the other hand, thus, similarly, at the same time.*

◆ **The conclusion**
   Every essay should have a brief conclusion, which should have three or four convincing sentences. It should:
   - refer back to the question
   - briefly summarise the main points from the main body but without restating them
   - clearly state your position with regards to the question.

The business letter

The following is a suggested letter layout. Invent any detail as necessary.

```
                                              Your full address
                                                 Telephone No.
                                                        E-mail

The address of the person/firm to whom you are writing        Date


Dear Sir/Mrs Brown*



Yours faithfully/sincerely*

Signature

Your name
Position
```

* Use *faithfully* if you have written to Sir or Madam; use *sincerely* if you have used the person's name

The memorandum

The main content of a memo should be presented in three parts:

◆   State the background of the problem simply and clearly

◆   Describe what you are doing or have done to solve the problem

◆   State the purpose of writing the memo and forecast what is to come – for example, 'This memo presents a description of the current situation, some proposed alternatives, and my recommendations.' Always begin with the most important findings or recommendations. Think of an inverted pyramid. Start with your general information and move to your specific facts.

If you are asked to give your answer in the form of a memo, this layout would be recommended:

```
                M E M O R A N D U M

To       Insert the name and job title of the person to whom the memo is being sent.

From     Insert the name and job title of the person sending the memo.

Date     Insert the date.

Subject  Insert the subject of the memo.
```

The report

A report should be:

◆ **Short**

◆ **Clear**

◆ **Relevant.**

If you are asked to write a report, you are advised to use the following layout.

◆ **Brief title**
Give the report a meaningful title. You should also briefly express the purpose of the report and say why it is being written.

◆ **A brief summary of the report**
This should state the aims of the report, what has been done, what has been found and what action is called for. Only mention important points.

◆ **Introduction**
The introduction should be brief. The aim should be to set the scene of the report, capturing the attention of the reader. Include the aims and objectives, the problem that caused the report to be written and also what it intends to achieve. You should also define any terms you think necessary.

◆ **Main body**
This is where you present all the facts and evidence. Use specific section headings, which should be numbered.

◆ **Recommendations**
This is where you describe a clear course of action. It should be short and simply state facts. There should be no doubt about the recommendations being made, for example that the number of staff in a particular department be reduced.

◆ **Conclusions**
The conclusions should draw out from the main body the implications of the report.

◆ **Date/Signature/Name/Position.**

Syllabus

Commercial Relationships

Aim
To examine ways in which supplier and customer relationships are created and managed in connection with both inter- and intra-organisational activities. To understand supply chains for both goods and services as value streams.

Rationale
Purchasing and supply is concerned with making available goods and services from external providers to meet the needs of internal and external customers. In undertaking the activities necessary to achieve this availability, interactions take place between functional staff, suppliers and customers. These interactions take many forms, from the straightforward exchange transaction of simple buying or selling, to long-term strategic alliances between organisations with complementary resources and goals. Developing concepts such as supply chain management and value stream analysis recognise the fact that many interactions do not exist in isolation, but form part of a longer series of relationship beginning at the origin of primary ideas or materials, and ending with the satisfaction of the needs or wishes of the ultimate consumer. This syllabus contributes to the overall scheme by providing insights into the developing recognition of the importance of commercial relationships, and the need to develop and adopt appropriate strategies and policies. The planning, direction, assessment and control of relationships are also considered.

1. Relationships in context *weighting 25%*
a) Strategic considerations in relationship formation
b) Supply chains, value streams and related concepts and their impact upon commercial relationships
c) The main types of relationship
d) Intra-organisational relationships
e) Relationship issues in public procurement

In the assessment the candidate may be required to:
1.1 Evaluate the need for appropriate strategies for relationships in different contexts
1.2 Evaluate the relationship implications of emergent supply system philosophies
1.3 Assess the circumstances in which short-term relationships might be appropriate, and analyse such relationships
1.4 Assess the circumstances in which partnership relationships might be appropriate, and analyse such relationships
1.5 Identify and explain the circumstances in which co-destiny relationships might be appropriate and analyse such relationships
1.6 Explain 'open book' philosophies
1.7 Analyse joint ventures, partnerships and other permanent alliances and discuss the 'relationships' aspects of such arrangements
1.8 Appraise the cross- and multi-functional aspects of corporate management, and the relationships implications of these ideas
1.9 Analyse relationships in the context of public procurement

2. Relationship strategy, policy and practice *weighting 30%*
a) Tools of analysis in relationship selection and determination
b) Risk assessment and evaluation in relationship decisions
c) The contribution of appropriate relationships to organisational success
d) Factors impacting upon relationships
e) Relationships and supply chain policy

In the assessment the candidate may be required to:
2.1 Propose and justify the use of appropriate tools of analysis in relationship determination
2.2 Assess potential risk and uncertainty in commercial relationships
2.3 Comment critically on the need for transparency in relationships
2.4 Evaluate potential wastes in the supply chain and suggest approaches to their elimination
2.5 Evaluate the supplier characteristics appropriate for the main types of relationship
2.6 Appraise appropriate sourcing policies from a relationship perspective
2.7 Assess the impact of lean supply, agile supply and power issues upon commercial relationships
2.8 Evaluate ethical, technological, legal, environmental and other relationship constraints and enablers.

3. Relationship management
weighting 25%

a) Structural issues
b) The role of the internal customer
c) The role of the supplier
d) Supplier development
e) The relationship life cycle
f) Relationship assessment
g) Management of supplier risk

In the assessment the candidate may be required to:

3.1 Appraise the role of supplier associations, buying consortia, joint buying arrangements and other groupings in commerical relationships
3.2 Appraise supply base tiering, and relationship implications of this practice
3.3 Evaluate the role of the internal customer, including the concept of the intelligent customer
3.4 Evaluate the potential and practicalities of supplier development from a relationship perspective. Recommend appropriate actions in relation to supplier development and upstream management. Explain the relationship life cycle
3.5 Recommend appropriate approaches to the termination or suspension of relationships
3.6 Evaluate the implications of relationship failure
3.7 Comment critically on developing theory and practice in relation to relationship assessment and management

4. Contracting and relationships
weighting 20%

a) The role of contracts
b) Relationship aspects of contracts
c) Relationships in the service context
d) Relationships in connection with hire or lease contracts

In the assessment the candidate may be required to:

4.1 Evaluate the role and value of contracts in relationships
4.2 Propose alternatives to contracts where appropriate
4.3 Determine appropriate approaches to the management of contracts, including payment methods. Explain and demonstrate the use of clauses employed for incentivisation purposes
4.4 Propose appropriate clauses employed for the purpose of accommodating changing costs
4.5 Evaluate the use of leasing or hiring arrangements as an alternative to buying
4.6 Assess the relationship issues particularly relevant where relationships are concerned with service provision

Author profile

Peter Stannack is an internationally respected consultant, educator and academic in the fields of supply chain strategy, organisational development and service quality. He has worked internationally with a wide range of large organisations, in both the public and private sectors, to help them manage their supply chains effectively, reducing costs and improving network performance. Peter is the author of many articles and academic papers on strategic supply chain management, as well as the author of the CIPS *Commercial Relationships* study guide, and joint author of the CIPS *Project and Contract Management* study guide. He is also the Chief Examiner for *Commercial Relationships*.

Reading

Note that the Professional Stage of the Graduate Diploma is at the same standard as a degree-level programme. It is therefore strongly recommended that you read as widely as possible. This will help consolidate information, provide other perspectives on topics (from which arguments can be constructed) and ensure that you are up to date with current practice, initiatives and legislation.

Although not essential, candidates may find is useful to consult the 3rd edition of the *Gower Handbook of Purchasing Management,* edited by Marc Day, 2002. Other useful supplementary reading is *Commercial Relationships* by Mark Moore, 1999.

These titles can be obtained from the CIPS bookshop on 01780 761467 or email bookinfo@cips.org, or can be ordered online at www.bookshop.cips.org.

Relationships in context

bjectives

When you have completed this section you will be able to:

◆ **Evaluate the need for appropriate strategies for relationships in different contexts**

◆ **Evaluate the relationship implications of emergent supply system philosophies**

◆ **Assess the circumstances in which short-term relationships might be appropriate, and analyse such relationships**

◆ **Assess the circumstances in which partnership relationships might be appropriate, and analyse such relationships**

◆ **Identify and explain the circumstances in which co-destiny relationships might be appropriate and analyse such relationships**

◆ **Explain 'open book' philosophies**

◆ **Analyse joint ventures, partnerships and other permanent alliances and discuss the 'relationships' aspects of such arrangements**

◆ **Appraise the cross- and multi-functional aspects of corporate management, and the relationships implications of these ideas**

◆ **Analyse relationships in the context of public procurement.**

Section 1 comprises subsections:

a) **Strategic considerations in relationship formation**

b) **Supply chains, value streams and related concepts and their impact upon commercial relationships**

c) **The main types of relationship**

d) **Intra-organisational relationships**

e) **Relationship issues in public procurement**

Introduction

Relationships are central to the way in which we do business. 'Good' relationships with customers, suppliers, shareholders, regulators and a whole range of stakeholders allow us to continue trading activities, whereas 'bad' relationships have a negative impact on business processes, profitability and jobs. Nonetheless, understanding relationships is often difficult and too often we rely on simple explanations that do not help us in maintaining and managing within our relationships.

This study guide has been written to help you understand some of the main issues that may impact upon commercial relationships between enterprises and individuals. It offers a perspective on a developing body of knowledge and practice and also provides some thoughts on the way in which that knowledge will develop over time. In contributing to the management of commercial relationships, the purchasing and supply professional may often move from managing the supply of goods and services to managing business processes and relationships. This calls for a variety of new knowledge, skills and attitudes.

Strategic considerations in relationship formation

The syllabus learning outcome for this subsection states that you will be able to:

◆ **Evaluate the need for appropriate strategies for relationships in different contexts.**

This subsection will cover:

◆ **Challenges**

◆ **Functional aspects of relationships**

◆ **Relationship management.**

Challenges

When we talk about 'relationships', there are often real difficulties in both language and subject matter. The words that we use to describe relationships often mean different things to different people or organisations, and the body of knowledge about relationships is both limited and fast changing. The meaning of terms and concepts, such as 'partnership', change rapidly in the commercial world and this changes the way in which individual and organisational actions impact on that way of organising a relationship.

Relationships are also problematic in that we often do not know 'what causes what' in the relationship. People and organisations have relationships with other people and organisations of whom we might know nothing and these relationships may well impact upon our relationships.

The study of relationships is in may ways in its infancy, and many of the ideas, concepts and practices described in this study guide will vary from organisation to organisation. If you think of your own studies and consider the complexity of a single organisation, you can imagine just how complex matters become when two or more organisations start to interact.

One source of difficulty is the fact that organisations do not act as individuals. Trying to reduce the complexity of an organisation by thinking about it as an individual or a thing is very tempting because it makes it much easier with which to deal. Many purchasing practitioners talk about the 'chemistry' or 'culture' of an organisation when, in fact, they are talking about their own personal perceptions and like or dislike of individuals. This leaves the student and the practitioner with a whole range of difficulties in developing an effective commercial relationship with a supply organisation, as we will see later in the study guide.

To get an idea of how complex commercial relationships can be and to consider how many different factors can impact on the level of satisfaction with the relationship, or its commercial value, consider the diagram in figure 1.

Figure 1: Decision makers

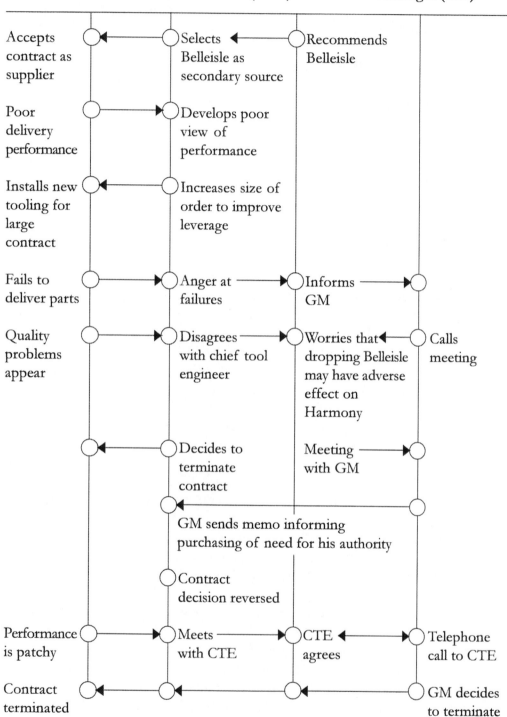

Belleisle Fabrications	Harmony Purchasing	Harmony Chief Tool Engineer (CTE)	Harmony General Manager (GM)
Accepts contract as supplier	Selects Belleisle as secondary source	Recommends Belleisle	
Poor delivery performance	Develops poor view of performance		
Installs new tooling for large contract	Increases size of order to improve leverage		
Fails to deliver parts	Anger at failures	Informs GM	
Quality problems appear	Disagrees with chief tool engineer	Worries that dropping Belleisle may have adverse effect on Harmony	Calls meeting
	Decides to terminate contract	Meeting with GM	
	GM sends memo informing purchasing of need for his authority		
	Contract decision reversed		
Performance is patchy	Meets with CTE	CTE agrees	Telephone call to CTE
Contract terminated			GM decides to terminate

As can be seen, there are many different decision makers involved in this commercial relationship, some of who have had no personal contact or relationship with the supplier. Each of these decision makers will be influenced by a whole range of factors including experience, enterprise policy or commercial pressures. All of these factors impact upon the relationship.

This becomes even more complex when we consider the factors at work in figure 2. This shows the process from the supplier's viewpoint.

Figure 2: Supplier's viewpoint

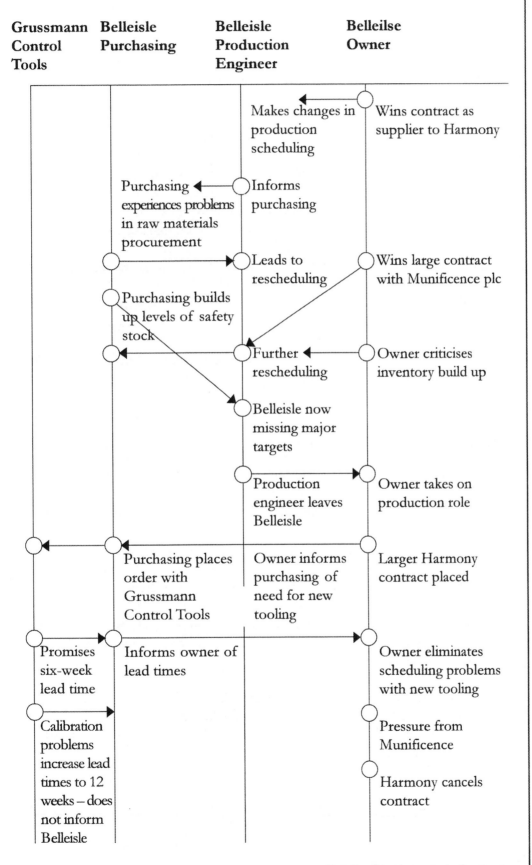

As can be seen in the figure, the supplier here is influenced by relationships with other suppliers and customers. This caused the difficulties that led to the loss of the contract. As proved when we talk about relationships, we often think only of how they effect us. In order to understand relationships we need to adopt a systems thinking approach which attempts to understand what is happening from the viewpoints of all the parties involved. This can be difficult, but it delivers a number of benefits.

The management of commercial relationships is a critical skill for the purchasing and supply professional. There are many ideas, skills and tools which can be used to manage these relationships, but one issue is paramount – commercial relationships rest upon clarity and robustness in:

◆　The way in which we think about relationships

◆　The information available within the relationship and about the relationship

◆　The quality of communication which rests upon the quality of information available. If information is poor, communication must be poor

◆　The understanding of one's own and others' role within the relationship

◆　The understanding of the way in which other relationships impact upon our own relationships

◆　The comprehension of the way in which relationships shift over time and in response to changing contexts.

Levels of relationship analysis

People have always been interested in relationships. Most of the books that we read, the TV programmes that we watch and radio programmes that we listen to are about relationships between people. There are, however, several problems with studying relationships:

◆　There is no real overall theory of what a relationship actually is and no single explanation that makes them work and makes them fail

◆　Individuals often think that they know a great deal about personal relationships and transfer that assumed knowledge into commercial relationships

◆　Relationships are unstable – they can change their response to factors which are invisible to the observer such as thoughts about what a customer or supplier might do. This makes explaining relationships and making rules on how to manage them very difficult.

One way of looking at relationships is to consider different levels of analysis. These may best be considered in the light of examples such as the following:

Individual or organisational behaviour

Your organisation decides to launch a new product on the basis of a technical breakthrough made by R&D. It carries out extensive market research with consumers. The returns are very good. Senior managers are very excited – sales have been falling off and they feel that they need a new product to win back some of the market share. On the basis of this research, 'production' implements a pilot programme to ensure that it can scale production to meet the expected demand. HRM recruits new production staff and 'finance' dedicates budgets to marketing and sales. 'Logistics' and 'warehousing' create extra distribution capacity. A major advertising programme is created and the product is launched in a blaze of publicity.

Sales are disappointing. Retailers do not stock the product because they associate it with falling sales of complementary products. Those who agree to stock it are unable to obtain supplies because the enterprise's own suppliers have been unable to gear up for the launch. After several months the product is abandoned and the organisation issues a profits warning.

Organisational interaction

R&D has stumbled onto a new product which seems, on first view, to offer the consumer dramatic benefits. Senior managers commission extensive market research with both consumers and customers. Pre-sales activity is carried out with customers to raise awareness of the benefits of the product. Feedback is mixed from customers whose past experiences with the organisation have caused mistrust, and these reports create misgivings among senior managers. Feedback is, however, good from consumers and, after a lengthy debate, a small pilot programme is agreed and limited success achieved. A major launch is planned and different functions gear up. Unfortunately, in the interim, a competitor launches a similar product and consumer attention shifts to this product, causing losses in development and market share. Suppliers, who had been told to increase inventory holdings on the basis of advanced forecasts from the pilot, are told that these orders will not materialise. The enterprise is embroiled in legal actions by suppliers. After several months the product is abandoned and the organisation issues a profits warning.

Organisational relationships

R&D has identified a breakthrough product which offers real added value to consumers and which senior managers expect will make a real impact on the market share. It approaches customers and suppliers with whom it has enjoyed a close working relationship for many years. Early customer and supplier involvement allows marketing and procurement to obtain good information about likely sales forecasts and turn these into hard order and production data. By working closely with suppliers it is possible to rationalise SKU ranges and this has a knock-on effect for post-sales support which makes the product more attractive to customers. One customer offers an idea that makes the product even more effective and creates a market for supporting products. The excitement of being part of such a radical new product launch is communicated to staff in different organisations and, after a successful product launch, the relationships begin to move to more formal, longer-term agreements.

Network relationships

A new product has been identified that cannot be brought to the market under existing cost structures. Your organisation needs to optimise the input of all the organisations within the supply chain in order to bring this product to the market successfully. Although the organisations use advanced planning and scheduling tools to manage inventory and costs into the first tier of the supply base, a major decision is made to identify the contribution of the whole network before further development can take place. A series of supply base mapping programmes take place with suppliers in lower tiers being identified and brought to workshops which show them the contribution that their own organisation makes to the final product. These workshops are successful and the lower tiers of the supply base are given access to the organisation's intranet, which improves transparency and information exchange. This electronic network is still reinforced with face-to-face meetings and problem-solving teams. Secondments from the organisation are often placed with lower-tier suppliers and vice versa. Unnecessary costs such as distribution are identified and eliminated, and a gain-sharing programme is introduced to ensure that all involved experience the benefits of the newly developed market.

From these examples, we can see that there are both risks and opportunities in the type and nature of relationships that we choose to pursue. This is not to say that network relationships will always be 'better' than intra-organisational relationships. Projects of this nature can be very time- and resource-intensive and may not give the organisation the return on investment that they require.

It is possible to optimise results and contribute to the maintenance of the relationship if you can:

◆   Choose the right type of approach that will help engender an appropriate relationship for the circumstances

◆   Choose the right framework which will help make that relationship work effectively

◆   Put in place the right type and level of resource to contribute to relationship development.

So, one way of classifying relationships is through the level of effort involved in maintaining the relationship and the extent of the individuals involved. This, however, begs the question of the function of a relationship. *What does a relationship do for us?*

Functional aspects of relationships

Functionally, relationships offer us a range of benefits and obligations. They represent a way of accessing the resources available. One way of looking at relationships is to see them as a gateway to other resources. We will look at this in more detail later in the study guide. These resources may be:

◆   Tangible in the shape of goods, services or money

◆   Intangible in the form of time or effort as more people are brought into a project or programme

◆   Informational in the shape of data and knowledge about inventory, sales, capacity or innovation

◆   Power-based in that the existence of large-scale customers or reliable suppliers give both status and potential advantage

◆   Emotional in the shape of a shoulder to cry on when things go wrong.

We can say that the strength and nature of the relationship will control and be controlled by the way in which that gateway opens and closes, the nature and quantity of the resources that pass through it and in what direction these resources pass through.

Process aspects of relationships

Another way of looking at this gateway was developed by Mari Sako and Ronald Dore. Sako described and compared commercial relationships in Japan with those in the United States and Western Europe. She identified a continuum of relationships which at one end were labelled 'ACR' or arm's length contractual relationships and 'OCR' which were obligational contract relationships. ACR relationships, which were mostly employed in the West, were characterised by adversarial win-lose style negotiations, short-term contracts and lack of communication. OCR contracts, on the other hand, were characterised by collaborative win-win style negotiation, longer contracts and effective communication. Sako's theory was that longer-term contracts enabled the growth in what she termed 'reciprocity', which is a feeling of obligation to return similar outcomes to those you have received. We will look in more detail at how reciprocity is a key element of influence in section 2 of this study guide.

Another process view of relationships was developed by the International Marketing and Purchasing group (IMP) who created a dynamic model of buyer-supplier relationships in industrial markets (the interaction model) and illustrated its applicability through comparative studies of buyer-supplier relationships in a number of European countries (France, Germany, Italy, Sweden, UK). The main conclusion of these studies was that buying and selling in industrial markets could not be understood as a series of disconnected and serially independent transactions.

Instead, transactions could only be examined as episodes in often long-standing and complex relationships between the buying and selling organisation. These relationships seemed to be fairly stable when studied over long periods of time, but turned out to very dynamic when looked at in more detail. The IMP group identified a number of factors which impacted upon the relationships including the personal relationships between actors, the types of activity carried out by the organisations within the relationship and, as with functional explanations, the type and nature of resources which could be mobilised internally or through the relationship.

Relationship models

As well as process and functionally based relationship models, we can also identify a number of descriptive models, all of which outline a relationship based on behaviours and concepts such as:

- Collaboration
- Commitment
- Communication
- Trust
- Openness
- Cooperation
- Power use and power sharing
- Intimacy
- Mutual investment
- Responsiveness
- Flexibility

- Adaptability
- Speed
- Joint total asset visibility
- Real-time management
- Process synchronisation
- Partnering
- Nurturing
- Symbiosis
- Risk assessment
- Risk management.

Most of these terms are about desirable concepts. Unfortunately, they are outcomes which are difficult to measure. In many cases there is little practical information about how individual firms or organisations can actually achieve these objectives. It is possible to consider a range of processes within a relationship which may bring about these desired outcomes.

Processes may include:

- Nominated staff for contract management
- Joint problem-solving teams
- Cross-functional coordination
- Early supplier involvement in design
- Early buyer involvement in design
- Electronic communication tools
- eMarket places/eCommerce/enterprise portals
- Desktop purchasing solutions
- Collaborative workflow tools
- Collaborative procurement, management and scheduling packages (based on advanced planning and scheduling (APS), enterprise resource planning (ERP), electronic data interchange (EDI) and extensible markup language (XML))
- Complementary business processes (for example, use of the same forms, same software, same ordering methods or inventory recording)
- Performance analysis
- Relational analysis
- Supply base reduction programme
- Supplier recognition programmes
- Supplier associations
- Third party logistics' solutions
- Logistics planning and management systems
- Kaizen teams
- Longer-term contracts
- New forms of contract

cont...

- Performance contracts
- Outsourcing contracts
- Adversarial purchasing
- Partnerships
- Co-destiny agreements
- New forms of negotiation
- Development of shared standards
- Collaborative business process redesign
- Collaborative business process re-engineering
- Value analysis and value engineering
- Activity based costing
- Total costing
- Total quality management (TQM)
- Purchasing skills development
- Marketing skills development
- Supply and value chain mapping
- Supply and value chain analysis.

And probably many more. Unfortunately, because commercial relationships is a developing field, we have only a general idea how different combinations of these processes actually lead to the types of relationship we want, although our understanding of how these processes might be implemented is more comprehensive. But perhaps the first question is 'why bother?'. What is it that drives the development of commercial relationships within the supply chain?

What drives relationship development?

There is a growing interest in the subject of relationships in many functional disciplines. In the field of marketing, customer relationship management (CRM) and relationship marketing (RM) initiatives have been introduced within many organisations.

CRM is designed to capture customer data and record external sources and consolidate the information in a central warehouse. If used properly, this helps enterprises to better understand and anticipate the needs of their current and potential customer base.

Once the enterprise has that understanding it can create better customised communication and persuasion strategies – aimed in some cases at individuals and not merely at demographic or psychographic market segments. These strategies are driven by the need to configure both communication (marketing or advertising) and production in response to increasing competition and increased customer volatility.

It is interesting to note that in the field of purchasing there has also been a shift towards an increasing reliance on relationships. In many industries, the role of the supplier has radically expanded. In many cases, this has been the result of increasingly sophisticated approaches to supply chain management, but it has also been the result of a range of drivers including the need to eliminate waste in the purchasing and production process across the whole supply chain.

In the case of integrated product design and development, for instance, the whole of the design process may have been outsourced to a new type of supplier that can manage a turnkey project. This type of early supplier involvement means that, in some cases, suppliers have gone from being made aware of the designer's decision, to being invited to the design team meetings and then on to becoming the design team.

In the case of lean or agile supply, the role of the supplier has also been changed by the need for assured supply. More outsourcing, higher levels of product complexity and operations such as the use of vendor-managed inventories have all increased the risk that a critical component may not be available when it is time to make an original equipment manufacturer's delivery. If this happens to a major product line, it can lead to an enterprise missing its financial targets for the quarter and a resulting impact on its annual performance and profitability.

This can mean that there has been a fundamental power shift between the supplier and the purchasing organisation. Suppliers are no longer simply supplying; instead they have become critical players in the success of the business. The interdependence of an enterprise with its supply network has never before been so explicit. If a supplier fails to develop and deliver competitive features or fails to allocate adequate supply, it can have a major impact on the enterprise.

Of course, the penalties for failure can be heavy for the supplier too, but where the relationship is strongly interdependent, such penalties cannot be used too often. Increasingly, purchasing and SCM needs to walk a tightrope balancing strategies and tactics that simultaneously reduce cost and risk. In such a situation, the purchaser-supplier relationship is critical.

Relationship management

It is, of course, difficult to select or manage a relationship. Relationships are, as noted above, co-created by two or more parties and the fact that one of those parties chooses to adopt a particular strategy does not necessarily mean that the second one will. Indeed, by adopting a particular strategy of openness or disclosure, one party may cause themselves serious damage if the second chooses to take advantage of this.

This uncertainty about other players' intentions is at the heart of the contracting process which has grown to structure relationships and protect the parties involved. Nonetheless, as we have seen, enterprises sometimes need to move beyond the contracting model or supplement this with some type of 'relationship management' strategy.

When considering the type of relationship required with a supplier, there are a number of factors which can be taken into account including:

◆ The current situation and needs of the enterprise

◆ The future situation and needs of the enterprise.

It is very easy for purchasing and supply staff only to consider the immediate needs and situation and then to find, when those needs change, that they have chosen the wrong type of relationship with a supplier. It is important to remember that although contracts can be drafted and redrafted fairly easily, relationships can be much more difficult to change.

Within a longer-term view there are a number of other factors which will impact on the nature of the relationship that grows up between the parties involved. These include:

The nature of the goods and services being supplied

It is very easy for purchasing and supply professionals to become over-focused on the nature of the goods and services being supplied. This is understandable in a manufacturing context where getting the right goods to the right place at the right time and for the right price is critical. In service environments, the goods may be less important. There are a number of ways of classifying the supply of goods so as to 'match' them with the appropriate relationship. The figures below describe some of these ways of classifying the supply of goods.

Figure 3: Classifying the supply of goods (1)

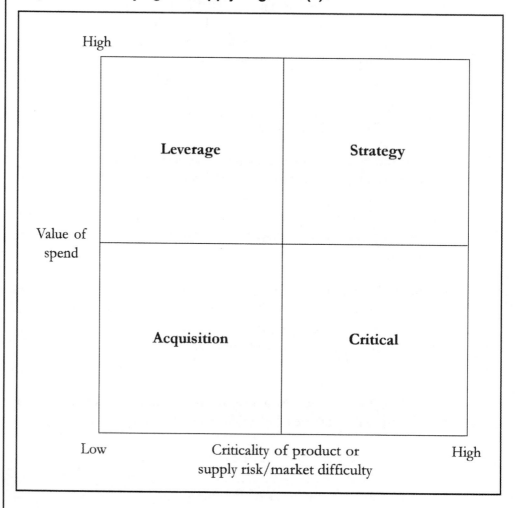

Relationships in context - Section 1a

This is Peter Kraljic's relationship positioning matrix which seeks to classify suppliers on the degree of spend (which can be translated into the customer's leverage or control of the supplier) and the degree of risk to the customer. Kraljic's matrix has a number of weaknesses as it assumes that the larger the spend, the larger the customer's power over the supplier. This, of course, only occurs when the spend is a large proportion of the supplier's total turnover, and there are few other customers for the product. The matrix also assumes that risk comes from within the relationship whereas, in fact, risks can come from a variety of sources.

According to this matrix, you would choose a relationship based upon the degree of risk and leverage available. However, the nature of supply, and the needs of the customer can change rapidly, and such an analysis often needs to take other factors into account.

Another way of considering relationships is to consider the way in which purchasing and supply relates to the overall strategic goals of the organisation, and the length of the relationship. This gives the matrix shown below:

Figure 4: Classifying the supply of goods (2)

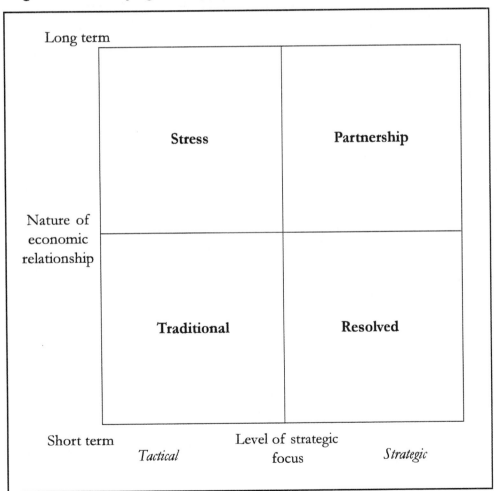

Here, a high strategic focus combined with a longer-term relationship would indicate the use of a partnership strategy. Of course, there are also drawbacks with this method, as we shall see later in the study guide.

As well as the factors just identified there are a whole range of other issues that might impact on the choice of a relationship and, more importantly, the ability to put that choice into action. Some of these issues might include:

The geographical location of the parties

In addition to the nature of the goods supplied, the geographical location of the supplier may have an impact on the type of relationship. Many Japanese manufacturing enterprises traditionally built business parks close to their main plants and required suppliers to build or occupy plants within these parks. Geographical closeness mitigates risk in shipping and also enables increased transparency as purchasing and engineering staff can easily visit a supplier to see work in progress and 'chase' production.

The information and communication systems and processes used

People often say that technology is designed to eliminate the problems of distance, and tools such as the telephone, the fax, EDI and the Internet can go a considerable way towards replicating geographical closeness. More recently, in the manufacturing sector, advanced planning and scheduling or supply chain optimisation tools can help the purchasing and supply function track production and inventory using shared tools coordinated through virtual private networks or the Internet. In the service sectors co-design or service scheduling tools can serve a similar function.

The business processes used

In addition to technological support, there are also issues with regard to the types of business process used, and whether these are aligned across the purchaser-supplier interface. Where supplier business processes fit closely with customer processes, there is likely to be less risk of supply breakdown. These processes may involve production, invoicing, organisational structure, account management or nature of contract.

Relative power

The nature of the market and the relative positions of the customer and supplier within that market will also have an impact on the nature of the relationship. Where customer orders represent a significant element of the supplier's total turnover, and where there are few alternative customers, this will have a major impact on the relationship. We will consider the question of purchasing power in more detail later in the study guide.

The nature of interpersonal relationships

More often than not, commercial relationships may spring out of personal relationships with people met on the golf course or elsewhere. Even where so-called 'handshake' deals are not the norm, the quality of personal relationships can have a major impact on the commercial relationship itself. In many cases purchasing and supply management programmes which may have involved a great deal of effort can change because the senior manager with whom the agreement was made moves on. Contracts can fail simply because the people involved do not 'get along'. We will look at the reasons for this later in the study guide.

Many of these factors are underpinned by the quality of information available to the contracting parties. Choosing the right type and level of information exchange is often critical to the relationship.

Figure 5: Communication and relationships

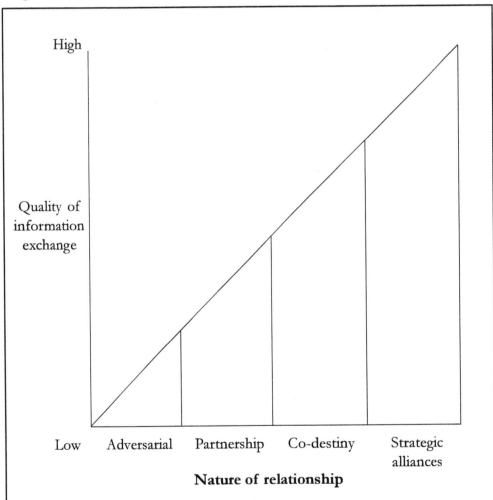

All of these factors might have an impact on the type of relationship which is likely to develop at the organisational, commercial and personal levels. As we will see later in the study guide, there are other factors which impact upon relationships. Broadly speaking, we can see that many of these factors are related to risk, which we will also consider in more detail later in the study guide.

Summary

Relationships are difficult to analyse and describe. Understanding these difficulties is an important task for anyone who seeks to develop effective commercial relationships. In fact, the study of relationships is in its very early stages. In order to understand relationships it can be useful to consider a number of different levels of analysis and identify the risks and benefits of each one.

It can also be useful to consider exactly what it is that relationships do and how they do it – what function they carry out for the purchaser and how they carry out that function.

For the purchaser, there are a number of strategic considerations with regard to relationship formation and maintenance, and many of these are connected with risk exposure, risk analysis and risk management. Factors that will impact upon this include the nature of the goods supplied, geographical location or integration of business and information processes.

Of course, there is no point in knowing the type of relationship that might develop unless there is some way of using that knowledge to create competitive advantage.

Supply chains, value streams and related concepts and their impact upon commercial relationships

The syllabus learning outcome for this subsection states that you will be able to:

◆ **Evaluate the relationship implications of emergent supply system philosophies.**

This subsection will cover:

◆ **Challenges**

◆ **Defining supply chain management (SCM)**

◆ **Role of SCM.**

The concept of the supply chain is perhaps best illustrated by the figure below, representing the exchange of goods, services, information and cash between groups of customers and suppliers.

Figure 6: Levels of exchange

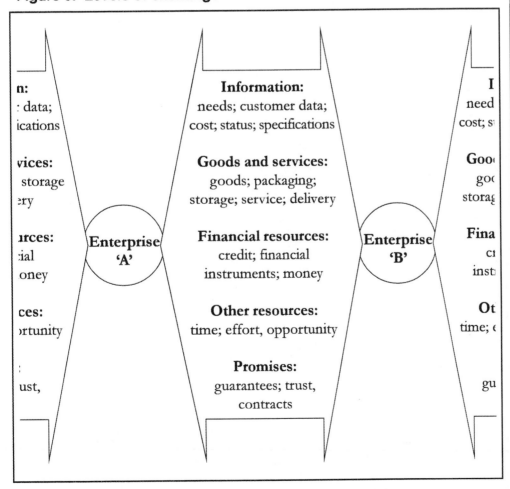

Effective supply chain management can be very difficult to achieve. It requires the practitioner to think beyond the boundaries of the organisation and in some cases beyond the boundaries of interaction with first-tier suppliers. In a global marketplace enterprises are increasingly finding that quality problems do not arise in first-tier suppliers (direct suppliers) to their own business. Instead they are finding that quality problems can begin with suppliers who are some distance along the chain.

These suppliers are not aware that they supply the enterprise in question. They may have no idea of the overall purpose of the component that they supply. A good example of this is where Chrysler had to recall its Jeep Grand Cherokee because the fuel gauge showed half-full when the fuel tank was empty. The fault was traced to:

1. A manufacturer of electrostatic coating who supplied.

2. A rheostat manufacturer who supplied.

3. The manufacturer of the fuel sender unit who supplied.

4. The manufacturer of the fuel tank assembly who supplied.

5. Chrysler Motor Corporation who made and sold the vehicle.

The original supplier had changed the specification on the coating, and the impact on Chrysler in terms of recall costs and lost sales was considerable.

Challenges

Figure 7: Complexity of supply

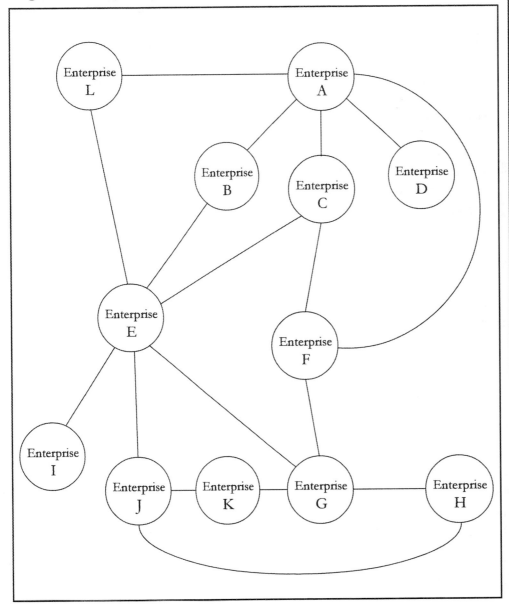

As we can see, the sheer scale and complexity of supply chain management is daunting. Traditionally both upstream and downstream portions of the supply chain have interacted as disconnected entities transferring sporadic flows of information, materials, services and cash. In the face of problems such as outlined above, there is clearly a need for a better approach to coordination between firms.

Within manufacturing supply chains, inventory has been described as the physical evidence of poor information exchange. In order to compensate for this lack of information, supply chains would contain costly stores of inventory, guaranteeing the ability to meet customer demand which, in itself, was difficult to predict. This unpredictability in customer demand could often lead to inventory build-up, although noone could easily see where this build-up took place. Lack of transparency meant that costs were incurred or expensive expediting projects had to be used throughout the supply chain.

Successfully operating an integrated supply chain requires continuous, good quality information exchange leading to transparency within every member of the chain. This, in turn, helps optimise product or service flows. Today, consumers are very aware of their ability to switch suppliers, and suppliers respond by trying to attract customers with new product launches or by customising products to unique market segments. This means that the demands on the supply chain can often change from order to order. Creating a customer-responsive system requires that enterprises within the supply chain process information in an accurately and timely manner. Retailers and distributors, who are closest to the point of consumption, have an important part to play by providing real-time, accurate consumption data using techniques such as bar coding and point-of-sale scanning.

This data can be used in conjunction with advanced planning and optimisation software to provide the projected replenishment needs for the supply chain and the production planning information needed by the manufacturers or the demand forecasts required by the service providers.

Before creating an integrated supply chain architecture, the supply chain management team have to diagnose what the problems are that prevent implementation. These may include:

◆ A lack of understanding about the need for an end-to-end demand planning function, which can cause frequent changes in the production schedule and can lead to costly expedited shipments

◆ Inconsistent or out-of-date data, due to a lack of integration with or lack of availability of enterprise resource planning (ERP) systems. This can result in planning being based on inadequate information or reactive decisions based on late information

◆ Inventory management has become more complicated as retailers and distributors seek to reduce costs and improve margins by replenishing inventory on a just-in-time basis. But until efficient process integration across all partners is in place, inventory management plans are hard to execute well.

Historically, planning, demand and inventory management systems in the supply chain have consisted largely of separate types of application software or manual systems that have been developed and modified internally over many years or licensed from third parties. For many enterprises they represent a considerable investment in money, time and commitment, and are difficult to change.

Imagine, if you will, that you approach a supplier and ask them to:

1. Change their ERP system from System X to System Y and also

2. Ask their own suppliers to ensure that they use System Y to ensure interoperability.

It can be even more difficult to ask them to install ERP from scratch. Suppliers will often see no reason to change a system that has been beneficial in the past, and they may not understand that these systems don't have the flexibility to support diverse and changing operations within an extended enterprise's business, nor can they respond effectively to changing technologies. Additionally, these applications have targeted only distinct levels of the supply chain and thus cannot provide the full benefits of integration which allows information to be distributed effectively.

However, this situation is changing with the advent of specialist software vendors. Solutions available are now developing handling large volumes of transactions. They possess a high degree of reliability and can rapidly capture and analyse data and distribute information throughout the enterprise, as well as link with other partners in the supply chain.

In service supply chains there are fewer products available, although the field is growing. As opposed to scheduling tasks, service supply chains require information on process design, re-engineering, management and integration. Supply chain information flows are much harder to define here, although demand planning information is critical. Here, however the supply chain manager may be more concerned with information flows about people, parts and interactions than inventory levels and build-to-order.

Defining supply chain management (SCM)

The terms 'supply chain management' and 'value chain management' are often difficult to define. Such terms are often used interchangeably to describe internal business processes, external processes between organisations, groups of organisations and relationships between customers and suppliers. In addition the phrase supply chain management has often been used in manufacturing supply chains and neglected in service supply chains. In this subsection we will consider both types of supply chain.

One of the important tasks in supply chain management is understanding exactly what is meant when the term is used. Words are only useful when they hold a common meaning and, unfortunately, SCM is a phrase with a wide range of meanings. Adding to the large number of definitions and redefinitions of distribution, logistics and other words associated with supply chain management does not always help. Having a common lexicon throughout the enterprise and across the business network is almost always necessary in selling the vision, institutionalising and standardising processes, systems and databases.

Use of terms

The terms used in supply chain management often mean different things to different people. It may help here to define the terms that we use. In this case we may call a self-contained enterprise, a 'firm' and its line of business, an 'enterprise'.

Trading partner

A trading partner is any organisation external to the firm that plays an integral role within the supply chain, and whose business fortune depends on the performance of the supply chain. The enterprise might represent a significant element of the trading partner's total revenue. Speciality retail outlets, distributor warehouses, contract manufacturers, sole source technology suppliers and logistics service providers are typical examples of trading partners.

Nominal trading partner

A nominal trading partner is any organisation external to the firm that provides an essential material or service, but whose financial success is largely independent of the financial success of the supply chain. The enterprise might represent a much less significant element of the nominal trading partner's total revenue. Suppliers, parts distributors, wholesalers, retailers, carriers, freight forwarders, customs brokerage services, international procurement organisations and value-added-network service providers are common examples of nominal trading partners.

Supply chain

A supply chain is the cross-organisational network used to deliver products from raw materials to end customers through an engineered flow of information, business processes and cash. A supply chain may also be known as an 'extended enterprise' or when links are electronic rather than physical, it may be known as a 'virtual enterprise'.

Value chain

The early 1990s saw the introduction of the idea of the value chain. This can be defined as a series of organisations extending all the way back to firms which extract raw materials, perform a series of value-adding activities and fabricate the finished good or service which then extends out to the ultimate consumer. The supply chain is the upstream of the organisation's value chain and is responsible for ensuring that the right materials, services and technologies are purchased and delivered at the right price, at the right time, in the right quality.

Of course, who defines these 'rights' and how these 'rights' are defined is open to question. We will look at these issues in more detail later in the study guide when we consider intra-organisational working. 'Rights' should also be considered in the context of performance measurement and measurement against standards or competitors.

SCM in manufacturing

Selecting the right definition is not an easy task because there is still a lot of confusion among enterprises of all sizes as to what SCM actually is. When some major enterprises refer to SCM they can mean:

♦ Inbound logistics

♦ Inbound and outbound logistics

♦ Logistics and distribution

♦ Logistics, distribution and transportation

♦ The above, plus materials handling and warehousing

♦ The above, plus manufacturing

♦ The above, plus procurement

♦ The above, plus order management

♦ SCM as a synonym for the order-to-cash core process.

In these circumstances SCM is more or less 'anything you want it to be' which leads to problems in management. However, in a manufacturing setting it can be viewed as the management of supply chains, which are defined as:

♦ The processes from the initial raw materials to the ultimate consumption of the finished product linking across supplier-user enterprises

♦ The functions within and outside a enterprise that enable the value chain to make products for the customer.

SCM in services

Supply chain management is typically focused on manufacturing but many supply chains hold 'no finished goods inventories' such as those typically associated with many service industries. Without finished goods inventories, customer demand can only be managed by adjusting the level of resources required to process them, such as, labour and capital equipment, or by redesigning business processes to eliminate waste. A good example is that of a mortgage services supply chain. Once generated, a customer order (mortgage application) queues up at each stage (credit check, appraisal and surveying and title check) for service because no service is, or can be, prepared in advance of the order's arrival at each stage. The way in which this process is managed is very much a supply chain.

Many other services including insurance, consulting, professional services and health care have a similar process structure. Service-based supply chains are not, of course, limited to the services sector. For example, custom-manufactured products produced by capital equipment manufacturers are similar to services because production may only begin after an order, including specifications for both final product and supplier components, has been placed.

In addition, recent advances in technology and increased competition means that many other industries are designing supply chains that hold no finished goods inventories. Enterprises such as the Dell Computer Corporation use direct sales and mass customisation to achieve supply chains that contain virtually no finished goods inventories. On the other hand, supply chains in some service industries, such as fast foods, essentially have inventory supply chains that are more similar to that of automobile production than to those in the mortgage, consulting or insurance industries.

In services we can suggest that supply chain management is about the integration of business, and cross-business processes, to deliver customer satisfaction in a consistent fashion across customer delivery systems.

---

activity 1

Consider the following questions and make an attempt to obtain answers to them. If you need to, speak with colleagues in other departments.

1. Does your organisation share a clear, well-defined definition of supply chain management?

2. How well is this definition shared by all staff in all departments?

3. Is this definition supported within your organisational structure?

4. Is there a nominated person to address SCM issues within your organisation?

5. Does that person have board-level responsibility?

6. Does that person have budgets and other resources to coordinate activities within the enterprise?

Role of SCM

Instead of providing a new definition for SCM, it may better to highlight some key points within SCM:

- SCM is enterprise-wide. It cuts across functions and business units requiring a cross-functional view

- SCM can cover the enterprise, the virtual enterprise and the extended enterprise requiring a cross- or inter-enterprise view

- SCM represents the infrastructure for a value chain; SCM is not limited to one set of linear connections but actually could cut across several value chains, especially in industries where supply chains are converging

- SCM manages all conduits and flows in an integrated, expeditious and synchronised manner

- SCM is driven by strategy, customer and market demand

- SCM could be viewed as a core process which, by definition, cuts across all functions of the enterprise including certain functions of the extended enterprise.

There are two other important questions that emerge from viewing SCM as a core process. The first is whether or not the executive in charge of the SCM core process is the same individual as the CEO of the enterprise. In reality, there is no option but to have only one executive in charge of SCM, regardless of whether SCM is treated as a core process or not.

Deploying SCM in manufacturing

Using SCM in a manufacturing context will often include the integration of functions such as:

- **Inventory:** control of parts, components, raw material and finished goods

- **Production:** control including shop floor scheduling along with the materials handling, storage and movement necessary to reach work-assembly stations

- **Subcontracting:** or deciding what to make, what to buy and what to outsource

- **Procurement:** or the purchasing of raw materials, subassemblies and maintenance, repair and operating supplies (MRO). It does not normally include the purchase of capital equipment

- **Transportation:** of incoming and finished goods

- **Salvage:** or the disposal of surplus and scrap.

For manufacturing then, SCM is the coordination of material flows, information flows and financial flows between all the participating organisations so as to ensure that the right product is in the right place, at the right price, at the right time and in the right condition.

- **Material flows:** involve physical product flows from suppliers to customers through the chain, as well as the reverse flows via product returns, servicing, recycling, and disposal

- **Information flows:** involve demand forecasts, order transmissions, delivery status reports and contracts

- **Financial flows:** involve information such as credit card details, credit terms, payment schedules, letters of credit and title ownership arrangements.

Deploying SCM in services

In a service supply chain the supply chain manager may be required to carry out:

- **Accountability audits:** identifying and training staff to achieve the right type of role and the correct levels of responsibility

- **Benchmarking:** business processes and process bundles to ensure optimum service delivery

- **Work-flow analysis:** to ensure the correct mix and level of task is carried out

- **Process mapping:** ensuring business processes are effectively integrated

- **Metrics:** selecting, implementing measures that reflect best practice

- **Model development:** to enable service testing

- **Cross-functional teams:** selecting, leading and supporting cross-functional teams

- **Implementation:** launching new processes and ensuring commitment

- **Training:** in using new processes

- **Best practices:** identifying and assessing best practice for service development

- **Documentation and systems:** supporting service processes through systems development.

For service supply chains, the task of the supply chain manager is to ensure that all business processes are integrated within organisations and across organisational boundaries and that the flow of information, money and processes are carried out effectively.

◆ **Process flows:** include customer and strategy supporting processes including order to cash, service delivery, customer satisfaction and demand assessment

◆ **Information flows:** as previously stated, involve demand forecasts, order transmissions and delivery status reports. Frequently information is represented by paper documents

◆ **Financial flows:** as for manufacturing, involve information such as credit card details, credit terms, payment schedules, letters of credit and title ownership arrangements.

Objectives of SCM

The objective of a supply chain is to ensure that multiple enterprises function as efficiently and effectively as a single enterprise, with full information visibility and accountability, which makes service to the final customer the output of the process. At the heart of this integration are:

◆ **Information systems:** which share long-term demand schedules and release dates with all members of the channel. Such systems obviously require long-term partnerships – contracts with the trust necessary to the sharing of sensitive information

◆ **Activity systems:** which integrate processes and work-flows across organisational boundaries

◆ **Relationship support systems:** which support both of the above.

Drivers for SCM

In order to maintain and increase market share, many enterprises are trying to redesign supply chains to drive out unproductive work and complexity and thus, eliminate delays, errors, excessive costs and inflexibility. Manufacturers and distributors are being forced to become more responsive to retailers and consumers, which has created a need for improved planning capabilities. At the same time, competitive pressures are forcing manufacturers to reduce costs, decrease order cycle times and improve operating efficiencies. These pressures include:

◆ **Cost pressures:** better information is replacing inventory. The capabilities of supply chain software applications are growing to manage inventory that enterprises 'can't see' and 'don't own', but which represent costs within the chain. Other costs and wastes can be identified and driven out. Good information management allows enterprises to identify costs, lower inventory and better utilise existing assets

◆ **Time pressures:** the need for faster and more customised deliveries has disrupted traditional production management policies and transportation choices. The lead times provided to customers has a 'knock on' effect, directly affecting their subsequent lead times and thereby the velocity and flexibility of the entire value chain. By decreasing the lead time, businesses can gain competitive advantage

◆ **Reliability pressures:** when promising delivery dates or product quality to customers, enterprises need to ensure that they are capable of delivering on that date and to that quality. Customers are becoming less tolerant

◆ **Response pressures:** customers are increasingly demanding real-time information into capabilities, products, configurations and availability as a way of managing risk. The ability to provide that information automatically is increasingly necessary

◆ **Transparency pressures:** the ability of a supplier to provide visibility into their order status is critical. Turning the supply chain into a 'glass-pipeline' will allow customers to identify current states, anticipate future states and proactively manage their inbound supply chain

◆ **Globalisation pressures:** the increasing complexity and globalisation of the interactions among suppliers, manufacturers, distributors, retailers and consumers requires sophisticated coordination of multiple distribution channels.

Relationships in SCM

To achieve supply chain optimisation, enterprises are having to rethink their relationships with suppliers, manufacturers, distributors, retailers and customers. Market leaders realise that the more efficient their relationships are with their partners, the greater the edge they have over their competitors. This interdependency is creating changes in the competitive landscape, forcing enterprises that want to remain competitive to solidify relationships with their own partners. But this involves a new relationship management approach based on higher levels of trust, communication and win-win negotiating strategies.

As these relationships become more efficient, they also become more dependent on information flow leading to increased interdependence. Improved interpersonal and activity linkages and software integration with suppliers are necessary as controlling uncertainty in customer demand, manufacturing processes and supplier performance are critical to effective SCM . The challenge lies in the integration of internal systems to each enterprise and to those of its suppliers, partners and customers to improve efficiency and distribution effectiveness.

SCM optimisation

The ultimate objective of the integrated supply chain is 'sell one, make one.' Market share and revenue growth are increasingly dependent on getting the right mix of products to the right place at the right time, or the right services to the right customer in the right way (remembering how 'right' is defined). SCM optimisation is driven by the widespread adoption of new technologies in the field such as:

◆ Data acquisition such as point-of-sale devices and bar coding

◆ Data storage and manipulation tools such as data warehousing and data mining

◆ Data sharing using advanced planning and scheduling tools

◆ Data analysis using sophisticated statistical packages.

Enterprises that have already made the necessary investments in ERP systems to integrate functions, such as purchasing, inventory management, production scheduling and finance within the enterprise need to leverage their sunk ERP investments by integrating up and down the value chain. This integration requires process optimisation, in other words, minimising the total cost of the order-to-delivery process by trading off the costs of inventory, transportation and handling.

Traditional optimisation solutions may minimise a single cost, but they cannot handle the complex interdependencies that real-life situations often create. Also, the business applications of manufacturers, distributors, transporters and retailers concentrate on controlling costs under an organisation's direct control, rather than controlling the combined costs of end-to-end operations. Consequently, until recent developments in SCM applications, no one player has had the information visibility needed to synchronise the entire channel. The result is that the typical supply chain contains far too much inventory.

The new generation of supply optimisation tools provides an integrated approach through which demand prediction, inventory stocking and transportation decisions are made together. In managing supply chains, the new generation of applications optimises not only cost, but also service, quality and time factors that can strongly influence customer satisfaction.

Key processes

Optimising SCM requires a detailed review of the underlying business processes. It is possible to identify a number of key processes that provide the infrastructure for an integration approach to SCM. These include:

- **Customer service management:** customer service becomes the key information process. Customer service provides the customer with real-time information on promised delivery dates and availability through contact with the organisation's production, distribution and service delivery operations

- **Product development:** customers, distributors and suppliers must be integrated into the product-development process in order to reduce time to market

- **Demand management:** the role of the demand-management process is to balance the customer's requirements with the firm's supply or delivery capabilities. Part of managing demand involves attempting to determine what, when, why and how customers purchase or use services. A good demand-management system is continuously modelled using point-of-sale and other customer data to reduce uncertainty and provide efficient flows throughout the supply chain

- **Procurement:** strategic plans are developed that include suppliers to support the manufacturing or service delivery processes. The purchasing function develops accurate assessment and rapid communication mechanisms to transfer requirements quickly. These tools reduce time and cost spent on routine transactions

- **Manufacturing flow management:** manufacturing processes may be lean, agile and flexible to respond to rapid order changes. Systems are pull-based on demand. Modular manufacturing can provide individualised products based on the principles of mass customisation

- **Service process management:** service processes must be streamlined to ensure cost-effective service delivery

- **Service support processes:** managing the service support channel as a business process offers an opportunity for sustainable competitive advantage.

Implementation

In the midst of supply chain planning it is easy to take relationships into account. In putting the supply chain into practice, relationships can be damaged as the realities of implementation begin to impact on both supplier and customer. In order to implement the extended enterprise it is vital that certain elements are in place. The elements are:

◆ An effective strategy for implementation that is flexible but robust with clear objectives that are jointly developed or can be shared

◆ Senior management understanding and commitment – although this may be a truism for all new programmes, integrated supply chain management starts at the top through linkages with key partners

◆ Change-management skills

◆ Commitment to development – the word 'magnificent' was originally meant as someone or something that was committed to 'magnifying' those people that he, she or it came into contact with. Organisations which will successfully achieve integration are those which will create the desire and ability to embrace improvement within every member of the supply chain

◆ A mechanism for turning that commitment into practice

◆ Effective and efficient communications – as noted above, good communications rest upon good quality information. This can be supported by real-time electronic communications with shared information at all levels. The entire service and manufacturing chain operations require effective forecasting which requires good information

◆ An understanding of the complexity of the supply chain and the way that the elements interact in different situations

◆ A set of agreed standards for performance

◆ A way of measuring performance

◆ Cross-functional integration – this may involve policies, teams or communities of practice within the firm

◆ Flexible relationships – think of relationships as a product and ask yourself what you might want that product to deliver. Good relationships require, among other things, commitment, congruence (doing what you say you will do), empathy, honesty, creativity, communication and trust. Building such relationships takes time and effort.

Differentiation strategy

In manufacturing, traditional make-to-stock supply chain models operate on the principles that production quantities and dates are provided by the demand forecast. Customers then receive shipments from the finished goods inventory. This means that any irregularities in the demand flow can be smoothed using so-called buffer stocks in warehousing. Resource utilisation with make-to-stock models is often less than optimal due to inefficient purchasing, poor asset utilisation or expensive and slow inventory pipelines.

Michael Porter has suggested that revenue may be grown by differentiation offering customers something unique that the competition doesn't have. Many enterprises, in an effort to differentiate themselves, focus their energy on products or services which will be better or cheaper than those offered by competing firms. More recently, however, we have seen some enterprises take advantage of the opportunity to differentiate themselves through the design and management of their supply chains.

Supply chain differentiation adds value in that most enterprises are part of an interlocking network of supply chains. This means that it is very difficult for competitors to replicate a supply chain differentiation strategy. Some ways in which manufacturing enterprises can differentiate include:

◆ **Integrated make-to-stock:** enterprises are now attempting to eliminate some of the problems associated with make-to-stock by using information to improve coordination of end-to-end activities. One recent innovation of make-to-stock is configuring the actual finished product while it is in the distribution channel. This is called postponement. Some products are destination-driven (particularly those for international customers) – these are also best handled in the distribution channel

◆ **Continuous replenishment:** to create a customer demand-driven pull system that stretches across several enterprises, new methods such as efficient consumer response (ECR), collaborative planning, forecasting and replenishment (CPFR) or quick response (QR) have been introduced. These methods vary in the level of integration, but they all aim at coordinating activities in an integrated manner by crossing inter-organisational boundaries

◆ **Build-to-order (BTO):** as the world moves from mass production to mass customisation, the supply chain requirements also change. The basic goal of build-to-order is to trigger the entire production/supply cycle only when a buy demand is sent by a customer.

Summary

Defining SCM is difficult. However, SCM is unquestionably a critical and core business process. SCM is used in both manufacturing and service settings. Although the activities used may be different, the principles are the same.

Integrated SCM is about optimising business processes and business value right across the extended enterprise. This 'extraprise' extends from the supplier's supplier to the customer's customer. To be truly effective, SCM needs to make use of a range of concepts and new technologies to manage beyond the organisation's internal boundaries. Reaching both upstream and downstream in the supply chain is accomplished a lot more efficiently and effectively with electronically enabled systems. The enterprise and its suppliers can, therefore, share sales forecasts, manage inventories, schedule production, optimise deliveries and, thus, improve productivity all along the value chain.

Relationships within the supply chain are, however, about much more than just integrating software. They require a range of tools and approaches which themselves must be integrated into an overall strategy which supports integration.

Supply chain management can be used as a differentiation strategy which can lend an organisation significant competitive advantage.

Self-assessment question

SAQ 1.1

Identify five pressures that are driving integration within the supply chain.

The main types of relationship

The syllabus learning outcomes for this subsection state that you will be able to:

◆ **Assess the circumstances in which short-term relationships might be appropriate, and analyse such relationships**

◆ **Assess the circumstances in which partnership relationships might be appropriate, and analyse such relationships**

◆ **Identify and explain the circumstances in which co-destiny relationships might be appropriate and analyse such relationships**

◆ **Appraise 'open book' philosophies.**

This subsection will cover:

◆ **Challenges**

◆ **Describing relationships**

◆ **Classifying relationships**

◆ **Adversarial/transactional relationships**

◆ **Partnering relationships**

◆ **Open book, target costing and transparency approaches**

◆ **Co-destiny relationships.**

Challenges

Any integrated body of knowledge about commercial relationships must rest on a firm basis of description and classification. Sciences, such as chemistry, rest in great measure upon the table of elements. Unless you can describe and classify elements, experiments are impossible to reproduce. Biology became a science when Darwin's theory of evolution provided a basis for the work of taxonomists who began to understand and classify the variety of species and identify the relationships between them.

In the case of commercial relationships, it is probably impossible to complete an exhaustive list of the 'types' of relationship. This is simply because commercial relationships are so complex. Not only can they change rapidly – what was seen as a 'good' relationship can turn into a 'bad' relationship overnight – but the patterning of interactions within them is often unique to the individuals and enterprises involved.

Nonetheless, despite such a list being incomplete, it is useful to consider different types of relationship. It is possible to take two approaches in identifying types of commercial relationship. These are:

◆ Describing the relationship so that you have some idea of what the relationship looks like

◆ Explaining the relationship in order to be able to understand and make use of it.

Describing relationships

When we describe relationships, we use dimensions in order to differentiate one type of relationship from another. Purchasing and supply staff will often describe their relationships with suppliers as 'good' or 'bad'. This might be useful to the purchaser involved, but because these measures are so subjective, it is much less useful to anyone else.

Broadly, we can identify two ways of describing commercial relationships:

♦   The first relates to the type of relationship

♦   The second is the nature of the relationship.

Types of relationship

We have a range of different types of relationship in our lives. Broadly, within our personal lives we can have relationships with friends, family, neighbours or individuals with common interests. These might be classified as communal relationships. In our commercial activities different relationship types might include:

♦   Agency   ♦   Licensing
♦   Distributor   ♦   Private labels
♦   Contract manufacturing   ♦   Franchise
♦   Supplier partnerships   ♦   Joint research and development
♦   Original equipment manufacturer ♦   Equity participation
      (OEM)   ♦   Joint venture
♦   Joint marketing   ♦   Mergers and acquisitions.

Agency

An agency is basically an agreement in which a enterprise or an individual acts on behalf of another to perform certain specific services such as marketing, customer support and product sales.

Distributor

A distributor is an individual or an enterprise that has the rights (sometimes exclusive) to sell goods or offer services on behalf of a producer in a particular market or geographical area. The distributor imports directly from the exporter.

Contract manufacturing

A contract manufacturer manufactures a product or component for another enterprise (the principal). The contract manufacturer provides labour, production capacity and some technical expertise. Marketing and distribution are controlled by the principal. The contract is usually for a fixed duration of time and can be terminated.

Supplier partnerships

In this form of relationship, a customer forms a collaborative relationship with the supplier for a project or for a specific purchase agreement. The partnership calls for the sharing of information and commitment from both parties.

Original equipment manufacturer (OEM)

An OEM produces products or components for another manufacturer who resells the products or components to the end users under its own brand name.

Joint marketing

Joint marketing occurs when two or more parties enter into an agreement to share marketing expertise and conduct joint marketing in the host or third country market.

Licensing

A licensing arrangement is given when an enterprise with a well-known product or technology allows the licensee to manufacture the product, usually for a country or region. The licensing enterprise collects royalties based on a fixed sum or the quantity produced.

Private labels

In the case of private label, the brand stands for the name of the distributor or retailer rather than the manufacturer. This practice is common in the garment and food industries.

Franchise

Franchising is an arrangement where a party which has developed a proven way of running and managing a business successfully licenses another party the rights to operate that business format under the trademark(s), service mark(s) or trade name(s) of the first party. The business arrangement involves a formal legal contract between the two parties.

Joint research and development

Organisations may choose to work jointly in particular areas, such as research and development, where the costs of such projects are too high for one organisation to bear.

Equity participation

In some business relationships one party purchases equity shares in another enterprise due to strategic reasons – for example, a principal may purchase shares in a supplier. This type of business relationship is called an equity participation. Equity participation usually does not result in a management takeover, although the enterprise would be represented on the board of directors.

Joint venture

Under a joint venture a contractual relationship is established between two or more enterprises to carry out a specific business or project. Joint ventures are often proposed in order to enter an industry for which the enterprise has some, but not all, of the critical capabilities. This creates scope for synergy. For example, an enterprise may have the technology but lacks the distribution networks – the enterprise may then enter into a joint venture with a distributor.

Mergers and acquisitions

Merger takes place when the assets and liabilities of one enterprise are combined with the assets and liabilities of another enterprise. If a merger is between two enterprises in the same line of business, we have a horizontal merger. If the merger is between two enterprises in the same business but participating in different stages of the value chain, a vertical merger develops. Finally, if the merger is between two enterprises in different businesses, it is known as a conglomerate merger.

Within each of these commercial relationships there are also a number of different types of exchanges which may take place.

Types of exchange within relationships

There are clearly a large number of potential types of exchange within relationships and we have already looked at some of the things being exchanged – money, goods, services and information. Broadly, however, we can suggest that there are five classes of exchange:

◆ **Contractual exchanges:** where goods and/or services are exchanged for money

◆ **Barter or countertrade exchanges:** where goods are exchanged for other types of goods or services

◆ **Asset exchanges or loans:** where assets such as tools or information may be exchanged

◆ **Asset hire and leasing:** where assets may be borrowed for a fee

◆ **Equity exchanges or acquisition:** where ownership is exchanged or acquired.

Relationships in context - Section 1c

The different combinations of exchange types used can be useful tools for the purchasing professional and can have a major effect on the nature of the relationship. For example, a combination of contractual exchange, asset loan in the form of tooling, and equity acquisition can be used to manage risk and develop supplier compliance.

Nature of relationship

Once we turn from the type of relationship and the exchanges within it, we can then begin to consider the nature of the relationship. This is when things become a lot more confusing. As we saw in the previous section, there are a number of different terms used to describe the nature of relationships. These include:

◆ Collaboration
◆ Commitment
◆ Communication
◆ Trust
◆ Openness
◆ Cooperation
◆ Power use and power sharing
◆ Trust
◆ Intimacy
◆ Mutual investment
◆ Gain sharing
◆ Responsiveness
◆ Flexibility
◆ Adaptability
◆ Speed
◆ Joint total asset visibility
◆ Real-time management
◆ Process synchronisation
◆ Partnering
◆ Nurturing
◆ Symbiosis
◆ Risk assessment
◆ Risk management.

Although many or all of these terms are instinctively appealing, they are less than useful when we try to use them in analysing a relationship, and even less useful when we set them as a contract term. As we have already seen, there are a number of processes which may support these outcomes. We will consider how these processes might lead to these desirable relationship outcomes later in the study guide when we consider how we assess and measure relationships and consider the factors that affect a relationship.

Classifying relationships

As well as describing relationships we also need to classify them. Understanding the differences between relationships is useful. Mostly we classify relationships in terms of what the participants do together and how they do it, but there are exceptions such as holding enterprises where relationships are classified by means of the ownership of assets. There are a number of models for classifying relationships, one of which was developed by Robert Fiske who suggested four classes of relationship:

- **Communal sharing:** in which individual needs are subsumed into a greater objective. Elements of this model are incorporated into the idea of 'shared destiny' across the buyer and supplier organisations, and which originated within some Japanese models of partnership sourcing

- **Equality matching:** based on reciprocity and fair exchange between the parties involved in the relationship so that fair value is always given in return for what is received, and no single party obtains advantage from the other party. Elements of this model are used in the employment of open book costing approaches and joint asset visibility exercises

- **Authority ranking:** is an approach where the relationship is based on the hierarchical status of the parties involved and where one party may be dominated by the other. Elements of this type of relationship can be found where large-scale buyers can use leverage to dominate smaller suppliers

- **Market pricing:** where the relationship is based on calculations of cost and benefit and optimising return from activities. Elements of this type of relationship might be seen in a completely free market where supply and demand interactions are not influenced by buyer power. The Internet was seen originally as a free market of this type where small enterprises could trade across market boundaries. This has, of course, not yet come to pass.

Within the specific field of supply chain management a number of models of commercial relationships have been developed which seek to define relationships by the use of a range of approaches placed along a continuum from adversarial/ transactional/short-term through to so-called co-destiny approaches. Research into these models is far from complete and there can be a great deal of overlap between them. For example, an adversarial/short-term relationship may be repeated over time and a series of short-term contracts turn into a longer one. Partnership relationships may have periods when they are challenged and adversarial techniques are used. Co-destiny approaches may shift into partnerships.

It is important to remember when considering relationships that the relationship is not always the starting point of the analysis and that we may need to start with the context and type of interactions that create the relationship.

Adversarial/transactional relationships

The focus of traditional purchasing was to build a large competitive supply base. This supply base was managed using short-term contracts and win-lose negotiation strategies where the objective was to obtain the best possible price, safeguarding budgets and maximising revenues.

Advantages

There are a number of advantages to this strategy including:

◆ Offering an abundant potential supply base to encourage competition which the purchaser can exploit to negotiate favourable terms

◆ Providing a shelter against supply interruptions due to unforeseen circumstances, for example industrial action or plant failure

◆ Offering flexibility in sourcing without the need for a longer-term commitment.

Disadvantages

So-called adversarial relationships have received a great deal of criticism in many industries including construction and automotive assembly. Reasons for this adverse comment can be seen in a number of business drivers which demonstrate:

◆ The increasing share of purchased goods and services as a proportion of the manufacturing costs. In many industries this could be between 60 and 80% of the cost of manufacture

◆ The current trend of focusing on the core capabilities of the organisation. This, in turn, results in more outsourcing and increasing reliance on suppliers

◆ The dependence of successful implementation manufacturing techniques such as just-in-time (JIT) on acceptable purchased inputs of consistent quality

◆ The shortening of a product life cycle and increased need for rapid product development and introduction

◆ Consumer pressure for increased production variety and thus complexity.

Disadvantages include the amount of resource used in vetting and contracting with suppliers, other administration costs in managing a large supply base and the lack of accurate information sharing across organisational boundaries to permit effective planning and coordination.

Implementation

Short-term transactional approaches to purchasing may, however be useful in a number of circumstances. One of these is in the field of indirect purchases – those not directly associated with end products or services. These may include a number of major expenditure clusters such as: advertising and marketing, technology, overheads, human resources and those specific to the business such as store fixtures or collection agencies. Three problems prevent most enterprises from managing these purchases effectively:

1. **Inadequate information:** enterprises have confusing, inaccurate data about indirect purchases

2. **Insufficient resources:** the people negotiating purchases lack skill or have other incentives in making purchasing decisions

3. **Improper techniques:** few enterprises gather sufficient information or solicit competitive proposals

Short-term approaches for improving purchasing in this area may include:

◆   **Measuring pragmatically:** managers should be extremely selective and focused when defining pricing data for purchasing

◆   **Assigning resources selectively:** enterprises should increase the resources assigned to indirect purchasing and clearly define the roles of people assigned to administer supplier relationships

◆   **Demystifying business requirements:** enterprises must establish precise quality requirements for indirect purchases

◆   **Clarifying the pricing basis:** lax pricing practices work to the buyer's disadvantage. In order to compare prices, the buyer must establish discipline in pricing by creating and enforcing a standard vocabulary

◆   **Leveraging the free market:** buyers must be willing to use free-market competition to reduce costs and must take business away from suppliers if necessary.

Such approaches, however, run counter to the prevailing 'partnership' purchasing model. In a supplier partnership some authorities suggest that enterprises give up their right to investigate alternative sources by making a commitment to work with a partner through good and bad. Such partnerships may be appropriate when there are few viable alternatives or when changing suppliers would be difficult. In many cases, enterprises could establish free-market competition as their standard operating procedure and form partnerships only on an exception basis.

Partnering relationships

Increasingly, in many sectors enterprises are considering, or have ventured into, a partnership agreement with suppliers. In the face of rapid changes occurring in drivers, such as cost management and increasing competition, suppliers have made drastic changes in the way they conduct business. Changing regulations, a consolidation of the supply base and changing consumer demands are some of the market forces that have played a role in the growing number of partnerships between an enterprise and its trading partners.

Partnership models

Supplier partnerships are either defined as a formal partnering activity or a more informal partnership arrangement. Formal partnerships include such ventures as mergers, acquisitions, joint ventures and licensing agreements. More informal partnerships include strategic alliances. Although many suppliers have formed relationships with other suppliers, truly strategic alliances are characterised by:

◆ Synergy, whereby customers and suppliers seek to identify opportunities that arise from joint activities

◆ Collaborative strategy development

◆ Risk and gain sharing

◆ Joint problem -solving activity

◆ Mutual incentive to improve products and processes

◆ Creation of common goals

◆ Trust

◆ A long-term commitment

◆ Increased information sharing

◆ Increased communication.

Forms of partnership

Partnership can take a number of different forms and can, in itself, be used as a tool for the management of relationships. One method of managing relationships through partnering is to create different levels of partner (or classes of contractor) and incentivise progression through the different levels.

In setting up such a programme the lowest level of partner might be a commodity supplier. In this pre-partnering relationship, which is on the borders of the transactional relationship, bid specifications and requests for quotations are the norm within a normal framework of contractual and legal requirements.

The next level up might be the preferred supplier, typically on a short list of enterprises recognised for providing superior competences to other suppliers. However, the framework for this relationship remains framed by administrative processes and legal requirements.

Next is the value-added supplier which is recognised for distinctive competences which are particular to the customer's own needs or capabilities. Customising a service may be value-added parts of such a relationship. An enterprise might outsource functions like telecommunications or information systems to such a supplier. Product performance may be required as opposed to product features. However, contracts are still an important feature of these relationships.

Advantages

Partnerships have a number of advantages including:

◆ Better information exchange for improved planning

◆ Reduced costs in administration and sourcing

◆ Potentially decreased risk as purchasers are able to focus on and manage risk more effectively

◆ Increased potential responsiveness from suppliers with whom a long-term relationship helps increase reciprocity.

As we have seen, in some cases, partnerships are 'need to have' because they allow the introduction of new technology for integration.

Disadvantages

Partnerships also have a number of disadvantages including:

◆ The fact that longer-term relationships can lead to less flexibility where suppliers are unable to respond sufficiently quickly to changing needs

◆ Problems where customers may find that partnerships reveal many more problems within the supply base than were previously thought to have existed. Sometimes supply base reduction can concentrate problems that were previously hidden. In other cases, partnerships can hide problems by pushing non-partnership suppliers into lower tiers.

Implementing partnerships

As already noted, it is very difficult to 'implement' a relationship. Relationships are co-created by two or more entities (people, organisations and departments). Nonetheless, some organisations have experienced significant success in implementing effective partnerships with their suppliers. Some of the factors which seem to lead to success are:

◆ Enterprises involved in partnerships, where partners have equal decision-making control, tend to report a higher level of success

◆ Effective and frequent communication among partners (a critical element in a partnership agreement)

◆ Enterprises with distinct cultures and managerial styles. The key is the ability to manage and monitor these differences prior to and during the partnership. It is also important to position these differences as strengths to complement the other partner's weaknesses

◆ Partnerships can be formed between traditional rivals who have approached the partnership with 'cautious trust'

◆ Enterprises who form partnerships to expand their product line, increase their global capabilities or become full service suppliers report the highest success rates

◆ Enterprises involved in successful partnerships tend to conduct thorough up-front research on their potential partner(s)

◆ Enterprises taking on the additional workload that often comes with a partnership

◆ Successful partnerships tend to have top executives who actively support the partnership

◆ Successful partnerships often have core groups to manage and monitor the partnership.

Obviously, when market competition is eliminated in a longer-term relationship, cost management may take a different form. One element sometimes found within partnerships is so-called 'open book' costing approaches. This is more often linked to target and activity based costing approaches which are designed to optimise the trade-off between cost and the benefits of partnership.

Open book, target costing and transparency approaches

Perhaps the first thing to think about when attempting to implement open book costing is the degree to which the supplier knows their own costs. In some cases it is possible to implement open book costing only to find that the figures available do not give an insight into costs. Where supply bases have been reduced and partnership agreements exist, purchasers no longer have the negotiation flexibility which a large supply base gives. This means that purchasers need to find a different way of managing down costs within partnership arrangements. The three methods that are broadly used in manufacturing, and particularly manufacturing with a JIT emphasis, are target costing, activity based costing and open book costing.

Open book suppliers

Open book costing is generally perceived as being very desirable from the point of view of the purchaser and often perceived as being very undesirable from the point of view of the supplier. Implementation of open book costing can be very difficult to achieve. Often, it is useful to think about implementing such programmes in stages and help educate the supplier in activity based costing, followed by target costing, before thinking of open book.

It may be seen that open book accounting provides the enterprise with the data to assess how cost reductions might be made. However, the prevalence of absorption costing systems in multi-product suppliers may make the cost model of the particular purchased part somewhat opaque even if the books are partly open. If, for example, the overhead allocation rules to pools or to products are changed infrequently, then the cost as assessed may change due to volume and mix. Cost reduction in these circumstances is more an art form than a science.

Suppliers to many enterprises are ranked according to tiers which give rise to different types of agreements. 'Open book' supplier arrangements enable cost identification and reduction (CIR) teams to identify and tackle cost problems. Without such agreements, teams use observations on matters such as machinery or number of operatives. In rare cases, it may be that an enterprise will even intervene in a supplier's cost allocation decision.

One advantage of the open book approach is that a more trusting and harmonised relationship may develop so that purchasing enterprises may allow renegotiation in the event of uncontrollable price increases. Suppliers may also receive help in benchmarking exercises. The negative aspects are that buyers may use cost data to press for price reductions which are not necessarily linked to suggestions on how to reduce costs.

Target based costing

Target costing offers an alternative to the conventional costing approach. The traditional method is to estimate the cost of design and production, add in profit and that becomes the product's price. The target costing method determines the market price requirement, the price required to win the customer's business, then subtracts the target profit to arrive at the target cost.

A number of factors influence target costing, including senior management's objectives and long-term profit objectives. Although context effects target costing implementation differently, there are two factors that tend to influence target costing efforts. These are:

◆   The type of customer

◆   The type of product made or service offered.

Target costing means that enterprises and suppliers need to match activities to customer requirements. This means evaluating products as they relate to customer requirements, and enhancing those factors, but reducing costs in areas that aren't as important to the customer.

This means that customers' needs must be translated into clear statements of work and specifications in order to help identify the right factors. Often in creating product functions that reflect what the customer wants, costs can become too high to hit targets. This means customers and suppliers need to work together to find other areas less important for customer satisfaction and try to reduce those costs. If the process doesn't work the first time around, try again. Sometimes, target costing needs many iterations to carry it through.

Product development cycles also influence target cost. Generally, the longer your product development cycle from the design stage to the production stage, the more difficult it may be to establish firm target costs early on. For instance, if your cycle is up to four years, which is how long it can take in some industries, the target cost you establish may need to be revised over the years.

Some companies with a long product development cycle take the process in incremental steps. They have an allowable cost for each component function, then the total allowable costs of all the functions for making the product are added to arrive at an expected cost of manufacturing the product. It's usually impractical for a company with hundreds of design and production components to evaluate all of them so a representative sample of allowable costs is taken and applied to all components. From these costs comes an updated target cost. Companies with shorter product development cycles may find they can stick to their initial target cost more easily because they are not as susceptible to the changes that time can impose.

Target costing means sharing information across functions. If a company using target costing finds that an engineer needs to look at an alternative design in order to hit the target cost, that engineer will need costing information immediately to stay on track. If engineers have to search for that information themselves, they may give up on the target costing process, figuring they don't have time to spend investigating less expensive design alternatives because they're under a tight deadline. It's up to purchasing and target costing teams to provide the engineer with costing information.

Target costing is not about cutting costs by 15% across the board. Its purpose is to target money where it will have the greatest impact on meeting customer needs and paring back expenses in other areas that are less critical for winning their business.

The advantages of implementing and maintaining an effective target costing system include:

- Determining an expected cost of manufacturing a product or providing a service

- Achieving greater cost efficiencies

- Spending money where it will have the greatest impact

- Identifying customers' real needs

- Matching activities to customers' requirements

- Increasing customer satisfaction

- Giving suppliers and colleagues a better understanding of cost objectives

- Allowing suppliers and colleagues to participate in setting quality, cost and time targets

- Transforming a 'policing' role and image into that of a valued partner working on everyone's behalf

- Becoming more globally competitive.

It may seem obvious to tie the cost of products or services to the needs of your customers. But target costing makes more of a defined effort to achieve this objective than traditional costing methods.

Activity based costing management

Target costing communicates customer needs with activities, but there is another stage in the cost management process, and this involves understanding which types of activities actually link to customer needs and which do not. This inclusion of the entire supply chain network as a task to be managed demands that purchasing staff and management accountants become familiar with the value chain concept in contrast with the internal focus that is typically adopted in management accounting.

Management accounting usually takes a value-added perspective and this fails to recognise the potential for exploiting linkages with the firm's suppliers and customers. Finance staff can become important members of a team which looks at the whole of the value chain.

An important part of value chain analysis is the diagnosis of cost drivers that explain variations in costs in each value activity. The way in which activity based approaches fit into the value chain concept is well illustrated. It is possible to argue that third-generation activity based costing (ABC) systems are used to enhance the enterprise's competitive strategy through value chain analysis.

It is possible to link ABC management to business process re-engineering, learning organisations and strategic cost management. The important point here is the need for a perceptual shift in the nature of internal and external boundaries with work processes becoming more simultaneous and cross-functional.

Activity analysis and re-engineering are important elements in value chain analysis and have implications for information systems within organisations. Like purchasing and supply, accounting is also a growing and developing function. It is, for instance, no longer limited by a lack of capability to deliver accounting information for organisational units in relation to the programmes that spanned them.

Increasingly, it is possible to identify a need for management accountants to introduce horizontal information systems to match the new cross-organisational and cross-functional developments. In many ways the old vertical management structures and information systems, for example divisions as hierarchies, should be turned on their side and replaced with horizontal information systems which are directed horizontally towards the customer. There have been claims within the accounting literature that old style accounting systems are holding organisations back, and limiting their competitive effectiveness. In this view, horizontal systems can bring activity based management systems into life:

> Horizontal systems provide managers with a new framework for measuring the real performance of the business. Strategy, satisfaction, quality, work, innovation and time rarely appear in the accountant's lexicon. But they must now be added.

Increased horizontal integration is typical of many enterprises and, for such organisations, a highly effective cost management programme is a necessity, not a luxury. In addition, the fact that much activity based information may be non-financial needs to be recognised.

Co-destiny relationships

So far we have talked about adversarial and partnership approaches to the management of relationships. Both of these approaches have utilised contracts and negotiation to obtain resources which can be specified. The style or nature of the tactics used will vary on a contract-by-contract basis, but there is another level of approach where desired resources cannot be specified, and where environmental uncertainty means that the risks and benefits cannot be easily quantified as to the skills and competences required. In such cases, there is room for considering what might be called a group of co-destiny approaches.

Types of co-destiny approach

Alliances

Alliances call for a higher level of performance which cannot be specified by a contract. Here the relationship may consist of two or more enterprises, who may decide to partner together on a single product or project. Although alliance partners share goals and information, the relationship is typically limited by the project which has an end point. However, an alliance might be spun off or integrated into a new enterprise. This has happened often in the computer industry.

Cooperation

Cooperation implies a more open-ended relationship. Partners jointly understand certain market requirements and are committed to joint problem solving and joint growth or co-evolution. The partners share information and ideas and commonly coordinate activities for mutual benefit. Intel and Microsoft are a notable example. United Airlines and SAS are another.

Strategic partnership

Strategic partnership is the most mature, valuable and difficult type of these relationships. The partners have a broad understanding of each other's needs and visions and share important values. There is a high level of trust and mutuality with open information sharing, gain sharing and concern for mutual well-being. Because the partnership shares so much, it is adaptable to change and transcends tactical difficulties.

Characteristics of co-destiny approaches

Within the above relational structures, members often state that the relationships between the partner firms are based on trust and co-destiny (that they cooperate because they have some common goals). This is probably true, but is not very helpful for someone trying to start up or manage a relationship. There are still major questions to be answered. How is trust created? What types of partner should be contracted? How do you manage within this relationship? How long should the contract last and what type of contract can be used?

We saw earlier in the study guide, when we looked at the types of exchange within a relationship, that equity acquisition or exchange might be one approach which the purchaser might use. Share ownership and mutual directorates are one way in which Japanese enterprises have achieved co-destiny within their supply networks.

However, as well as ownership mechanisms, co-destiny also relies on 'softer' elements such as culture. Toyota, the automotive maker, for instance, relies heavily on cultural aspects of the relationship, some of which we identified in talking about partnership, and some of which we will look at in more detail.

Co-destiny

Partners in a co-destiny relationship find themselves in a situation in which they are so closely tied that they win together, but also lose together.

Shared vision and shared goals

If no bureaucratic mechanisms for integration exist, an implicit coordination by shared goals and, even better, by a shared vision allows the partners to move in the same direction.

Equity

A co-destiny relationship relies on a specific code of conduct and on a specific professional sense of fairness whereby one party does not feel that it is unfairly controlled or dominated by the other.

Advantages and disadvantages of co-destiny and co-makership approaches

Co-destiny approaches provide many of the same type of advantages and disadvantages as a partnership, but perhaps more intensely. This often means that parties to the relationship can experience the type of cultural problems experienced within enterprises seeking to complete a merger. Co-destiny relationships may often have a huge impact on the people and organisations involved. Many fail to deliver their potential value because the motivation of staff and workplace culture suffers during the integration process.

Implementing co-destiny and co-makership

Although organisations often speak of aiming for a co-destiny culture which is the 'best of both worlds', there is rarely a successful strategy in place to make this happen. Successful management of the integration process requires careful examination of a wide range of issues relating to corporate strategy, industry analysis, finance, accounting and post-integration management.

Integration strategy and value delivery activities are the activities associated with determining the level of integration and establishing exactly how the value from the relationship will be created. These are closely related to the processes of identifying the overall deal logic and determining where the value will be derived.

The strategy for integration needs careful consideration of a range of options from 'absorb' at one end to 'preserve' at the other end. In between lie a multitude of blended options taking the best from both sides. There is no 'one size fits all' solution when it comes to the degree of integration. Companies must determine where along the spectrum from 0 to 100% is most appropriate for the case in question.

In many cases, the purchasing and supply function may well be focused on improving access to and control of the manufacturing facility. There may, however, be other elements which accompany the relationship. For example, where the logic for an acquisition is to obtain a new technology, the core focus will be on integrating the team that has developed the new technology with the acquirer's own R&D team.

In many cases the setting of integration objectives is a process that requires close contact between the two companies and will span the planning and execution phases of integration. This ensures consensus between the two organisations on objectives and early buy-in and leads to more realistic and achievable targets.

Summary

Within commercial activities there is a range of relationship types. This range includes many possible relationships and it is difficult to 'choose' one relationship. Instead, it is possible to create an environment in which certain types of relationship will flourish. Within this it is possible to identify three main approaches which offer a number of advantages and disadvantages. These three approaches are:

◆ Adversarial, short term and transactionally focused

◆ Partnership

◆ Co-destiny.

Each of these relationships requires a range of tools and approaches which range from costing to strategic integration planning.

Self-assessment questions

SAQ 1.2

Identify five types of commercial exchange within relationships.

SAQ 1.3

Identify the approaches to open book costing and some of the drawbacks to its implementation.

Intra-organisational relationships

The syllabus learning outcomes for this subsection state that you will be able to:

◆ Analyse joint ventures, partnerships and other permanent alliances and discuss the 'relationships' aspects of such arrangements

◆ Appraise the cross- and multi-functional aspects of corporate management, and the relationships implications of these ideas.

This subsection will cover:

◆ **Challenges**

◆ **Cross-functional relationships**

◆ **Supporting intra-organisational relationships**

◆ **Policy deployment approaches**

◆ **Objective setting**

◆ **Analysis**

◆ **Development**

◆ **Implementation**

◆ **Cross-functional teams**

◆ **Collaborative technology**

◆ **Communities of practice**

◆ **Service level agreements**

◆ **Training and the intelligent customer**

◆ **Recognising cross-functional working**

◆ **Evaluating intra-organisational relationships.**

We looked in the last section at the external supply and value chain and how these concepts impact upon the nature of the commercial relationships employed. However, for many enterprises, the supply chain begins with the coordination of business activities and processes within the organisation.

Challenges

Traditionally, enterprises have been organised along functional lines. Historically this made perfect sense. By clustering activities together the organisation benefited from minor economies of scale and learning effects as people in accounting or production learned how to solve problems collectively.

Operating externally, the purchasing and SCM department has all the traditional tools available. It can aggregate expenditure, develop contract strategies and negotiate advantageously with suppliers. However, the supply chain does not start at the door of the organisation. Instead it runs through the organisation and across traditional functions. This is often where strategic SCM can face difficulties. The management of interfaces between different functional departments within the business is a critical task in SCM. There are a number of paths which can be employed in managing relationships within the organisation. These are:

◆   Policy development and deployment

◆   Service level agreements

◆   Cross-functional teams

◆   Collaborative working tools

◆   Communities of practice

◆   Training and the intelligent customer.

But, before we go on to consider these, it may be useful to look at why cross-functional relationships are increasingly important within the enterprise and the supply chain.

Cross-functional relationships

It seems odd to say that intra-organisational relationships (relationships within organisations) are something that we need to even think about. Membership of an organisation means that people will work together to a common goal. However, this is often less than true. Cross-functional collaboration, when individuals attempt to integrate their diverse knowledge and experiences into solutions that provide synergy more than the sum of the parts, or add value, is often difficult.

Cross-functional working involves a complex set of factors. These factors have been identified in a range of disciplines including:

- Psychology

- Management

- Social psychology

- Computer science

- Design

- Architecture.

Concepts such as team, group, cohesiveness, group maturity, creativity or decision making cross these boundaries and influence each other in complex ways. Different individuals and groups have diverse, often conflicting, perspectives and insights on the process.

As we have seen, one of the common approaches to organisational design is the bureaucratic organisation in which managers coordinate the work of multiple functional specialists on various tasks which are then integrated into a common whole. Traditionally, the most common attitude used is 'you do your job, and I'll do mine'. An assumption was made that if all the parts are done right, they will fit together into an effective whole.

Of course, there are good reasons for this. A great deal of our civilisation's economic success has come from dividing complex tasks into simpler ones which could be done by less talented people. Adam Smith tells the story of pin making, where dividing the work formerly done by master craftsmen into simple steps done by people with far less training allowed a quantum leap in productivity and profitability.

However, this situation is changing in response to a variety of driving forces. These include the need to control costs in the face of higher levels of competition and increasingly demanding customers. They also include the introduction of new technology such as enterprise resource planning (ERP) systems which, as we have seen, have a major impact on accountability and the elimination of the 'you do your job, and I'll do mine' mindset.

Supporting intra-organisational relationships

Challenges

The success of cross-functional working depends on a range of factors and decisions. The first of these decisions relates to the way in which intra-organisational relationships are supported.

Policy deployment

If the purchasing and supply function chooses to use a purchasing policy, there are a number of challenges. Effort is often spent in introducing and agreeing purchasing policies which are designed to eliminate maverick buying and optimise spend aggregation to deliver best value savings.

As well as being time, and resource, consuming to introduce, these systems can also be very difficult to regulate. The purchasing department may find that much of its time is spent dealing with disparate staff groups who feel that purchasing and supply is trying to erode both their authority and autonomy, and are resisting attempts to ensure that they optimise spend, or even adhere to purchasing policies. In addition, these policies can often become outdated very quickly, which makes the work of the purchasing and supply function even harder.

Of course, this situation is changing as more and more enterprises install electronic procurement systems where spend limits can be preset and all procurement takes place through a desktop buy side system, but principles still apply.

Cross-functional teams

Here the purchasing and supply department might wish to consider the operational stimulus for cross-functional working. Is the process going to be based around and focused on:

◆ Quality?

◆ Customer service?

◆ Innovation in product or service design or delivery?

◆ Cost reduction?

◆ Delivery improvement?

◆ Improvements in product or service flexibility?

The objectives of cross-functional working need to be fairly well defined because these objectives will dictate its operation and structure. It is important to remember that when the team is organised you are asking members to move from a traditional role, which they may of occupied for years, into a new role. If that role is not adequately defined, they will tend to fall back into their old role and the cross-functional team will be a team in name only.

In addition, teams can become just as limiting as departments. Sharing learning across teams involves more than project post-mortem briefings or documenting lessons learned. To convey the depth of people's insights in a way that's valuable to others, learning needs to be an exchange in which people build enough relationship to understand and make sense of each other's ideas.

Collaborative working tools

Where intra-functional relationships are supported by information technology, there are still issues that relate to both structure and information. Project teams, whether temporary or permanent, are increasingly used in many industries to organise and produce work. In spite of the importance and widespread use of such teams, there is often no proven basis for the modelling and sharing of information to support decision making by cross-functional and multi-organisational teams.

By their nature, project teams bring together participants from many disciplines that use discipline-specific information formats, modelling, analysis and visualisation tools for their work. It is a challenge to combine these discipline-specific sets of information and representations to support cross-functional access, interaction and decision making.

However, essentially all decision making by project teams is cross-functional and needs to consider large, disparate data sets. Furthermore, many parties coming together on projects have only a casual working relationship because they are from different disciplines and often also from different organisations. They need, though, at least some access to each other's information, which is typically embedded in discipline-specific legacy applications or paper-based systems which may be robust, but are frequently time-consuming and inflexible.

Little support exists today to share relevant information easily and flexibly because it is difficult to predict who needs to see and work with what information. Today's approaches to exchanging electronic and paper-based project information (e.g., standardised semantic models, software wrappers and electronic or paper-based sharing of visualisation and documents) do not scale to the information interaction challenges of project teams. They can often overwhelm meeting participants with the amount of information that is exchanged or require too much software overhead for project teams whose composition changes frequently, where participants come from many different organisations, and where participants bring many diverse sources of information to a meeting.

Communities of practice

Communities of practice rest upon the idea that individual relationships support group relationships and vice versa. Rather than sharing information from one whole team with another, it links individual team members with people from other teams in networks and communities of practice. Communities of practice can help create the levels of trust and understanding that allow people to share mistakes as well as accomplishments and half-baked ideas as well as brilliant insights. However, such communities are often long-term projects which rely on a stable operating system and long-term relationships within the organisation. They cannot grow in organisations where high staff turnover exists.

Service level agreements

In some cases, where purchasing and supply offer an internal consulting service, there may be a service level agreement (SLA) where a customer and purchasing as a service provider agree about the types of services to be provided and the levels at which those services are to be provided. It is often difficult to give SLAs 'teeth' as internal penalties are insufficient or non-existent.

Training and the intelligent customer

Finally, another method of working internally is to use training in procurement to create 'intelligent customers' who have a range of key procurement competences in sourcing, acquisition or managing contracts.

Implementing cross-functional working

Often within purchasing and supply departments the effort involved in integrating disparate functions and creating a coherent approach to the management of the supply chain leaves little resource for the actual management of supply.

The section below will consider some of the ways in which cross-functional relationships critical to supply chain relationships can be created.

Policy deployment approaches

In carrying out activities, individuals typically follow a set of rules. Tennis players are taught a set of rules allowing them to hit the tennis ball in a fashion which will cause the ball to cross the net landing in the opponents' court. Students follow rules (some formal, others informal) which allow them to score well in their classes. Rules are ubiquitous. They are, to some extent, a vehicle for representing structured knowledge. They can be used for passing on knowledge on how best to carry out some task, function or activity; or what we ought to do or not do; about what ends are worthwhile and what are the best means for achieving them; and so on.

Advantages

Policy has been perhaps the most popular way of coordinating relationships within firms. Many large organisations have extensive purchasing policy procedures which are embodied in guidelines or handbooks that can run into thousands of pages. It is often useful to consider both what function these policy procedures fulfil and how purchasing policy can be best developed.

Policy procedures carry out a number of functions to:

◆ Record and store existing knowledge about what works and what doesn't in purchasing within particular organisations

◆ Create a set of rules to replicate best practice

◆ Ensure that purchasing activity produces best value within an ethical and possibly environmental context.

Disadvantages

As noted above, purchasing policies can become outdated very quickly and it is, therefore, important that such policies are introduced and reviewed effectively. Where purchasing policy is not implemented effectively, the cost of maintaining and policing the policy can be very high.

Implementing policy

There are a number of steps in introducing a purchasing policy within an organisation including:

◆ Objective setting

◆ Analysis

◆ Development

◆ Implementation.

Objective setting

In introducing a purchasing policy it is important that clear objectives are developed at the inception. Without clear objectives the policy will often run into difficulties at a later stage, either in implementation or use. Policy objectives should always be SMART:

S pecific

M easurable

A chievable

R ealistic

T imed.

They should also recognise the fact that purchasing objectives will have a major impact on many other areas of the organisation's activities.

Analysis

The objective of analysis is understanding. The technique involves a series of interactions between examination of the details and overall observation (pattern recognition). Having identified the basic facts related to the issue at hand, the analyst shifts through them to identify the key elements that will lead to a diagnosis of the problem, a clarification of the goal or objective and an understanding of the constraints on any proposed solutions. Analysis usually involves the examination of four interrelated aspects which are:

◆ The current situation

◆ The expressed objective

◆ The perceived options

◆ The barriers to getting there.

To a considerable extent, these aspects are interdependent and subjectively defined. Resolving the problem may involve changes to all four aspects. The current situation could change due to the passage of time or as a result of better information.

The expressed objective may change with greater understanding of the issues. The perceived options could be modified as a result of a better understanding of the current situation or theory. The barriers can be removed, avoided or modified.

Considering policy development analysis of the situation must be as well formulated as possible. This includes consideration of:

The issues

Is the organisation ready for a purchasing policy? What issues are current within the firm or organisation? How are these likely to change? Look at the issues from various perspectives. Ask others what they believe are the most important issues and focus on those most often identified. Try to rank the issues by importance as seen by each of the major parties involved. Be ruthless – limit the number of issues to the essentials. Don't try to solve everything.

The scope of the policy

How far will the policy range and what will it affect? Purchasing policy issues rarely exist in isolation. What may appear as one issue, tends to be part of a constellation of issues. Action on this issue may be seen as a precedent for others or may lead to a string of decisions on related issues. Policy proposals without powerful backers are usually more successful if they are related to general issues or positions for which there is strong public support or hooked onto another proposal with strong backers. It is therefore important to analyse the policy issue in its relationship to other policies and positions.

The parties involved

Who are they? What are their fundamental interests? What is their history within the organisation? How do they make decisions? What are their previous dealings with the purchasing department? Does the issue affect one or more groups in the organisation in a different manner? Are there differences in the impact on women and men? Document how different groups would be affected by the current problem and the proposed solutions.

The relationships between the parties

Identify the relationships between the parties. Are they good, bad or distant? How will this policy issue affect the relationships? What kind of relationships do the parties want in the future? Which parties are allies and which are enemies?

The people

Decisions are taken by individuals. Most organisations have a limited number of people who make the final decision with respect to policy. You need to identify the key individuals related to the policy issue at hand. What do they think about the issue? What is their background and experience? What are the relationships between the key players? Identify how the individuals involved are likely to affect the way the issue is seen or decided.

The interests

These are the more fundamental desires of individual groups or organisations that give rise to the positions they are taking. Try to look behind the positions that the major parties may have expressed about the policy question and try to identify their fundamental interests. Analyse the interests of the various parties to see what there is in common.

The timing

Analyse the time frames that are relevant to the policy question at hand. Issues around timing can be as important as the substance itself. Note when a decision is needed. When do we need to effect a new policy? Are there any deadlines that are relevant? What are the major events or milestones that can affect the proposals to deal with this policy question? Are there external events that will affect this issue? Is the issue a crisis or an anticipated crisis? Are we dealing with a current problem or a problem that is likely to arise unless some changes are made? Timing may be more important to some parties than others.

Hidden agendas

Policy development can be based on a host of theoretical assumptions that are never stated. It is a good rule for the implementation team or group to be explicit about the major theoretical assumptions that are being made in the analysis. Try to identify the most important theories that are relevant to the issue at hand and then check to see what the latest academic research has to say about them. Are they still valid? Being explicit about the theoretical underpinnings of the policy will sharpen the examination of cause and effect relationships between the factors at play. It will also help avoid the trap of basing analysis solely on the 'current wisdom'.

Organisational climate

In some organisations the general opinion held by staff is a key factor in any policy decision even though senior managers are often prepared to take decisions that the 'majority' does not support. Policy is not created in isolation, consequently different groups should be extensively consulted throughout the whole process of policy development and implementation.

Costs

Document the quantifiable costs and benefits relevant to this policy and flag potential costs that can't be quantified. Who will have to pay and how much? Is there a source of funding for proposed incremental costs? What is the time frame for the required expenditures? Are there opportunities to recover the costs from users? Determine whether there are costs that will be imposed on others because of the policy decision. Are these direct or indirect?

Development

Having subjected the issue to such an exhausting analysis, the purchasing policy maker may feel that the job is done. However, it is only half over. Analysis and diagnosis should lead to alternative options that could address the expressed objectives of the purchasing and supply function. The options should be a set of realistic choices. In developing options, it may be helpful to consider three types of option:

1.   Paradigm shifts.

2.   Conventional substantive options.

3.   Process options.

Paradigm shifts

Paradigm shifts refer to a change in perspective. Often these changes may be radical. In such circumstances purchasing may wish to consider a range of very different ways to deal with the current problem which may result in innovative and unconventional, but realistic options. Even if no 'paradigm shift' options emerge at the end of the process, trying to develop them may help to develop more effective conventional approaches.

In pursuing 'paradigm shift' options, the purchaser may wish to start with technological training or even theoretical considerations. Is there any way of achieving objectives that would lead to radically different solutions? Could any of the operational parameters be altered that would change the nature of the problem dramatically?

Conventional options

The purchaser could attempt to create a set of possible optional approaches that could satisfactorily resolve the problem or reach the intended objective. At the initial stage of option generations it may be helpful to 'brainstorm' or list all the possible approaches without critically evaluating the choices. Try to develop broad ideas about what could be done. Focus on being creative. Try to develop options from the position of each of the major players or affected departments. Try to collect proposals that have been put forward in the past. Are any still relevant?

Having developed a wide range of options to begin with, try to narrow the choice. Group the ideas into categories to help you understand and compare them. Identify the major differences between these choices.

Process options

Frequently, the issue at hand cannot be resolved without further research consultation or public attention. At times, the impact of other issues (e.g., market shifts, mergers and acquisitions or expansion) may preclude senior management from taking a decision. In these situations, the purchaser may wish to identify process options. These can range from consultancy projects to informal discussions among the principal parties. There may be a need for significant research and fact finding. Often enough, the basic facts are not available and a considerable amount of work will be needed before any substantive decision can be taken. In other cases, purchasing and senior management may want to identify a preferred option, but only proceed if there is substantial support indicated through consultation, for example the 'white paper approach'.

Implementation

The implementation of purchasing policy will vary from organisation to organisation, so there are no fixed rules. Generally speaking, as well as consultation in developing a policy, there also needs to be a considerable amount of training and consultation during the implementation process.

Consultation

Consultation should:

◆ Inform robust and practical policy advice to policy and decision makers

◆ Inform stakeholders as part of an ongoing relationship with them.

Consultation involves actively seeking information or views before making a recommendation or decision. It normally involves providing information about a particular issue or proposal to stakeholders, and gathering their input or feedback. The information circulated often includes options or proposals that are being considered.

The background information that the purchasing department communicates in a consultation process advises interested parties of what is under consideration, how an issue is being defined by policy or decision makers (the intellectual or philosophical framework), and even which issues are considered high priority by policy or decision makers. Stakeholders may wish to have input at this level of issue definition in addition to any questions posed by policy or decision makers on a specific, narrower issue.

In order to work effectively consultation must:

◆ Be genuine – it must inform a decision not yet made

◆ Adequately inform the parties of relevant information upon which the proposal is based

◆ Allow sufficient time for those parties to respond.

Policy or decision makers must:

◆ Consider the responses received with an open mind, without predetermination.

Training

Training should:

◆ Explain why the policy is being implemented and the benefits it brings to the organisation and the individual departments or groups

◆ Explain how the policy works and the part which different departments and groups have to play in making it work so as to maximise ownership of the policy.

Training may include coaching in using the policy guidelines but, in order to be effective, should emphasise the role of non-purchasing staff in the process. In some organisations it may be difficult to implement a coordinated purchasing policy, or the need for such a policy may have been overtaken by new technology. In other cases, policy may not in itself be enough to coordinate activities across functional departments. In such cases, one of the possible paths to the development of intra-firm relationships is the use of cross-functional teams.

Cross-functional teams

Cross-functional teams can make it much easier to coordinate activities and information. Where such teams share the same physical location, team members can informally stop by and discuss the timing of key aspects of a project, the interpretation of results or the logic behind a conclusion. Team members can immediately communicate information they used to have to wait for team meetings to share.

But they also lose some of the advantages of functional organisation. When team members are located with other specialists in a particular field, they can discuss a whole range of discipline-specific issues, which can be difficult to achieve in cross-functional working.

Team working

In many enterprises, teams are the building blocks of the organisation. In manufacturing, teams of multi-skilled operators may build a whole product or major subassemblies of a product. In new product development, people from sales, marketing, research, engineering and manufacturing team up to design products and bring them to market quickly and cheaply. In professional service firms, accountants, tax specialists and risk analysts may team up to provide a full range of services to a client. In oil exploration, teams of geologists, geophysicists, reservoir engineers, petro-physicists and other disciplines team up to find and assess the potential value of an oil prospect.

A team can be defined as a group of people with a common goal, interdependent work and joint accountability for results. In team-based enterprises, teams are composed of people from different professions or jobs so that all the knowledge and skill needed to manage a complete process to completion is represented. They are frequently responsible for producing key products or services. Their business directives, common goals and joint accountability tie them together into a cohesive unit. They may be located in the same place and report to the same manager.

Advantages

There are a number of advantages to team working. Because they are located together and share common goals, team members easily share the information and thinking that fell in the 'white space' between traditional functional 'silos'. Teams improve focus. Cross-functional teams can focus on a single output and the connected processes. This may be a major subassembly in the production of a car or the management of a merger between two multinational corporations. This focus can help teams develop a real sense of common purpose and focus. By working together in close proximity over an extended period, they can develop a rhythm, a rapport and a common identity. This, in turn, leads to higher levels of trust which vastly improves their ability to build on each other's ideas and solve business and technical problems.

Teams can be excellent vehicles for learning. To learn effectively, people need both time to reflect and a safe environment. They need time to think about their experience and its implications and incorporate new insights into their current mental models. They need safety to explore new ideas and challenge their own assumptions. Within the trust and rapport created in a team, people can feel safe enough to share their thinking, the reasons behind their conclusions, the questions they have about their conclusions and even their half-baked ideas. When they take time to collectively reflect on their experience, they can build on each other's ideas and deepen the richness of their thinking and insights.

Disadvantages

All of the above rests upon proper team selection and effective team leadership. However, in some cases this cannot take place, for instance, where expertise within a team is required but the people involved are unable to work together.

Teams can also become new 'silos'. People in team-based enterprises often complain that they have trouble getting information from other teams. They find out too late or not at all about work done by people in their own discipline who are assigned to other teams. They reinvent tools, analyses or approaches developed by their peers on other teams. They waste time searching for information they know is held by one of their colleagues. The very thing that makes teams work well – common goals, shared focus, physical proximity and working rapport – can easily lead to two related learning disabilities: isolation and team myopia.

Teams can get isolated. Team members naturally focus inward, concentrating on team goals and connecting with fellow team members. When Pepsi Co expanded internationally, teams charged with building the business in Eastern Europe, Russia, the Middle East and the Pacific Rim had no planned way to share experiences, insights and ideas with teams working in other regions. The result was that every single team started anew, repeating the same mistakes and following the same blind alleys already explored by their predecessors. This sort of isolation is common for cross-functional teams. Even when team members fully intend to share insight and information with other teams, team goals often pull so strongly on people's time, that they simply cannot find the time to do so.

Isolation can lead to team myopia. When teams have very little contact with other teams or are isolated for extended periods, they can get into the habit of rejecting ideas from outside and lose their ability to generate new ideas, that is, they can become myopic. Research in creative thinking has long shown that new ideas usually come from the intersection of disciplines, perspectives or ways of thinking. Scientists often do their most creative work a few years after they changed fields. Small enterprises working at the edge of a field often develop new technologies. Teams' most creative ideas often come when they see how people in other enterprises or industries perform similar processes. When teams lose touch with other teams, they often get into a rut of using the same approaches, tools and ideas repeatedly. This can be particularly hard for technical specialists on cross-functional teams. When they lose touch with colleagues from their own discipline, they have trouble keeping up with developments in their field.

These are often symptoms of what has been called 'groupthink' and include:

◆ Overestimation of the group where the team members believe that the team can do no wrong

◆ Closed mindedness where the team refuse to listen to new ideas

◆ Rationalisation where failure is blamed on factors outside the team

◆ Self-censorship as people refuse to say anything that will disturb the team image of itself.

Teams can also easily neglect long-term capacity building. Most organisations need to balance the tension between short-term production goals and long-term capacity building. On an organisational level, this is the tension between production and product development. On an individual level, it is the tension between focusing on current projects and taking the time to develop and share knowledge. Because teams are typically tasked with output goals (producing a product or service) they tend to pull people toward the production side of this tension. They tend not to see the value of building capacity beyond their team. Frequently, they even have trouble preparing their members for the next generation of technical development.

Implementing team working

There are a number of models and approaches in implementing cross-disciplinary team building. These rest upon effective selection, an understanding of group processes, effective leadership, team membership and support. Skills which might be used to manage and work within effective cross-functional teams include:

Managing a team

◆ **Recruitment and selection:** ensuring that the right blend of personalities and skills are selected; making sure that the recruitment process makes team members value the team

◆ **Management of conflict:** understanding the uses of conflict; separating issues from people; understanding feelings and positions; using the right approach

◆ **Leadership:** setting goals and standards; understanding processes; creating vision; communicating effectively

◆ **Development:** helping the team grow and develop.

Working as part of a team

♦   **Initiating:** proposing tasks, goals, or actions; defining team problems; suggesting procedures

♦   **Information sharing:** offering facts; giving expression of feelings; giving opinions

♦   **Information seeking:** asking for factual clarification; requesting facts pertinent to the discussion or activity

♦   **Opinion seeking:** asking for clarification of the values pertinent to the topic under discussion; questioning benefits involved in the alternative suggestions

♦   **Clarifying:** interpreting ideas or suggestions; defining terms; clarifying issues before the team; clearing up confusion

♦   **Orienting:** defining the position of the team with respect to its goals; pointing to departures from agreed-on directions or goals; raising questions about the directions pursued in team discussions

♦   **Summarising:** pulling together related ideas; restating suggestions; offering decisions or conclusions for the team to consider

♦   **Reality testing:** making critical analyses of ideas; testing ideas against data to see whether the ideas would be likely to work

♦   **Participating:** taking responsibility within the team; considering the ideas of others; serving as an audience in team discussion and decision making

♦   **Gatekeeping:** helping to keep communication channels open; facilitating the participation of others; suggesting procedures that support sharing information

♦   **Harmonising:** attempting to reconcile disagreements; reducing tension; getting people to explore differences

♦   **Compromising:** offering compromises that yield status when his or her own ideas are involved in conflicts; modifying in the interest of team cohesion or growth

♦   **Encouraging:** being friendly, warm and responsive to others; indicating by body language or remarks the acceptance of others' contributions

♦   **Consensus testing:** asking to see whether the team is nearing a decision; sending up 'trial balloons' to test possible solutions

♦   **Standard setting:** expressing standards for the team to attempt to achieve; applying standards in evaluating the quality of team processes.

Collaborative technology

We have seen that cross-functional teams may be located in the same physical location or 'co-located'. However, increasingly teams may be located at very different geographical points and may sometimes work many thousands of miles from each other. In some multinational companies central purchasing may be based in one country, while each factory has a local purchasing unit. Coordination between these units, and production, distribution and finance requires more than just an enterprise resource planning (ERP) system. It requires a range of computerised collaborative working systems (CCWSs).

The world of CCWS is often described in terms of the time and space in which a collaborative activity occurs. Collaboration can be between people in the same place (co-located) or different places (remote). Collaboration can be at the same time (synchronous) or separated in time (asynchronous).

The technology currently being used includes:

- Video teleconferencing

- Data sharing

- Document sharing

- Shared whiteboards

- Chat

- Instant messaging

- Online presence (for example, ICQ, Ding)

- Bulletin boards

- Threaded news and discussion group systems

- E-mail

- Mailing lists

- Voting/polling

- Virtual communities

- Virtual reality.

Implementing collaborative technology

When trying to build computer systems that will help people to work together more productively, we have to take into account a number of factors. These can be expressed by the following questions:

◆ What exactly is it that people do?

◆ Which activities can computers do for people?

◆ Which activities can computers help people do more effectively?

◆ Which new activities does the new technology allow people to do?

◆ How can we introduce new systems and ways of working without disrupting existing successful operations?

This is known as the socio-technical design challenge. It involves determining what should be built not merely by reference to what is technically possible, but what would be useful to the organisation and acceptable to the organisation. Collaborative work is by its very nature 'social'. It requires issues about the way in which people interact to be taken into account. Any collaborative working system that flouts social rules, norms or customs, even if it does useful things, may fail to be used.

The key to selecting or developing successful collaborative systems appears to involve an understanding of what is currently done, and designing systems that not only can mesh with that way of working, but can adapt gracefully as people change their way of working over time. One important lesson that has been learned from CCWSs implementation is to pay close attention to the distribution of costs and benefits resulting from a change in work practice. Although a new system may be beneficial for an organisation as a whole it can still fail. If the new system imposes extra work for many people in order to benefit others, there will be a natural reluctance to use it.

Sometimes this can be overcome if management determine that it is a requirement to use the system, but even so, it is sometimes possible for workers to sabotage such a disliked system by blaming it for all the inevitable problems that arise. If the system can be designed so that everyone using it benefits somewhat (by its improving their work problems), then acceptance and adoption will be far more likely to be successful.

Another approach to the introduction of new technology is to acknowledge that humans and computers are suited to different types of activity. Computers are good at laborious, repetitive and memory-intensive tasks; humans are good at creative, interpersonal things and tasks requiring broad knowledge, common sense and judgement. We believe that the most productive applications of computers in libraries will occur when computers do the boring jobs leaving the humans to concentrate on other tasks. This approach suggests that we should be aiming for supportive software rather than trying to replace humans with a computerised 'intelligent expert'.

Communities of practice

Some enterprises are trying forge cross-functional relationships in a way that blends policy, teams and computer-supported working. One way in which this can be carried out is through the development of communities of practice (COPs). Each COP focuses on a topic or discipline important to the organisation.

They are responsible for sharing knowledge and standardising practices. This approach links the organisation in two ways. Cross-functional teams focus on outputs, typical products, major processes or market segments. COPs focus on learning within functions or disciplines, sharing information and insights, collaborating on common problems and stimulating new ideas. Communities of practice are a way to preserve a discipline or technical focus, while cross-functional teams unite disciplines around common products. Teams weave the organisation together in one direction. Communities weave it together in the other.

A community of practice is a group that shares knowledge, learns together and creates common practices. Communities of practice share information, insights, experience and tools about an area of common interest. This could be:

◆ A professional discipline such as production engineering

◆ A skill such as machine repair

◆ A topic such as a technology, an industry or a segment of a production process.

Consulting enterprises, for example, usually organise communities of practice around both disciplines, such as organisational change and industries like banking, petroleum or insurance.

Implementing COPs

Unlike teams, communities of practice rarely have a specific result to deliver to the organisation. They are typically driven by the value they provide to individual members. Individuals share information and insights and discover ideas which will save them money, time, energy and effort. The value individuals derive from the community is typically what keeps community members involved. While a team delivers value in the result it produces; a community discovers value in many day-to-day exchanges of knowledge and information.

Starting and supporting communities of practice is very different from team building. Since communities of practice are organised around knowledge, not outputs, traditional team-building activities of setting goals, dividing tasks and developing workplans are not appropriate. Starting and supporting communities of practice follows a different set of guidelines:

◆ **Building communities around a few important topics:** organisations frequently cast 'too wide a net' when initiating knowledge management approaches and end up building stockpiles of underutilised information – information junkyards. To leverage knowledge effectively, start with a few communities of practice focused on topics important to the organisation. Focusing on strategically important topics will make it considerably easier to expand beyond the original communities

◆ **Finding and building on natural networks:** whether the organisation supports them or not, communities of practice arise naturally in most organisations. So don't create new communities. Once you have identified an important topic to form communities around, find the networks of people who already share knowledge about that topic. They are likely the seed of your community

◆ **Developing community coordinators and core groups:** a key success factor for intentional communities is to have a coordinator who organises and maintains the community. This coordinator is usually a well-respected, and well-connected community member. The coordinator invites people to participate, links people together, finds exciting topics for the community to address, connects outside the community and generally keeps the community vibrant. Coordinators usually rely on a core group of community members to contribute

◆ **Initiating some simple knowledge-sharing activities:** since intentional communities of practice are a new approach to organisational structure, they are difficult for people to really understand. Nothing conveys what they are about better than the experience of sharing insights in a regular forum, supported by a coordinator and/or facilitator. Rather than explaining or extensively designing communities of practice, engage people in participating in them by starting a few in your organisation

◆ **Supporting communities:** if the organisation values learning and sharing knowledge, it will provide a rich ground for growing communities of practice. But that means managers need to give people the time and encouragement to reflect, share ideas with other teams and think through the implications of other teams' ideas

◆ **Creating a community support team:** because they are organised and supported differently from teams, community development requires a different set of tools and approaches. Form a team to find, practise and use these new development tools

◆ **Being patient:** communities of practice often take time to develop. One of the most successful communities at Shell started as a group of six to eight people meeting weekly to discuss cutting-edge issues. It took six months for word to spread of the value of these discussions. Then attendance at the weekly meetings grew to about 40 people. Because they are organic, communities of practice need time to find the right kind of information to share the right level of detail, the right participants and the right forums. Support of the community in making these discoveries is needed quickly. But since this the information, level of detail, participants and right forums will be different for different communities, they will need to make these discoveries on their own.

Service level agreements

In the former examples of tools and approaches that can be used to manage internal relationships, we have looked at the way in which policies, cross-functional working, collaborative technology and COPs can be used to bring about improvements in those relationships. There is another way of improving internal relationships which can involve changes in the purchasing and supply function itself. This involves the use of internal service level agreements (SLAs).

SLAs allow internal customers to state their service level needs clearly and unambiguously. In turn, suppliers are enabled to focus their resources into providing services at the required level. Key performance indicators (KPIs) measure the quality of the service provision to allow for remedial action where necessary.

Where services, over time, are not delivered to expected levels of quality and efficiency, two courses of action can be taken. Either the service capacity can be increased (often accompanied by a cost increase), or the customer's expectation as to the level of service can be decreased. This decision should be taken transparently so that both customer and supplier are aware of new expectations and/or service targets. Any additional costs would also have to be negotiated.

The starting point

Although an SLA is an excellent expectations-managing mechanism, it's important to recognise its limitations. In some cases an SLA can be used as a way of stifling complaints or quick fix for a problematic relationship. Using it for such purposes creates more problems than it solves. Instead, purchasing should think of an SLA as:

◆ **A communications tool:** the value of an agreement is not just in the final product; the very process of establishing an SLA helps to open up communications

◆ **A conflict-management tool:** an agreement helps to avoid or alleviate disputes by providing a shared understanding of needs and priorities. If conflicts do occur, they tend to be resolved more readily and with less gnashing of teeth

◆ **A framework for review:** this is one of its most important benefits. The agreement isn't a dead-end document consigned to the 'forget forever' file. On a predetermined frequency, the parties to the SLA review the agreement to assess service adequacy and negotiate adjustments

◆ **An agreed basis for evaluating service effectiveness:** an SLA ensures that both parties use the same criteria to evaluate service quality.

To be effective, a service level agreement must incorporate two sets of elements:

◆ Service elements

◆ Management elements.

Service elements

The service elements clarify services by communicating such things as:

◆ The services provided (and perhaps certain services not provided, if customers might reasonably assume the availability of such services)

◆ Conditions of service availability

◆ Service standards, such as the time frames within which services will be provided

◆ The responsibilities of both parties

◆ Cost vs service trade-offs

◆ Escalation procedures.

Management elements

The management elements focus on such things as:

◆   How service effectiveness will be tracked

◆   How information about service effectiveness will be reported and addressed

◆   How service-related disagreements will be resolved

◆   How the parties will review and revise the agreement.

Strengths of SLAs

An SLA can significantly improve the ability of purchasing to manage the expectations of internal customers. They can also help to establish service standards and to document and communicate them. In this sense, a service level agreement can be an extremely effective communications tool for creating a common understanding between two parties regarding services, expectations, responsibilities and priorities.

Indeed, the process of SLA development can be incredibly useful. The process of information gathering, analysing, documenting, educating, negotiating and consensus building can, in some cases, do away with the need for an SLA altogether.

Weaknesses of SLAs

Many people complain that SLAs have no 'teeth'. Penalties are difficult to identify and implement. The development of SLAs is also time-consuming. Often SLAs are introduced after a relationship has begun to fail and there is little time or patience for a proper introduction process.

Service providers sometimes want to create an SLA to suppress customer complaints. However, attempting to establish an SLA with complaining customers usually backfires because customers will see it as just one more thing to complain about. Before engaging in SLA efforts, the service provider should obtain customer feedback. Dissatisfied customers may hope to use an SLA as a sledgehammer with which to bludgeon the service provider whenever service slips.

There is no point in establishing an SLA when something less complex will suffice. For example, in many companies the division of roles and responsibilities between offices or departments is vague at best. Because achieving clarity about services, functions and responsibilities is essential to SLA success, it is a worthwhile starting point even if a full-blown SLA is not ultimately needed. If clarity solves the immediate problem, investing the additional effort to develop an SLA may be unnecessary.

SLAs are often initiated and unilaterally established by service providers. The customer is given little or no say about either the content of the SLA or the process by which it is established or managed. This is the wrong way to be successful with an SLA. Very simply, if the two parties have not agreed, it's not an agreement and it shouldn't be called an agreement. The resulting document may still serve a useful purpose, but it's not an agreement.

The very essence of an SLA is that both parties have a say. In practice, it is rarely practical or feasible for both parties to be involved in every step of creating the agreement. However, a successful SLA is one in which the two parties collaborate. When the process is truly collaborative, the resulting document can be filed away and largely ignored because the two parties have already succeeded in learning how to work together. That's the right way.

Key steps in establishing a service level agreement

A service level agreement is an excellent tool for helping two parties improve communications, manage expectations, clarify responsibilities and build the foundation for a win-win relationship. However, establishing an agreement is neither a quick nor a simple process and may include a number of stages:

Gathering background information

Both the internal customer and the service provider need to start by gathering information which offers a basis from which to negotiate. Before eliciting commitments from their service provider, customers should carefully review and clarify their service needs and priorities. Before making any commitments to customers, service providers should examine their service history and determine the level of service they can provide realistically. In addition, service providers should assess customer satisfaction so as to clearly understand customer concerns and establish a baseline for assessing service improvements.

Ensuring agreement about the agreement

The two parties often have different views about the role of the SLA and what it can realistically accomplish. Both sets of views may be valid yet sufficiently different as to cause a breakdown in negotiations. Before any SLA development work is done, it is advisable for the two parties to hold an open discussion to ensure that they have a basic level of agreement about the role of the SLA. If they don't, they may not be able to reach any usable, or successful, agreement.

Establishing ground rules for working together

In this critical, but often overlooked, step the SLA developers (those assigned to negotiate the SLA) focus not on the agreement, but on the process by which they will work together to create the agreement. Issues to be discussed include the division of responsibility for development tasks, scheduling issues and constraints and concerns regarding potential conflict.

Developing the agreement

As noted the actual process of developing the SLA is often more important than the SLA itself. Here, parties concerned may create a framework SLA document and then, over time, reach agreement about its contents. In doing so, they may each solicit assistance, input or feedback from others in their own department. This step may take some time depending on previous experience, the demands of parties, other responsibilities and the state of the relationship between the two departments.

Generating buy-in

The result of the previous is a draft agreement. Before implementing an SLA, all members of both parties who have a stake in, or responsibility for, the success of the agreement should have an opportunity to review the draft, raise questions and offer suggestions. Using this feedback, the developers can conduct further negotiations, gain the necessary approvals and finalise the agreement.

Completing pre-implementation tasks

This step includes the identification and completion of tasks that must precede SLA implementation. These might include:

◆ Developing tracking mechanisms

◆ Establishing reporting lines

◆ Developing responsibility charts

◆ Communicating service user expectations to staff

◆ Providing training.

Implementing and managing the agreement

An agreement that is not managed dies upon implementation. This is true of both contracts and SLAs. Management within an SLA may include providing a communication channel for problems related to the agreement, maintaining ongoing contact with the other party, conducting service reviews, coordinating and implementing modifications to the SLA and assessing and reporting on how the parties involved can develop their working relationship.

Training and the intelligent customer

There is a school of thought which suggests that procurement skills, as a core competence, should be shared across the whole organisation. This leads to the concept of the 'intelligent customer'. The characteristics of an intelligent customer will shift from organisation to organisation and industry to industry, but involve the development of a corporate viewpoint and an understanding of the nature of the marketplace and organisation as well as specific procurement competences such as:

♦ Sourcing skills and knowledge

♦ Specification development skills

♦ An understanding of the tendering process

♦ Supplier assessment and selection skills

♦ Negotiation skills

♦ Contract drafting and management skills.

Adopting the objective of creating an intelligent customer standard is a laudable and useful one. It offers the advantages of improving transparency in the procurement process and shares vital knowledge, taking pressure off purchasing and supply departments. The disadvantages are the loss of specialist knowledge and the fact that procurement may lie with staff who are increasingly multi-tasking, and do not have the time required to create and manage large-scale, high-risk contracts

Recognising cross-functional working

There are a number of ways of recognising an integrated, coordinated commitment to cross-functional working. Coherence is a word that pertains to arguments and means both internally consistent and easy to follow. Organisations now need to operate in a coherent way. Operating in this way, as opposed to a fragmented way means that:

♦ Customer needs and requirements are clearly understood in every corner of the organisation

♦ Work is viewed in terms of the whole of a business process, not merely as one department passing work from it to another department

♦ Business processes are clearly linked to customer critical outcomes

♦ Work groups with employees from several different functional areas take responsibility for making sure that all business processes are coordinated, and serve the customer and the enterprise

- Information is shared between work teams and functional departments

- Technology supports information sharing

- Policy and procedure changes are made only after consulting other functional groups to assess unexpected impacts on customers

- Problems that arise are viewed as opportunities to improve the process of serving customers; there is less of a culture of blame, which may be replaced by collaborative working.

Evaluating intra-organisational relationships

Cross-functional teams, collaborative working and communities of practice are all ways of improving intra-organisational relationships. Just as we might seek to improve the quality of our relationship with a supplier, we might also seek to improve the quality of our relationship with groups and departments within the enterprise.

However, in the same ways as the tools and methods that we choose to improve our relationships with suppliers need to be cost-effective, so do the tools and methods that we choose for intra-organisational relationships. This means subjecting all these methods to evaluation. Of course, the way in which we evaluate internal relationships may be different to the way in which we evaluate external relationships.

The criteria that we use to evaluate internal relationships will always contain some factors that are specific to the issue at hand. These may include asking questions such as:

- What is our primary objective? What is the key interest that we are trying to satisfy most?

- What is the absolute minimum that must be achieved?

- What are the desirable, but not essential aspects, that we want to satisfy?

- What are the key things to avoid?

- What are the consequences of continuing with the status quo, or doing nothing?

In working with internal stakeholders there are five general criteria that are usually helpful in determining the likely success or failure of a particular option. These are:

- Legitimacy
- Communication

- Feasibility
- Support.

- Affordability

Legitimacy

Options for developing intra-organisational relationships will be explicitly, or implicitly, examined for their legitimacy by the key players involved. Legitimacy can be measured against a range of factors, including conventional knowledge – the way we do things around here or opinion. Being able to support a particular option with an objective standard or an expert opinion can be important.

Feasibility

The feasibility of various options is frequently not intuitively clear. Feasibility is affected by technology, demographic and geographic factors and organisational and administrative considerations. Feasibility changes over time, and is affected by factors within government, by the general technology in society and by the attitudes and behaviour of staff within the organisation. Feasibility issues include:

◆ Is the proposed option feasible from a technical, organisational and administrative perspective? Is the proposal supported by the current theoretical and technical knowledge? Is it feasible with the financial and human resources that we have? If not, can they be acquired?

◆ What is the time frame required to implement the option? Is it consistent with the 'political' requirements?

◆ Will staff willingly cooperate in the implementation of the policy or programme?

◆ Can we force action on unwilling participants?

Affordability

At the heart of most choices is money. How much will it cost? Who will pay for it? Will the benefits outweigh the costs? These are essential issues that must be addressed in an analysis of the various options.

Communication

A large part of relationships is about communication: listening to what staff are saying and effectively communicating senior managements' policies and intentions. The key question is 'should a particular option be communicated by the department, by senior management or by external consultants to staff and other key stakeholders in particular?'

In assessing the 'communicability' of various options, the analyst should address these questions:

◆   Can we reasonably explain the policy choice to the major parties and the public?

◆   Will the proposed approach appear fair and reasonable?

◆   Could the department realistically defend the decision before colleagues, staff and other stakeholders?

◆   Is the proposal consistent with the principal policy positions of the enterprise in general and the department in particular?

◆   Will staff opinion be negative or supportive of the proposal?

◆   Will the proposal be linked to some other events or messages?

Support

Actions to develop internal relationships should be assessed on the basis of both the particular support they have and on their impact on the overall support of the government. Support and opposition needs to be analysed in relation to the likely reaction of certain groups and individuals and the reaction of the general public. Some issues attract the specific focus of well-organised interest groups who will actively demonstrate their support or opposition while other issues have a more diffuse impact and generate a less intense reaction from a large number.

Using criteria specific to the type of issue at hand and the general criteria of legitimacy, feasibility, affordability, communication and support, the purchaser should assess the likely options. Ranking of the options could be set out in summary fashion for each of the criteria. The assessment of a number of people is usually helpful. The process is never cut and dried nor completely objective. The purchaser will have to rely on experience and judgement in applying the criteria to the options. The importance or weight of a particular criteria will vary from case to case. In some cases, one criteria will dominate all others. In others, they will be evenly balanced.

Real value from the exercise will come from being bold. Don't try to downplay the negative assessment of an option against one or other of the criteria just because it is favoured by a powerful group. Be rigorous and try to be dispassionate.

Summary

Internal/intra-organisational relationships, although not strictly speaking commercial, can have a major impact on the way in which the supply chain works and the roles of the purchasing functions within that process. Overall, it is possible to identify a group of approaches to develop intra-organisational relationships. These include:

◆   Purchasing policy development and implementation

◆   Service level agreements

◆   Cross-functional team working

◆   Collaborative technology

◆   Communities of practice.

Each of these methods has advantages and disadvantages. Any approach should be evaluated carefully to ensure that it is the best option. In order to successfully work within the organisation, purchasing may often employ different combinations of these approaches to ensure that good working relationships support the value chain.

Self-assessment question

SAQ 1.4

Identify some of the functions of a purchasing policy.

Relationship issues in public procurement

The syllabus learning outcome for this subsection states that you will be able to:

◆ **Analyse relationships in the context of public procurement.**

This subsection will cover:

◆ **Introduction**

◆ **Responding to relationship challenges in public procurement**

◆ **The procurement life cycle in the public sector**

◆ **Procurement integration roles.**

Introduction

Impact of public sector purchasing

In the European Union the purchases of goods and of services by public authorities and bodies represent about 14% of gross domestic product (GDP). As we can see from these figures, public sector purchasing is a critical function that impacts on many different elements of society.

First among these are the buyers and buying entities within a public sector organisation who have responsibility to perform designated missions for the agency they represent and which require material and service support (for example, highways, social services, environment, leisure, education, finance or health). Within the public sector, these buying entities – whether they are subdivisions of the whole organisation or project-based operations – sometimes have a great deal of autonomy, which can present problems for purchasing coordination.

Then there is the business community of actual or potential suppliers to the public sector. Increasingly, we are seeing this group come to the fore in procurement planning, as some public sector organisations attempt to use procurement as a tool for economic development (see below for other public sector procurement objectives). Central government and the Scottish Executive also form a group with an interest in procurement with responsibility for ensuring best value in deploying these expenditures.

There are also academic, training and public interest groups, which have important views in how public sector institutions are to perform. The largest interest group is the general public, who represent a powerful, if largely unaware, constituency. We might expect this group to show satisfaction when they know that expenditures are being made through a procurement system which is performing in an economical, rational and fair manner.

Drivers of public sector purchasing

Because of the wider responsibilities of the public sector, we can also suggest that the nature of relationships is more sensitive. As a consequence, there is, in some ways, more scrutiny of purchasing in the public sector, with sometimes a wider set of goals and constraints.

Some of the contexts – and therefore key drivers – that have impacted on public sector purchasing in the United Kingdom over the past few years have included:

The modernising agenda

This ranges from the recommendation of the Byatt Report in local government, which strongly suggested that improving value for money in providing local authority services is to modernise the whole procurement process. This modernisation may include factors that range from the way in which elected members perceive and 'own' the purchasing function, through to the improvement and definition of the business processes underpinning purchasing.

The need for accountability

This ranges from the effects of the EU procurement directives in promoting transparency and equity in the supplier selection process, through to the introduction of more project-based purchasing and tools, such as the Office of Government Commerce's 'gateway process', which structures and opens to scrutiny the purchasing decision-making process in large project procurement, such as 'public finance initiatives' (PFIs) and 'public/private partnerships' (PPPs). In addition, we can also identify here the need for effective performance measurement to facilitate transparency.

The need for flexibility

As in the private sector, increasingly, organisations are being asked to 'do more with less'. This places more pressure on the supply chain, and also upon purchasing functions, as more complex partnering and purchasing arrangements come into being. These may include some of the PFI/PPP arrangements mentioned above. They may also include consortia purchasing or participation in a centrally developed eHub or eMarketplace.

The management of complexity

Although complexity is not limited to the public sector, it is fair to say that, in terms of variety and variability, the public sector purchaser can face a complex task. This may include the role of the purchaser, which may encompass manufacturing style purchasing through to the drafting and management of complex service contracts. It may also include the nature and complexity of the buying task which may include large-scale construction projects or the buying of maintenance, replacement and operations-type goods, such as stationery.

The coordination of purchasing

As we have seen and will see elsewhere in this study guide, organisations cannot really be said to have 'relationships'. People within organisations have relationships, and one key factor in defining those relationships is the degree to which purchasing is coordinated and communicated to suppliers. Without effective coordination of purchasing spend, relationship management can be very difficult.

This subsection considers the question of relationships in the public sector from a range perspectives. These are:

1.   Purchasing governance.
2.   Purchasing coordination.
3.   The tasks of the purchaser in the public sector.
4.   The roles of the purchaser in the public sector.

Responding to relationship challenges in public procurement

Making best use of good procurement governance

Effective procurement governance is a critical first step in improving procurement practice. A high level of commitment is required from the organisation as a whole to support good governance programmes. Such programmes require that public procurement improvements clearly support essential concepts and values. These should include:

◆   Accountability to establish clear lines of responsibility for procurement

◆   Transparency and accountability in decision-making structures

◆   Professionalism to improve individual and system performance

◆   Transparency to ensure that procedures and policies are understood and acceptable by buying entities

◆   Responsiveness to citizens and service users

◆   Responsiveness to the staff within other functions and divisions within the organisation.

A well-functioning public procurement system must seek value for money in meeting the needs of the public sector agencies for goods and services to support public missions. These needs must be reconciled with those of suppliers conducting commercial operations for their own profit when supplying goods and services to the public sector entities. This must be done within the bounds of public policies established to ensure that procurement transactions take appropriate consideration of the public good and political decisions in the allocation of resources.

An effective public procurement system allows users to balance supply performance (in dimensions, such as price, reliability, consistency, service quality, flexibility, timeliness and innovation) against commercial and compliance risks (such as, failure to comply with EU procurement directives and supply failure).

Although the formula is simple, it involves questions of accountability, integrity and value with effects far beyond the actual buyer/seller transactions at its centre. A serious and sustained review of such decisions is needed to properly manage the procurement function.

Improving transparency in procurement

Another critical issue is the degree of transparency within the procurement process. The degree of transparency helps to determine the effectiveness of the procurement system. Transparency, in the context of procurement, refers to the ability of all relevant participants to know and understand the actual means and processes by which contracts are awarded and managed. Transparency is a central characteristic of a sound and efficient procurement system and is characterised by:

◆ Well-defined regulations and procedures open to public and other stakeholder scrutiny

◆ Effective processes for sharing information across divisions and projects

◆ Clear, standardised tender documents and procedures

◆ Bidding and tender documents containing complete information

◆ Equal opportunity for qualified suppliers in the bidding process.

In other words, transparency means the same rules apply to all bidders and that these rules are publicised as the basis for procurement decisions prior to their actual use. It is an effective means to identify and correct improper, wasteful – and even corrupt – practices. Fighting waste and corruption and improving financial accountability are essential elements of good governance, needed to institute effective procurement policies and procedures.

Legal and compliance issues

Central to the design and deployment of an effective procurement system are the questions of adherence to European and UK law, as well as compliance with financial and contracting standing orders. In managing legal and financial compliance, it is useful to consider the principles involved:

Legislation

European public procurement legislation contains rules concerning the process of acquiring goods, works and services by public sector entities. Usually, it also includes institutional arrangements required to ensure the proper implementation of these rules. The word 'legislation' is used to signify primary legislation in the form of an Act of Parliament or subsidiary legislation to any such Act, in the form of regulations and directives.

Purpose

The primary purpose of such legislation is often to foster economy and efficiency in the use of public funds – to give value for money. The state and its subsidiary organs are normally obliged, under domestic law and various international agreements, to transact procurement in a fair, transparent and non-discriminatory manner. Public procurement legislation for this purpose normally:

◆ Makes open tendering the default procedure

◆ Describes in detail the steps involved in open tendering (preparation of invitations to tender and tender documents, advertisements, submission and opening of tenders, examination and evaluation of tenders, award and conclusion of contract)

◆ Defines the circumstances under which methods other than open tendering may be used (for example, restricted tendering and request for quotations)

◆ Describes those other procedures

◆ Lays down rules concerning essential elements in the process (for example, qualification of tenderers, technical specifications, records of proceedings and evaluation of tender).

Compliance issues

In considering issues with regard to compliance, we can suggest that there are two critical issues. The first of these is **accountability** in ensuring that public funds are properly spent. The second is **commercial freedom** in placing contracts for 'spot buys'. There is some degree of tension within any public sector organisation with regard to the above.

Coordinating procurement activity

A critical challenge faced by purchasers in the public sector is that of purchasing coordination. Although this is also a common problem in the private sector, public sector purchasers would probably argue strongly that their own case was more extreme. Purchasing can operate within public sector organisations to meet a range of organisational objectives. These may include:

◆ Provision of public accountability

◆ Achieving value for money in public spending in critical value dimensions of:
   - cost
   - delivery
   - reliability quality
   - consistency quality
   - service quality
   - flexibility
   - innovation

◆ Working within authority policies to ensure the contribution of the procurement function to overall strategic targets

◆ Ensuring contract performance

◆ Ensuring effective risk management in supply

◆ Operating within available or reduced resources

◆ Understanding the underpinning principles of, and meeting, central government performance management targets

◆ Using the procurement strategy to support economic development objectives.

Public sector organisations may wish to set a range of procurement objectives. The choice of objectives, in terms of range, scope and clarity will clearly have an impact on the overall effectiveness of procurement within a public sector organisation.

Policies

Policies which support these objectives may include:

◆ Placing responsibility for procurement clearly within the individual buying entities

◆ Forming some type of central procurement support unit (CPSU) to develop coherent procurement policy, rules and regulations and procedures across the organisation

◆ Taking steps to integrate existing legacy, purchasing and information systems across the organisation

◆ Developing accreditation procedures, supported by the CPSU, for procurement systems and skills within the individual buying entities

◆ Facilitating the use of standing orders and service level agreements to manage relationships between different buying entities.

Metrics

Measures used may include:

◆ Percentage of spend allocated via a competitive process in a defined time period

◆ Percentage of net spend delivered through partnerships, voluntary sector agencies, public sector agencies, private sector agencies in a defined time period

◆ Total number of customer orders

◆ Total number of contracts managed

◆ Total value of business including orders and contracts

◆ Cost reductions compared with other suppliers or a market basket of prices

◆ Delivery accuracy improvements

◆ Lead time reductions

◆ Quality improvement, in terms of warranty claim numbers, complaint numbers and types reduction

◆ Service configuration and support, in terms of properly measured and monitored customer or user satisfaction

◆ Flexibility, in terms of service changes or customisation.

The critical issue in selecting metrics for performance assessment is to ensure that those metrics accurately reflect the performance required and, also, accurately reflect the contribution of the purchasing function to the organisation as a whole, and the strategic direction chosen by the organisation, as a whole.

The coordination process

We will look later in this study guide at some of the tools that might be used to coordinate purchasing across the organisation. As we shall see, the development of a procurement policy or strategy that supports effective relationships is a process, which in itself, can offer a number of benefits. Developing a strategy can help raise awareness of the need for effective procurement. It can help explore issues around good governance and it can define the resources required, and risks involved, in moving from an existing to a desired state.

By considering alternatives, a public sector organisation can build a robust strategy, which is clearly defined and owned by a wide range of stakeholders.

Roles and responsibilities of the individual buying entities

Any procurement strategy must take into account both the role of the procurement function and, also, the role of the function within the individual buying entities. Individual buying entities currently have, and clearly need, a public sector organisation to undertake the procurement of the goods, services and works required in meeting their responsibilities with the funds appropriated to them. Officers of the organisation with delegated procurement authority should be accountable for the public procurement decisions taken by them.

To comply with accepted standards, the contracting, monitoring and auditing roles must be clearly separated. Such a separation of function avoids conflicts of interest, encourages competition and improves value for money spent.

The separation of the three roles can help ensure that the process is accountable and is seen to be accountable. This is important for developing trust between the public sector and its suppliers, as well as, funding bodies. A responsible officer within each entity should ensure this requirement is met. Audit procedures may wish to involve lay auditors in the auditing process. The individual divisions and other major buying entities may also wish to:

◆   Set themselves targets for savings

◆   Benchmark their performance against other public sector organisations *and* the private sector. At the moment, public sector organisations have no formal benchmarking system in place, with benchmarking currently being carried out on an informal basis across networks within other public sector organisations. This type of benchmarking is limited in scope and, therefore, effectiveness

- Collaborate with other departments/organisations. Procurement collaboration between divisions is apparently minimal with real scope for savings through aggregation and standardisation

- Share information on contracts and savings achieved. Although there are examples of good practice in public sector organisations, these examples are often only division or subdivision wide, and are not implemented across the whole of a public sector organisation

- Promote continuous contracting performance improvements and shared benefits.

Prioritising objectives and actions

There are a number of ways in which objectives and actions can be prioritised. Internally these can range from the identification of 'quick wins', in terms of resource use in areas such as telecommunications or utilities.

Externally they can range from simple 'Pareto' or 'Kraljic' style analysis of the supply base through to more comprehensive and robust category management strategies. Medium-term wins can be facilitated by the right level and type of spend analysis, coupled with contract aggregation and competitive dialogue with suppliers. It is important to remember, however, that contract aggregation needs to be supported by adequate category management strategies in order to maintain these wins over time.

Developing procurement operations in the public sector

There are a number of steps involved in improving both internal and external relationships in public sector organisations.

Organisation positioning

Perhaps the first issue, which merits consideration, is the positioning of the procurement function. In many public sector organisations purchasing is managed directly by the finance function. However, because the director of finance is also a buying entity, it may be that purchasing could be attached to other functions, such as the chief executive's office or legal section. Wherever the purchasing section is positioned, the perceived independence of the function and the establishment of a clear role is important.

It is impossible, of course, to establish a clear role for purchasing within the organisation, if its role is unclear internally. It is possible to identify a range of roles.

Primary purchasing roles

In coordinating procurement within public sector organisations, it is important that clear roles are established quickly. The size of a public sector organisation means that staff members within the divisions are often called upon to carry out tasks that are not within the 'normal' remit of the division. This 'blurring' of roles can also lead to a blurring of relationships, leading, in turn, to time and money being wasted in establishing roles.

Broadly, we can identify a number of potential roles for the purchasing function:

♦ **Direct buying:** the first of these is in carrying out the purchasing task. Here the purchasing function will directly buy goods and services on behalf of the organisation as a whole, using a variety of methods. This is often the most desirable role for the function as it eliminates much of the uncertainty and ambiguity in the role of purchasing. However, it is not always desirable to directly buy

♦ **Internal consulting:** the second role is to offer an internal consulting role within the organisation to ensure that buying entities carry out the purchasing task effectively. This may be done by providing expert advice on contracting or negotiation, or through the design and development of purchasing systems

♦ **Service provider:** where purchasing departments do not have the skills to offer internal consulting to the organisation, a fallback role is to offer services, ensuring that they take on purchasing administration on behalf of buying entities. This can often be an uncomfortable role if administrative systems are inadequately designed and supported, and roles unclear within the buying entities

♦ **Project procurement:** here the purchasing department may take on procurement responsibility for a project with a defined life cycle and budget. This might include a PFI/PPP role and the use of 'special purpose vehicles' for schools, roads, hospitals or other major projects

♦ **Purchasing policing:** a common, but sometimes undesirable, role for purchasing in the public sector, is that of the purchasing police. Here, in its desire to ensure European directive or other forms of compliance, the purchasing function or department attempts to 'police' the behaviour of the buying entities. This can be successful in some cases, but in others it worsens an already poor internal relationship.

In thinking about these primary roles (and we will look at the secondary roles that support them below), it is important to remember that many purchasing organisations and functions will carry out a mixture of these roles. It is important, also, to remember that the main role should be well defined so that individuals within buying entities know how to use the function effectively.

The procurement life cycle in the public sector

Roles depend upon tasks to a great degree, and it is possible to identify a number of tasks within the procurement function. These include:

Task 1: Requirements planning

This involves ensuring that procurement budgets are effectively coordinated. Underpinning information required here is detailed budgetary planning in such a form as to identify key expenditure forecasts by category. Historical expenditure data may also be used to prepare forecasts.

Decisions here might involve cross-functional mechanisms, which may take the form of full- or part-time teams for larger projects or 'groupware' planning mechanisms.

Critical success factors include:

◆ The right steps in budgetary design

◆ Both human and technological information-sharing mechanisms in place

◆ Accuracy and robustness of forecasting models employed

◆ Multiple communication channels to raise awareness of requirements coordination.

Risks here include the trade-off between forecast accuracy and budgetary control.

Task 2: The 'make or buy' decision

Ensuring that the right decision is made with regard to the procurement of goods and services.

Underpinning information required here includes a broader, cross-functional approach to decision making with possible reference made to external consultants for major procurement decisions.

Decisions here should involve more cross-functional coordination of the type identified in the section on requirements planning.

Critical success factors include:

◆ More 'blue sky' thinking within make-or-buy decisions

◆ Creativity training for staff involved in these decisions

◆ Structured decision-making processes

◆ Improved market information and awareness.

Risks in this area include insufficient technical know-how and poor market information.

Task 3: The sourcing decision

This involves the decision about how to find the right type of suppliers. There is often no coherent policy for sourcing across public sector organisations, with many buying entities having their own 'unofficial' lists of suppliers.

Underpinning information required here is a list of approved and pre-qualified suppliers, which is properly maintained and monitored, as well as consistent performance measurement of suppliers.

Decisions here should involve effective performance measurement.

Critical success factors include:

◆   Development of an approved supplier database

◆   Development of a disqualified supplier database

◆   Adoption and adaptation of a method of standardising high-level performance measures

◆   Adoption and adaptation of a method of comparing supplier performance over time.

Risks in this area include choosing suppliers for reputation rather than performance. These may not always be the same thing.

Task 4: Specification development

This task involves developing the right level and type of specification to communicate the needs of the organisation to the supplier. This may, again, involve cross-functional working or coordination. Where possible, specifications should be developed and checked against guidelines.

Underpinning information required here pertains to the user needs definition, both at the point of specification development and in the future.

Critical success factors include:

◆   Clear specification writing guidelines

◆   Specification development and writing training on understanding different types of specification and their use

◆   Effective staff/user feedback

Relationships in context - Section 1e

- ◆ Reference to other elements of the procurement task

- ◆ Clear market information

- ◆ Accurate market information.

Decisions here could involve cross-functional information and external consultancy in key markets.

Risks in this area include poor specification development, leading to contract disputes and poor performance.

Task 5: Supplier qualification

This task involves ensuring that the right suppliers are chosen from the pool developed as part of the sourcing decision. Choosing the right methods for the qualification of suppliers is a critical part of the decision support process in awarding contracts.

Underpinning information required here is similar to that required in task 3.

Critical success factors here include:

- ◆ A method of standardising high-level performance measures

- ◆ A method of comparing supplier performance over time

- ◆ An approved supplier database and, potentially, a method of weighting supplier performance with regard to user needs and preferences

- ◆ A disqualified supplier database

- ◆ Market information on price and delivery for benchmarking.

Risks here include supplier failure, poor comparative costs or delivery performance.

Task 6: Contract drafting

Advising and working with the legal department to develop the right type of contracts to support overall strategy. This may include the use of performance- or incentive-based contracts or newer forms of contract, such as the 'new engineering contract' (NEC), to reduce transaction and contract drafting costs.

Underpinning information required here is the nature of existing contract forms.

Critical success factors here include:

◆ An understanding of the nature and type of current contracts in place

◆ Development of standard forms of contract for a public sector organisation as a whole

◆ The development of a contracting strategy for different divisions within a public sector organisation.

Risks in this area include incorrect use of contracts leading to supplier failure.

Task 7: Defining the contract

As well as contributing to the contract drafting process, purchasing may wish to negotiate contracts on behalf of buying entities. These joint contracts may be in the form of:

◆ **Call-off contracts (or definite/indefinite quantity or indefinite delivery contracts):** these are contracts under which a defined quantity of goods would be produced by the supplier and held in stock for ordering as and when required by individual purchasers, usually within a defined period

◆ **Framework arrangements (or basic ordering agreements):** these are arrangements covering a given period during which a supplier will provide goods, services or works to an agreed specification at an agreed price with agreed service levels. Contracts are formed when individual orders are placed against the arrangement. For these contract arrangements to operate successfully, the participating buying entities must be part of the process. This requires their involvement in all contracting activities – from production of specifications through to contract award and performance monitoring. In practice, for each contract, only one entity will be responsible for letting the contract. This will usually, but not necessarily, be the largest purchaser. Whoever undertakes the process must agree on the contracting decisions with the other participants.

For the framework arrangements, an estimated quantity of requirements to be purchased during the contract period must be made known to the tenderers. Also, there should be a means for the contract arrangement to provide choice of product or service, if this is required by individual buying entities. The process will not work well if standards are dictated to individual purchasers.

Variable prices for different purchase quantities, different geographical locations and different service levels may be established. However, for this arrangement to work, there must be a clear commitment to use the contracts by the participating entities.

Underpinning information required here is a clear understanding of the internal and external markets.

Critical success factors might include:

◆   Clear contract targets

◆   Adequate benchmarking of new contracts against existing contracts

◆   Adequate understanding of the benefits of using contracts by staff within internal buying entities

◆   Clearer roles for suppliers

◆   Clearly understood contract performance measures.

Risks in this area include inadequate monitoring of contract performance.

Task 8: Managing the contract mix

This task involves ensuring that the right type and mixture of contracts are employed to balance supplier performance with risk management. At the moment many public sector organisations have no way of establishing what proportion of contracts are performance based, and how these contracts fit into an overall strategy.

Underpinning information required here is the nature of contracts used and the expenditure through each contract type with each supplier.

Critical success factors here might include:

◆   Higher profile for contracting within a public sector organisation

◆   Adequate contract selection and drafting

◆   Joint supplier/authority workshops prior to contract award.

Task 9: Post-contract negotiation and competitive discussion

Because of the nature of competition in the supplier selection process in public procurement, there is often less attention paid to post-contract negotiation. Nonetheless, ongoing negotiation, with regard to performance, can be a critical element of the procurement task.

Critical success factors in this area include:

◆   Advanced negotiation skills within the CPSU

◆   Negotiation skills within the buying entities.

Task 10: Aggregation and standardisation

Within some public sector organisations, many individual buying entities purchase similar goods and services. If these purchases could be aggregated, it would result in prices that are more competitive, lower operating and maintenance costs and improved service for the buying entities. It could also encourage domestic manufacturers to invest in plant and equipment.

Purchasing has a role in facilitating aggregation and standardisation where procurement responsibilities remain within the buying entities. Joint contracting should take place where appropriate and beneficial to the parties involved. Experience in other organisations has shown that for joint contracting to be successful, buying entities must work together to rationalise requirements, agree on contract specifications and determine who will be responsible for the contracting process.

Experience has also shown that challenges must be overcome for this rationalisation to occur, including:

◆   Concerns about loss of responsibility and control

◆   Concern that the larger users will impose their standards on the smaller purchaser

◆   Time and resource constraints

◆   Lack of information.

Critical success factors here include:

◆   Identification products or services purchased by more than one buying entity that would benefit from joint contracting

◆   Development of groups of advisers to form contracting working parties and invite members from the participating buying entities

◆   Adequate technical and organisational support to the working parties

◆   Clear reporting on results, including performance improvements achieved.

Task 11: Tendering and addressing legal compliance

This is part of the policing role referred to above and as such, requires careful planning. Again critical information needs and critical success factors are:

◆   Accurate spend information

◆   Timely spend information

◆   Further development of spend planning mechanisms

◆   Improved information granularity to facilitate monitoring.

Task 12: Alternative dispute resolution (ADR)

Another task group for a purchasing department or function might include the management of disputes and the development of an alternative dispute resolution mechanism. Although there is often little evidence of dispute with suppliers within many public sector organisations, this is likely to be as much a result of low expectations and poor or non-existent performance measures, as the lack of potential for dispute.

Critical success factors for setting up an ADR system include:

◆ Accurate performance measures

◆ Higher expectations within the buying entities of supplier performance

◆ A mechanism for handling escalation

◆ Reference to competent external agencies

◆ Good cross-functional coordination.

Task 13: Payment management and purchasing administration

The management of payment in terms of both **responsiveness** – getting payments out on time – and **strategy** – using variations in contract terms supported by payment management to manage supply relationships are both important tasks.

Information required here includes information on current agreed payment terms and payment clearance rates.

Critical success factors might include:

◆ Redesign and re-engineering of payment and purchasing administration processes

◆ Use of appropriate terms and conditions.

Task 14: Disposal

Sustainable waste management is, increasingly, on the public sector's agenda. This involves a range of tasks involved in reducing resource inputs, maximising the efficient use of resources and minimising the final impact of resource use on land, air and water. The public sector faces enormous challenges in making real progress on developing sustainable waste management.

Procurement integration roles

As well as tasks that the purchasing function might carry out on its own behalf, there is also a clear need for a coordinating role.

This includes the provision of sustained management advice and assistance to support budgetary considerations in the area of expenditure for procurement. Potential responsibilities/roles for a procurement function could include:

Role 1: Developing procurement policies

A critical function is the development and issuance of policy. As we will see in this study guide, the process of consultation which supports the framing and drafting of policies is often as important as the content of the policy itself. Polices here may include:

◆ Policies at the macro level covering matters like participation in consortia, use of internationally accepted technical or performance standards, such as ISO 9000/9002, application of electronic commerce, preference for firms in the local economy and the application of environmental purchasing

◆ Policies covering professional practice, including contracting procedures, measurement of performance by the buying entities, measurement of supplier performance, supplier qualification procedures and supplier relationships and organising notices of tender opportunities.

Role 2: Developing procurement regulations and procedures

The implementation process involved in developing procurement regulations and procedures often makes an important contribution to the subsequent effectiveness of these procedures and regulations.

This function includes:

◆ The development, maintenance and updating of procurement law, regulations and procedures

◆ The dissemination of legal and regulatory updates and amendments

◆ The development of training materials on the legal and internal compliance requirements of procurement

◆ Compliance with procurement law, regulations and procedures

◆ Developing and maintaining standard tender documents and standard conditions of contract

◆ Providing help and advice to the contracting entities

◆ Establishing financial thresholds as required by law or regulation.

Relationships in context - Section 1e

Role 3: Promoting professional practice

There is a need for a coordinated approach to procurement, if the public sector is to achieve best value in its use of public funds. This coordination can be provided within a central policy unit which, while recognising individual authority in the buying entities, works with these entities to:

♦ Develop and disseminate recommended procurement policies

♦ Set professional standards

♦ Monitor professional standards

♦ Develop a code of business ethics

♦ Provide professional advice and support to the individual buying entities

♦ Issue good-practice guides in relation to procurement

♦ Undertake research into the needs of buying entities

♦ Undertake research into domestic and international sources of supply

♦ Develop a database of information on which to base procurement decisions

♦ Operate a professional development scheme for staff with purchasing and contracting responsibilities, including adherence to proper ethical standards

♦ Promote economies of scale through the use of volume purchasing for the public sector requirements and intra-public sector contracting, by means of call-off contracts (definite quantity and indefinite delivery contracts) and running/framework contracts (indefinite quantity/indefinite delivery contracts)

♦ Rationalise standards for the procurement of information systems and equipment.

Role 4: Carrying out or supporting the re-engineering of procurement processes

Within many public sector organisations there are often different ordering systems in place. Multiple systems, however, militate against effective coordination of both spend and procedures. In addition, the growing use of electronic purchasing systems in the public sector means that processes need to be stabilised. Purchasing might here map existing ordering and procurement processes and work with the buying entities to develop a system which can support eProcurement, whether in the form of a desktop solution or an eMarketplace.

This will also assist in the possible introduction of purchasing cards linked with an eSolution, to reduce transaction costs.

Role 5: Management of consortia performance

Public sector organisations often make use of consortia to source goods and offer procurement advice. However, it was clear that take-up is often much higher in some buying entities than in others. These differences seem to rest upon a number of factors including:

◆ Availability within the consortium suppliers catalogues

◆ Complexity of the buying decision

◆ Perceived value for money.

Role 6: Management of internal relationships

As we see again and again, effective external management of supply relationships rests upon effective internal relationships. Purchasing might employ SLAs to manage these relationships.

Role 7: Helping professionalise existing staff resources

All staff with a responsibility for contracting should be trained in professional procurement and its associated activities. This training should include purchasing officers plus legal, financial and technical staff involved in contracting. The responsibility for developing a procurement training and staff development scheme could be situated within the purchasing department or function.

Role 8: Ensuring internal consulting support to the contracting process

Buying entities should train and develop professionally qualified staff for the public sector procurement. To do this, it may be necessary to maximise the use of existing resources, possibly by developing a specialised multidisciplinary contracting team that could provide professional advice and assistance to individual buying entities for major contracts.

The responsibility for the contracting process, the contract award and the contract performance would remain with the buying entity. It would be a central function to coordinate this process.

Role 9: Promoting effective competition by qualified suppliers

To obtain best value, quality and service, it is good procurement policy to encourage the most competitive and able suppliers to tender for your contracts. To achieve this objective, the CPSU and buying entities should emphasise:

◆ Procedures which are fair, non-discriminatory and transparent

◆ Compliance by the purchaser with its obligations under the contract, including the terms of payment

◆ Standard conditions of contract

◆ Requirements which are clear – using performance and international specifications where possible

◆ Rationalisation of needs and aggregation of demand to facilitate economic manufacture

◆ Use of framework and call-off contracts

◆ Use of longer-term (two- or three-year) contracts to encourage investment.

Role 10: Developing management information

A constituent part of any purchasing department or function must be the collection and management of information.

Among the data that buying entities should provide routinely are:

◆ The number and monetary value of contracts awarded during the year (or for a shorter period of time)

◆ The extent of competition, and the types of articles purchased.

Role 11: Promoting ethical buying

One major step in developing professional buying within the workforce in the public sector is for the organisation to adopt a code of ethical conduct. This code should apply, not only to those who make purchases, but also for all employees.

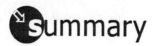# Summary

We have seen within this section, some of the challenges faced by purchasing staff in managing relationships in the public sector, and some of the remedies that may help them meet and overcome these challenges. There is no doubt that in some sectors, such as local authorities, purchasing is being brought to prominence in that procurement is one central part of the government's Comprehensive Performance Assessment. Reports, such as Byatt's, have also placed purchasing in the forefront of the modernising agenda. Whatever the results of these initiatives, we can be sure that public sector purchasing will increasingly be recognised as a critical function in the same way that it is in the private sector.

# self-assessment questions

SAQ 1.5

Identify four key drivers for public sector purchasing.

SAQ 1.6

What are the five primary roles of the purchasing function in the public sector?

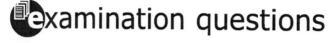# examination questions

Exam 1.1

Identify and discuss three methods of working across functions within an organisation. Illustrate the discussion with examples of the advantages and drawbacks of each method.

Exam 1.2

What are the key underpinning objectives of the EU procurement directives?

Exam 1.3

Discuss Sako's ideas of dependency and trust in both adversarial and obligational commercial relationships.

Exam 1.4

Summarise the principal characteristics of a transactional commercial relationship and indicate the circumstances in which such relationships with suppliers are likely to be most appropriate.

Exam 1.5

Compare and contrast the concepts of cost transparency and open book costing.

# saq responses

SAQ 1.1

Five pressures that are driving integration within the supply chain are:

◆   Cost pressures
◆   Time pressures
◆   Reliability pressures
◆   Response pressures
◆   Transparency pressures.

SAQ 1.2

Five types of commercial exchange within relationships are:

◆   Globalisation pressures

◆   Contractual exchanges where goods and/or services are exchanged for money

◆   Barter or countertrade exchanges where goods are exchanged for other types of goods or services

◆   Asset exchanges or loans where assets such as tools or information may be exchanged

◆   Asset hire and leasing where assets may be borrowed for a fee

◆   Equity exchanges or acquisition where ownership is exchanged or acquired.

SAQ 1.3

One of the key issues in attempting to implement open book costing is the degree to which the supplier knows its own costs. In some cases, it is possible to implement open book costing only to find that the figures available do not give an insight into costs. Where supply bases have been reduced and partnership agreements exist, purchasers no longer have the negotiation flexibility which is given by a large supply base. This means that purchasers need to find a different way of managing down costs within partnership arrangements. The three methods that are broadly used in manufacturing, and particularly manufacturing with a JIT emphasis, are target costing, activity based costing and open book costing.

SAQ 1.4

Policy procedures carry out a number of functions. These include:

◆ To record and store existing knowledge about what works and what doesn't in purchasing within a particular organisation

◆ To create a set of 'rules' to replicate best practice

◆ To ensure that purchasing activity produces best value, within an ethical and possibly environmental context.

SAQ 1.5

There are a range of drivers that impact upon public sector purchasing and therefore public sector relationships. These include:

◆ The modernising agenda
◆ The need for accountability
◆ The need for flexibility
◆ The management of complexity
◆ The coordination of purchasing.

SAQ 1.6

The five primary roles of the purchasing function in the public sector are:

◆ Direct buying
◆ Internal consulting
◆ Service provider
◆ Project procurement
◆ Purchasing policing.

Relationship strategy, policy and practice

 Objectives

When you have completed this section you will be able to:

◆ **Propose and justify the use of appropriate tools of analysis in relationship determination**

◆ **Assess potential risk and uncertainty in commercial relationships**

◆ **Comment critically on the need for transparency in relationships**

◆ **Evaluate potential wastes in the supply chain and suggest approaches to their elimination**

◆ **Evaluate the supplier characteristics appropriate for the main types of relationship**

◆ **Appraise appropriate sourcing policies from a relationship perspective**

◆ **Assess the impact of lean supply, agile supply and power issues upon commercial relationships**

◆ **Evaluate ethical, technological, legal, environmental and other relationship constraints and enablers.**

Section 2 comprises subsections:

a) **Tools of analysis in relationship selection and determination**

b) **Risk assessment and evaluation in relationship decisions**

c) **The contribution of appropriate relationships to organisational success**

d) **Factors impacting upon relationships**

e) **Relationships and supply chain policy**

Introduction

So far we have considered the nature of relationships and the way in which relationships impact upon purchasing and supply activities. In the next section we will consider some of the concepts and tools which support relationship formation and relationship processes.

Tools of analysis in relationship selection and determination

The syllabus learning outcome for this subsection states that you will be able to:

◆ **Propose and justify the use of appropriate tools of analysis in relationship determination.**

This subsection will cover:

◆ **Introduction**

◆ **Legal framework**

◆ **Supplier assessment.**

Introduction

This subsection considers how relationships might be analysed in order to give us the information we require to contribute to the formation of the optimal commercial relationship. It also deals with the issues you will face in choosing suppliers, once you have an acceptable pool to choose from. The process of choosing suppliers is perhaps one of the most difficult issues that the purchasing manager faces. It is possible to identify a number of stages in choosing suppliers and a number of issues that should be taken into account. By using a structured, evidence-based approach to choosing suppliers, purchasing managers and staff will be likely to avoid pitfalls that will cause you – or your company – problems once the contract is awarded.

Legal framework

If you work in public sector or former public sector bodies such as universities or utilities companies, you should be aware of the European procurement directives. These require that you observe certain safeguards. The legislation includes the General Agreement on Tariff and Trades which supports European directives preventing any public procurement body discriminating against a supplier on the grounds of location or ownership from a member state.

The European directives also support a range of legislation in the UK including:

◆ The Public Supply Contracts Regulations 1995 (SI95/201)

◆ The Public Contracts Regulations 1991 (SI91/2180)

◆ The Public Services Contracts Regulations 1991 (SI91/2680)

◆ The Utilities Supply and Works Regulations 1992 (SI92/3279).

In the latter case, utilities companies are not only barred from discriminating against suppliers, but have to have a system in place to prove that this discrimination does not take place.

Supplier assessment

The first stage in choosing a supplier is generally labelled 'supplier assessment'. Supplier assessment can be seen as one of the keystones of modern purchasing practice, and a variety of weighted 'models' are available to assist in the selection process. The second stage is decision making: choosing which supplier should be awarded the contract. Before we consider the actual choice process itself, however, it may be useful to consider just what we are trying to do when we assess a supplier.

The objectives of assessment

Assessment seems easy at first glance. We are looking to choose a supplier who can supply the goods or services to a certain specification. It is, however, not always this simple. Purchasing professionals use assessment for a variety of purposes. These include:

- The management of commercial exposure or risk

- The management of the supplier after contract award

- The supplier selection.

It is vital in assessment to be clear about objectives. This can be difficult as the objectives of a purchase can be less than clear to the purchaser, who may be buying on behalf of a user. Often large purchases can involve a multidisciplinary or cross-functional team, who can spend time drawing up general performance criteria as well as specification information.

In considering these objectives, the key issue is the degree to which the system is most appropriate to the environment in which it will be used. There is no point in having an assessment system that does not meet the objectives that you have set.

The objectives of supplier assessment are often wide-ranging (see opposite). These may also be multiple objectives that vary over time. Clearly, the better you are able to frame and define objectives, the more chance you have of achieving these objectives.

Objectives of supplier assessment

◆ To evaluate supplier reliability and capacity

◆ To select the right supplier

◆ To motivate suppliers

◆ To maintain defect-free supplies

◆ To maintain authority over suppliers

◆ To create an elite supplier 'club' within the existing supply base

◆ To improve transparency of decision making

◆ To improve visibility of competition

◆ To create a tiered supply base

◆ To engineer the market

◆ To help suppliers develop

◆ To test supplier's ability to stand up to stress and pressure

◆ To compare supplier with supplier

◆ To compare supplier with standards

◆ To give suppliers a sense of achievement

◆ To eliminate risk

◆ To provide information for other departments

◆ To give other departments a degree of confidence

◆ To give supplier feedback on progress

◆ To predict future supplier performance

◆ To give feedback on effectiveness of purchasing department.

The processes of assessment

As well as variation in objectives, there is also a degree of variation in the processes used. Some enterprises use formal assessment 'models' or tools. Others tend to use informal methods. Formal methods tend to be structured and have the advantage of transparency in decision support. This transparency improves both perceived and actual fairness in selection.

Assessment is simply about turning information about suppliers into quantitative measures and then comparing each supplier with the others to pick the best. Before we choose, we need to know what criteria we are going to use. Often in purchasing, these criteria will be out of the control of the purchaser. The criteria that we develop for choosing here can be simple: 'what's the lowest price?' Or complicated: 'will they be able to produce the sort of innovations that we need, will delivery be on time and will they be able to respond quickly to our changing needs?'

One of the most common measures used when assessing a supplier is its financial 'health'. A number of organisations offer financial status checks. Many of these are based on a company's Z score. A Z score is a calculation of relative financial ratios that give a reliable indication of the company's ability to keep trading. This gives the purchaser assurance in two areas:

◆ The first is that the supplier will still be trading after the contract has been awarded

◆ The second is the fact that the company is sufficiently solvent to make good any damage caused by its failure to fulfil the contract.

Some of these companies also offer an assessment system based on recorded quality, delivery accuracy and price.

The quality of information used in assessment is critical. Information gathered through the tendering process and financial assessment can be supplemented with site visits. Here the buyer may audit the processes in place within the supplier and consider how likely they are to lead to the outcomes required by the contract.

There are a number of possible indicators here, depending upon the nature of the industry. In manufacturing settings, we could look for the way in which staff are organised, the level of training offered to staff, the cleanliness of the workplace or whether an active maintenance programme is in place. In service settings we might look at issues such as service quality training, type of customer focus programmes in place or quality of service setting.

In addition it is often useful to look at the way in which supplier systems and processes will actually fit with the systems and processes of the buying enterprise. These systems may include tooling, delivery, order communication and processing or joint working arrangements.

Of course, these assessment methods can be expensive, and all assessments should be customised to take into account the nature of the contract and the nature of the supplier. You do, however, need information upon which to base your selection decision. The way you obtain this information is critical. Always attempt to make sure that the information is most appropriate for the circumstances.

Assessing assessment

Clearly, we know when we have made a good choice when our supplier delivers the right goods, in the right quantity, to the right place, at the right time and the right price. We also know that we have made a good choice when the supplier comes to us with innovative suggestions that save us money. Chrysler's SCORE programme has saved the company hundreds of millions of dollars through innovative suggestions.

Here suppliers are awarded points on the basis of the innovative suggestions which they make and the degree to which those suggestions save Chrysler money. Such suggestions may include new ways of eliminating waste.

Unfortunately, we only know this after the contract has been awarded, which can be too late. For every Chrysler, there are hundreds, perhaps thousands, of companies that lose money because of poor assessment methods and supplier selection decisions. This means that we tend, in selecting suppliers, to stick with whom we know. The problem with this strategy is that we may be disqualifying someone better.

One of the ways that you can consider the effectiveness of supplier selection decisions is by looking at the criteria that you have chosen and the way in which they will lead to the outcomes that you require. The stronger the links between the measures that you choose and the outcomes you require, the better. Perhaps a good example of this is the international quality standard ISO 9000 and its variants. ISO 9000 certification has been seen as a guarantee of consistent quality; indeed, in the Pacific Rim, ISO 9000 is mandatory to do business. Purchasers used to refuse to do business with companies that were not certified. There is, however, a growing recognition that ISO 9000 need not necessarily mean consistent quality, but merely consistency, which is no use to a purchaser.

Other criteria that you might use to check on the effectiveness of your assessment system or process are given in the table below.

Evaluating assessment

Element	Questions to ask
Accuracy	How well do the measures chosen reflect required outputs or objectives?
Predictive validity	How well do the measures chosen reflect future delivery of required outputs or objectives?
Stability	How well do measures chosen remain stable over time and across different suppliers?
Consistency	How well do chosen measures reflect outputs across different businesses/sites?
Operational validity	Can we manage these measures to vary the delivery of outputs?
Perceived relevance	Does the supplier and do other stakeholders see the chosen measures as relevant?
Verifiability	Can we communicate and express these measures?
Cost	How much does it cost to collect the information we need?

By using the evaluation criteria in the foregoing table you can improve the effectiveness of your supplier assessment and selection procedures. You can also customise these procedures for different circumstances where the contract involves low-value, low-risk items. Remember, though, that a low-value item can support high-value activity.

Summary

Supplier assessment and selection is a difficult task because many companies avoid the problem by using informal selection methods. This can lead to problems for the company as a whole and for the purchasing function in particular. A rigorous method of assessment and selection can improve the way in which suppliers are assessed and selected. This can, in turn, lead to a better fit between the needs of the business and the capacity and reliability of the supplier.

A rigorous method of assessment and selection means making sure that your information-gathering activities are appropriate and well structured. There are a number of factors that help ensure this including:

♦ Being clear about objectives

♦ Making sure that the measure you use corresponds to the outcome or objective you require

♦ Evaluating the effectiveness of assessment and selection criteria.

Once the supplier has been selected, the next stage is to monitor ongoing performance. We will look at this in more detail when we look at relationship assessment later in this study guide.

Risk assessment and evaluation in relationship decisions

The syllabus learning outcome for this subsection states that you will be able to:

◆　**Assess potential risk and uncertainty in commercial relationships.**

This subsection will cover:

◆　**Introduction**

◆　**Assessing risk.**

Introduction

Every day, we take chances as we go about our daily lives. Whether we realise it or not, virtually everything is risky to some degree or another. These risks can become even more problematic when we consider the commercial area of enterprise-wide activities on which our decisions can have a major impact. Recently Volvo cars had to recall large numbers of its S40 model because of a fault with the servo mechanisms on the power steering. Was this a supplier risk, a purchasing risk or a production risk? Risk allocation is, as we shall see, important as it helps avoid conflict and improve accountability.

Although some activities are more risky than others, parachuting as opposed to ping pong, for example, the potential danger in other activities is not so obvious. Choosing one supplier over another, choosing one type of contract and choosing a particular negotiating position are all risk-laden activities. Yet, unless we take some risks, organisations would not be able to make a profit.

The challenge is to determine whether we feel that the benefits outweigh the risks. This section has been written to help you better understand the concept of risk, how to look at the risks you encounter in a rational, analytical way and how to weigh up conflicting information to make decisions with respect to the purchasing activities we carry out.

So how do we evaluate risk and decide what is an acceptable level for us?

Assessing risk

There are a number of approaches to assessing risk. Broadly these fall into two groups. The first rests upon the belief that events in the past can be quantified (numbered) in such a way as to offer a platform upon which we can predict the future. The second rests upon a belief that the past cannot be quantified. It is just too complex, and therefore presents no safe platform for predicting the likelihood of future events. In the first of these views, risk assessment is a science. In the second it is an art.

If we are going to assess risk, we must agree that certain predictions can be made on the basis of past events. Assessing risk on the basis of this belief involves a set of steps. These steps are:

1.   Understanding the nature of the risk involved by creating a set off possible risks from each activity carried out. For parachuting, the risks are fairly easy to define: failure of parachute to open, individual fails to clear aircraft or unpredictable winds at landing.

2.   Calculate the probability of the risk occurring by looking at the frequency of an event happening in the past and the reasons for its happening.

A key aspect of managing risk is risk analysis – identifying and evaluating the sources of risk. Microsoft has a program of risk analysis based on a 'universe of risk'. This identifies 12 primary sources of risk which are:

1.	Business partners.	7.	People.
2.	Competitive.	8.	Political.
3.	Customer.	9.	Regulatory and legislative.
4.	Distribution.	10.	Reputational.
5.	Financial.	11.	Strategic.
6.	Operations.	12.	Technological.

Each new Microsoft product or business strategy is assessed on these risk factors. For example, in 1995 Microsoft was ready to license an innovative keyboard for production, charging a royalty for each unit. Just before issuing the contract, a risk analysis revealed a potential liability for repetitive stress injury, which had not been considered by the manufacturing or marketing departments. The royalty was adjusted to insure against the possibility that Microsoft would have to defend the keyboard design in legal proceedings.

Defining risk

Such risks are a frequent occurrence in the commercial world. The *Oxford English Dictionary* definition of risk is 'a chance or possibility of danger, loss, injury or other adverse consequences'. The National Academy of Sciences defines risk as 'a combination of the probability of an event – usually an adverse event – and the nature and severity of the event. So even if an event has a high likelihood of occurring, for example sneezing after you take a sniff of pepper, the consequences are pretty insignificant, and you may choose to take that risk. On the other hand, what if the chances of something happening are relatively high and so are the consequences? For example, in some European countries the possibility of being killed in a road traffic accident is one chance in 35. And yet people still drive.

Risk perception

Perception is a major factor in assessing risk. Many people are afraid of flying for fear of crashing. In the United States, for instance, there is a one in 250,000 chance an individual will die in a plane crash. But there is a significantly higher chance (one in 160,000) that the individual will choke to death on food. People rarely refuse to eat out in a restaurant because they are afraid they will choke. Some suppliers may seem riskier than others, but what causes these perceptions?

Because risk is very much concerned with individual perceptions, expectations and objectives, people evaluate risks in different ways. Some people may find parachuting from an aeroplane unacceptably risky. Others may find it an adrenaline rush. People, whether in purchasing or elsewhere, do not often evaluate risks solely by comparing numbers. Perceptions of risk, whether based on fact or not, are frequently people's sole means of evaluating risk. As Supreme Court Justice Oliver Wendell Holmes put it: 'Most people think dramatically, not quantitatively'.

Peoples' perceptions of what is risky are influenced by many factors. It is important not only to be aware that these influences are occurring, but to be able to sort out what is fact and what is feeling. Factors such as whether risks are voluntary or familiar, and the immediacy of the consequences, influence our perception of risk. When risks are familiar, when we can choose to take the risk and if the risk consequences are removed in time, can have a major impact on the way we look at risk.

The critical task for purchasing and supply is to manage risk appropriately. In many cases, there is little time for anything else but a snap decision based on minimal information and a gut feeling. In other cases, such as preparing an outsourcing contract, purchasing will need to invest time and effort before making a particularly risky choice that could have a major impact on company profitability.

When assessing risk, it is important here to think about the differences between risk avoidance, risk shifting and risk taking.

◆ **Risk avoidance:** allows one part to assess the risk and avoid it. If we can assess the likelihood of a supplier failing to deliver to quality standards or on time, we could probably reduce our risk by choosing another supplier

◆ **Risk shifting:** means passing the risk on to another person or organisation. Risk can be shifted to insurance companies who will assess the risk on our behalf and charge a premium for remedying the damage done. Risks can also be shifted on to suppliers. Inventory holding is a good case in point. In an industry with short product life cycles, inventory may become obsolete. Some organisations pass risk down the chain to suppliers who are forced to hold stocks on their behalf

◆ **Risk taking:** means assessing the risk and taking it because the value of the potential pay-off outweighs the risk. It is always useful to remember that although human beings as a whole are generally risk averse (they do not like taking risks), profit and risk are closely linked. Once it has been decided to take a risk, it is important that this risk is properly allocated. Joint venture agreements are often a way of allocating risk across two separate organisations. Within organisations it is equally important to recognise the risk and allocate it fairly between the individuals and groups involved.

When considering risks, it is possible to say that risk, as a whole, cannot be eliminated. There will always be factors beyond the control of governments, enterprises and individuals. Consequently the wise risk manager assesses and manages risk so as to optimise benefits against potential losses.

Types of risk

Because many risks are unforeseeable, it is impossible to categorise them all in a study guide. People and enterprises develop experience about risk over time. In commercial relationships risks may include:

◆ Failure to obtain the optimum price so that a competitor can deliver the same, or a similar product, much more cheaply to the end user

◆ Failure to deliver or complete a project on time when other projects, as part of a major programme, are contingent upon completion

◆ Physical risks to plant, machinery and other assets such as theft, fire or other loss

◆ Bad faith risks where a supplier or a buyer may have no intention of fulfilling the contract

◆ Risks from shifts in national or transactional policy which cause cost increases in a core business activity or lead to it being banned

- Intellectual property risks when a supplier may use trade secrets in developing a relationship with another customer

- Risks from contract misinterpretation caused by poorly drafted specifications or poorly drafted agreements

- Significant design or manufacturing shortcuts in the face of delivery or cost pressure leading to a serious health and safety problem causing injury or loss of life

- Ethical risks which may become shareholder or customer risks when enterprises employ transnational low-cost labour in poor conditions.

Some organisations do in fact keep a register of risks, which guides staff in making risk decisions, and such registers can be useful. However, to be able to make rational, informed decisions about risks, it is important to understand some basic concepts of risk, risk evaluation and decision making.

Risk terminology

To minimise the risk of misunderstanding, the first thing we can do is to become familiar with risk terms such as:

Uncertainty

People are faced with choices every day. Sometimes it is difficult for them to know what choice to take. Which road will get them to their objective? 'Uncertainty' just means there is something we don't know. Very seldom does anyone have all the information they need to make a decision. That is what makes decision making difficult. When you hear in the news that a new study shows that mobile phones can cause brain tumours, what researchers are really saying is that, based on the study they conducted, there is a high probability that mobile phones cause tumours. However, there is always a measure of uncertainty in any study because research is difficult, observations are often inexact and all studies have flaws. For example, researchers often use rats as their subjects because of the ethical obstacles of using human beings as guinea pigs. This leads to uncertainty about whether the study's findings hold true for humans. Scientists deal with uncertainty by measuring probability.

Probability

Probability is the chance that a given event will occur. Thanks to a 17th-century French monk named Blaise Pascal, there is now an entire branch of science concerned with the study of probabilities. This is something we deal with every day. When the weather forecaster reports a 50% chance of rain, that's a probability. In describing risk, probability is more likely as a number, usually a fraction, from zero to one. This number is a measure of the likelihood that something will happen.

A value of zero means we can be certain the event won't happen, while a value of one means it surely will. A toss-up (50-50 chance) is given a probability of 0.5 (the term 'toss-up' comes from coin toss), usually expressed as a fraction, which is the ratio of the number of chances of a specific event to the total number of chances possible.

For example, if you have four marbles in a jar, three reds and one blue, then the probability of drawing the blue is 1/4 or 1 in 4. There is one chance of a blue marble and four total chances (marbles).

It is also the number of expected successful events divided by the number of attempts. For example, if one rolls a single die 24 times, the expected number of '3s' rolled is 4 (24 divided by six sides to a die). Therefore, the probability of rolling a 3 is 6/24 or 1/4.

P value

Scientists and statisticians deal with uncertainty by measuring probability. A widely used way of doing that is through P values. P values measure the probability that an event or finding might have been produced by some random event. A P value is measured as the ratio $p/(p+q)$ where p is the probable number of occurrences and q is the probable number of non-occurrences. For example, if a researcher says the probability that a citizen of the United Kingdom or Ghana has A-type blood is 4/10, he or she means that 4 out of 10 people have this type.

A P value of 0.05 or less (reported as $p < 0.05$) is considered low, and also desirable. It is desirable because it means there are probably only five or fewer chances in 100 that a result could have happened by chance. It also means there are less than five chances in 100, or one chance in 20, that the statistics could have turned out this way by pure chance when really there was no effect.

A P value measures 'statistical significance'. When you see a study reported in the news, one of the things not mentioned is statistical significance. That doesn't mean the study is flawed or isn't important – it just means that you have to probe deeper for the information you need to decide whether to heed the study's results. Journalists are not usually scientists or statisticians and they, typically, don't have the training for assessing statistical validity. Understanding risk gives individuals the power to make informed decisions.

Sample

A sample is a relatively small subset of a population being studied. Because it's often not possible to gather information on an entire group (for example, all voters in a country), researchers (in this case, pollsters) often gather data on a sample. The quality of the sample is as important as its size and should be considered in evaluating a study's results. For results to be statistically dependable, a sample must be random (each unit has an equal chance of being selected) and the selection of one unit has no influence on the selection of other units. In the real world, completely unbiased, independent samples are hard to find. For example, surveying voters by randomly dialling phone numbers is biased because it ignores voters without a telephone and over-samples people with more than one phone number.

Relationship strategy, policy and practice - Section 2b

The fields of statistics and risk analysis have given us a variety of tools for quantifying risk. By describing risk in terms of numbers, we can compare relative risk – how risks stack up against one another. This means that, in theory at any rate, it is possible to assess the relative risk that a supplier will fail to make a delivery, produce a flawed part or become insolvent.

As you probably already know, numbers by themselves are usually not enough to make a risk assessment; values, perceptions and emotions also come into play. Plus, we often find that there simply aren't statistics readily available for the everyday risks we face.

Still, numbers are an important aspect of risk, especially to risk management professionals, so it is important to have a basic understanding of how risk is calculated. This knowledge helps us to make sense out of research results, news reports and perhaps what a supplier is telling us. Think of it like taking a taxi ride in a foreign country. If you don't know some of the language and how to use the currency, you may pay a lot more for your ride than you had expected.

Numbers also help us, as well as insurance companies, policy makers and lots of other people, make important decisions as to how to allocate resources, usually money.

Risk and decision making

Risk is inextricably linked with decision making. Every decision humans make and the actions that stem from that decision involve risk. Even everyday decisions such as what clothes to wear, what to have for lunch and what to do for fun, involve risk. Most of our decisions are made on the fly, in our head. In making these decisions we often rely on sets of unexamined rules. No one wants to reconsider all the factors that might be involved in, for example, a decision to go to a restaurant. Instead we use thinking 'short cuts' based on rules that we have developed through experience.

Sometimes, however, we transfer these rules into situations where the problem is more complex and the decision consequences are likely to have a higher impact on our careers, lives or organisational success. This can often increase the likelihood of a risk occurring.

In addition, decision making is becoming more complex for many purchasing professionals. Increasingly purchasers are being asked to move away from decisions that are based purely on lower costs and higher quality, and to make comprehensive assessments of supply organisations. One of the most valuable attributes of a purchasing professional is their analytical ability. The capacity to perform value analysis, cost analysis, supplier finance and performance, and business process analysis is increasingly a key to success in the profession.

When the purchasing and supply function is expected to act as manager of external resources, it requires the use of more effective decision-making tools which take into account a much broader array of factors.

To assist in making complex decisions there are a wide range of decision support systems available. These systems range from complex to simple tools to provide structure to the decision process and break down a large task into manageable parts.

Decision making can be divided up into several key steps:

Step 1: What's the decision?

This first step may seem obvious, but often just stating the problem can be complex. To begin the process of organising our thoughts we must clearly identify and state the decision to be made.

First, ask yourself, 'Who's decision is it? Is this an individual decision or the decision of a cross-functional team or other group?' By considering the ownership of the decision, it is possible to begin establishing the boundaries of the decision.

Once the decision owners and makers are known, conduct a risk assessment by identifying the risks and benefits associated with a particular path or option, calculating the chance of it occurring and the consequences of the result. Once the risk assessment is complete you can identify the important considerations or 'goals' of a decision. Goals are needed to show how much value one outcome may have over another.

Step 2: What should happen?

Now the decision maker should identify alternative courses of action, or options, in the decision. Each option should meet as many of the goals in Step 1 as possible. Next, identify the outcomes associated with each goal. Some outcomes are uncertain; we may not know exactly how an option will impact a goal, but we need to take this into account.

A useful tool for this step is a decision chart. A decision chart lets us see goals, options and outcomes all at once. It also allows us to add probability and value to the analysis.

To construct a decision chart, list goals down the left column and options across the top. Outcomes are the 'intersections' where goals and options meet. Each outcome can be quantified by calculating its expected value, which is the outcome's value (V) multiplied by its probability (P). Value is assigned according to how well an outcome fulfils a particular goal. If the outcome is 100% certain, $P = 100\%$ or 1, then the expected value is $V \times 1 = V$.

Step 3: What do we know?

The next step is to gather specific information in order to quantify the outcomes and fill in the holes in the decision chart. In most buying decisions, information is far from perfect. As a result, decision makers use best guesses and apply values to their evaluations.

Probability expresses the likelihood of a possible outcome. There are two ways to express probability which are:

1. **All-or-nothing events:** are events that either happen or don't happen. A candidate for an examination either passes or fails. A meteorite either collides with Earth or it doesn't. These all-or-nothing events are expressed as a percentage chance of the event happening (yes) or not happening (no). For example, the probability of rain today may be 30%; the probability of no rain is then 70%.

    When entering an all-or-nothing event in a decision chart, make two columns in the outcome box: Yes and No. Enter the probabilities and outcomes for each situation as stated above.

2. **Continuum events:** are events that happen to some degree instead of all-or-nothing. With events on a continuum, it is common to estimate the most likely degree and establish a confidence interval around that degree. Confidence intervals use a combination of real data and estimates to state the range within which an outcome is 'very likely' to fall (usually 95% probability).

Step 4: What's the answer?

Once this structured decision framework has been implemented the next step is to make the decision. There are a number of methods of decision analysis – techniques used by professional decision makers to simplify the information in order to weigh the possible options and determine the results. This study guide will consider two of these methods.

Method 1
To begin, ignore any uncertainties, leave out the probability estimates and consider which option has the better outcome for each goal. Each goal is first considered separately, and one option is said to have an 'advantage' over the other for each goal. Decide which option is best for each goal and put a (+) in that outcome cell. Put a (-) in the least preferable option for each goal.

The next step is to compare advantages across goals using only the best and worst options. This is where importance bars come into play – drawing lines of varying length to indicate the importance of the advantage, with the worst option on the left end and the best option on the right end. The longer the line, the more important the advantage it represents. Therefore, the longest line represents the advantage that seems most important across all goals. Line lengths can be translated into numbers.

Example:

Goal	Advantage	Importance bar *Worst* *Best*
Manage delivery risk	Ensure effective supply chain coordination	Option A ▬▬▬▬▬▬▬ Option B
Reduce costs	Improve market penetration	Option A ▬▬▬▬ Option B
Reduce defects	Increase customer loyalty	Option A ▬▬▬▬▬ Option B

If you carry out the exercise, you will notice that the combined advantages for Option B (the length of the two bars laid end to end) are a little greater than the advantage for Option A.

Once you have rated the importance and impact of the decision, the next step is to consider the probability of particular consequences. Where probability is expressed on a continuum, then use the most likely outcome and draw an importance bar based on that, ignoring the range of other probabilities. If the outcome box is expressed as an all-or-nothing event, then estimate two values (yes and no) separately by drawing two importance bars and then picking a value in between. Measure the two line segments that make up each importance bar and average the values. The average value should be closer in length to the more likely outcome.

Method 2

Using the first method, importance bars helped assign values to each outcome. Here, importance bar values and probability estimates are used to compute the total expected value for an option.

To obtain a numeric value for each outcome, use the importance bars and convert them to numbers. For each outcome box, enter the probability (P) and value (V) data. If an outcome box has more than one possible outcome (all-or-nothing events), put separate value and probability numbers for each. For continuum events, use the most likely outcome as though it were certain (P = 100% = 1.0). Multiply the P and V data for each outcome box and add up all outcomes for the option (column). This is the total expected value for the option.

The final decision should be the option with the greatest expected value. A common way to check your work is to perform a sensitivity analysis to determine if a particular uncertainty affects the decision as a whole.

It is possible to do this by asking: 'Would the same option still be the best if you assumed that the outcome least favourable to it occurs?' If you discover that an outcome by itself can change an option from being the best to second place (or worse), just by changing the outcome from the initial estimate to least favourable, then this indicates the need for further research on this particular outcome.

Once analysis is complete, the results of the analysis and gut feelings may not agree. In such cases, some considerations may be missing. Then again, there may not always be a logical answer when analysis and feelings don't agree. Sometimes people waver back and forth between preferences, depending on their mood or which consequences are uppermost in their minds at a given moment in time. One of the purposes of decision analysis is to get people to face up to such inconsistencies and try to decide which decision would best satisfy their goals in the long run.

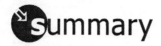Summary

The management of risk is a key part of the purchasing professional's responsibility. More complex decisions and activities require more effective analysis. Increasingly, sophisticated techniques of risk and decision analysis are becoming a part of the purchasing professional's toolkit. Often risk assessment requires a structured approach, which helps the professional to define the goals of the decision and the likely outcomes. This depends on an enhanced understanding of the concepts of probability and uncertainty.

self-assessment question

SAQ 2.1

Identify eight of the 12 sources of risk used in Microsoft's model.

Relationship strategy, policy and practice - Section 2b

The contribution of appropriate relationships to organisational success

The syllabus learning outcomes for this subsection state that you will be able to:

◆ **Evaluate potential wastes in the supply chain and suggest approaches to their elimination**

◆ **Evaluate the supplier characteristics appropriate for the main types of relationship**

◆ **Assess the impact of lean supply, agile supply and power issues upon commercial relationships.**

This subsection will cover:

◆ **Introduction**

◆ **Strategic background**

◆ **The contribution.**

Introduction

'Good' relationships offer a number of advantages to buyers and suppliers. They can reduce costs, improve information and communication quality, solve joint problems, identify opportunities and generally improve flexibility in commercial activities. Relying on self-interest is not enough in global markets that are populated by increasing levels of technological breakthrough and characterised by increasing competition.

However, defining and developing the right type of relationship is often difficult. Limited models of relationship lead to, or at least imply, limited strategies for managing within those relationships. In addition, as we have already seen, the tools used to manage within those relationships do not always clearly correspond to the relationships we require.

Strategic background

◆ 'Only the paranoid survive'

◆ 'This business is intensely, vigorously, bitterly and savagely competitive'

◆ 'Major sustainable competitive advantages are almost non-existent in the field of financial services'

◆ 'I don't believe in friendly competition. I want to put them out of business.'

The foregoing statements were all reported as having been made by the chief executive officers of major American enterprises. In reading these, it looks as though business has entered an age of new realities, global markets, technological breakthroughs and an increasingly 'educated' and demanding customer, all calling for a fundamental shift in thinking about business competitiveness.

Trading environments are increasingly characterised by rapidly escalating competition based on:

◆ Price – quality positioning

◆ Competition to create new know-how and establish first-mover advantage

◆ Competition to protect or invade established product or geographic markets

◆ Competition based on deep pockets and the creation of alliances with even larger war chests.

In such environments, the frequency, boldness and aggressiveness of movement by the players can lead to even more market instability. This, in turn, is made even worse by short product life cycles, short product design cycles, new technologies, frequent entry by unexpected outsiders, repositioning by existing competitors and radical redefinitions of market boundaries as diverse industries merge. In other words, environments escalate towards higher and higher levels of uncertainty, dynamism, differences between players and hostility.

The traditional sources of advantages no longer provide long-term security. Multinational corporations still have economies of scale, massive advertising budgets, the best distribution systems in their industries, cutting-edge R&D, deep pockets and many other features that give them power over buyers and suppliers and that raise barriers to entry that seem impregnable. But these are not enough any more. Leadership in price and quality is also not enough to assure success. Being first is not always the same as being best. Entry barriers are destroyed or circumvented using new ideas and technologies.

As enterprises struggle to sustain advantage, it becomes increasingly evident that no single organisation can build a sustainable competitive advantage. Every advantage erodes. So, in this changing environment, companies must actively work to disrupt their own advantages and the advantages of their competitors. One way in which enterprises can do this is through the management of the supply chain.

Commercial relationships and organisational success

There are many views about the contribution that commercial relationships make to organisational success. Perhaps the first is the need for both enterprises, and the supply chains that support them, to become more flexible. A number of authorities have noted that the manufacturing function within the United Kingdom has moved from manufacturing to 'design, sourcing and assembly'. Such strategies maximise organisational flexibility and shift the traditional role of purchasing.

The second of these drivers includes the need to secure competitive advantage through reduction of waste, and thus cost minimisation. The need to minimise cost dictates increases in process visibility and efficiency. Increases in process visibility facilitate the process and also the performance measurement. Performance measurement is a necessary component of cost minimisation.

Although the logical extension of this lean philosophy may have a number of drawbacks, it is firmly embedded within many organisations in the form of JIT systems and continuous improvement programmes.

The third driver is the need to deal with increasing complexity within the purchasing process. We can identify increases in complexity both in product/service specification and assembly in items ranging from manufactured goods to construction projects. Appropriate relationships are an important way of managing these drivers, and developing these relationships sometimes requires a shift in focus or 'mindset'.

Stage one

The first stage in such a process is the traditional approach. We will label this product-centred purchasing (PCP). Such an approach is concerned with the 'five rights' of Bailly and Farmer. These rights concentrated exclusively upon the purchasing of tangible products and the outcome dimensions through which this product can be described and managed. This purchase of tangible products has a number of drawbacks.

The first of these drawbacks is that product-centred purchasing is relatively inflexible. Product-centred purchasing means that the purchaser often receives ineffective notice of product or service failure, particularly in low-volume, low-turnover environments. Forecasting or quality assurance techniques, such as Motorola's 'six sigma' programme, are ineffective in such environments. Even in high-volume, high-turnover environments, the move towards 'assembly', noted above, means that manufacturers cannot effectively control the condition of finished goods because processes in second- or third-tier suppliers are all but invisible and therefore not amenable to control. Processes in first-tier suppliers may also not be as visible or as controllable as practitioners might like because of the very nature of control from beyond the organisational boundary.

Stage two

The next stage in the development of the purchasing function is that of process-centred purchasing. Process-centred purchasing moves beyond a concern with outcomes and begins to measure the process through which the outcome is delivered. Here we see the use of supplier assessment, and certification programmes to filter out unsuitable suppliers and to set specific process goals, many of which are quality related. Purchasing here begins to broaden in function as it begins to move away from a product focus towards a concern with the processes which will deliver that product. Process-centred purchasing also has a number of drawbacks. These include the cost of the assessment programmes to both the purchaser and the supplier.

Stage three

The third 'stage' in the development of the purchasing function is a relatively recent one. We will label this 'relational purchasing'. It involves a further broadening of focus to include the way in which the relationship between the purchaser and supplier might be used to manage the quality and nature of the supply. Here we can see the beginnings of the 'partnership sourcing movement'. It includes the concept of 'relational governance' in which suppliers are managed through relationships and reflects, in part, the work of John Kay (1992) on relationships as a foundation of corporate success.

We can expect that, at this early stage in its development, relational purchasing will also have drawbacks. The relational focus often means that the relationship is perceived as an outcome rather than a process which will achieve outcomes.

Stage four

This leads us to the last stage which we have been able to identify in the 'evolutionary' process: solution-centred purchasing. Performance-centred purchasing seems to have two main components. The first of these is that the purchasing function deals increasingly with 'abstracts'. Organisations are increasingly concerned with the purchase of 'service' rather than fastenings or protective equipment, and a power generating company may be concerned with the purchase of kilojoules of energy, rather than tonnes of coal, barrels of oil or cubic feet of natural gas. Such an approach has a number of advantages. It permits the purchaser to realise the complexity of the purchasing function and also to manage that complexity through increasing the abstraction of the perceptual process. Purchasers in this mindset no longer buy products but they buy the process that makes the product or delivers the service and the relationship between the supplier and themselves.

This means that the purchaser can gather information more broadly and thus manage risk more effectively. It also allows the purchaser to think more flexibly in devising specifications and aggregate certain functions which were previously bought separately. A purchaser in the electrical transmission and distribution industry, for instance, who may have previously bought a tree-felling service, a ditch-digging service, cable, jointings or planning permissions can now buy a cable-laying service which includes all of these. In the field of health care, a hospital purchaser who previously bought a patient transport service which specified vehicles, timing and journey costs now buys a service which moves its patients from home to clinic and back, including booking services, cancellation lines and general administration.

The second component is the degree to which purchasing acts as a responsive function or a 'proactive' function. Traditionally, purchasing has responded to the needs of production management or marketing. It has also responded to the flow of materials, goods or services from the supplier and attempted to ensure that this flow meets the shifting criteria for quality or performance within its own organisation.

The contribution

As we saw in section 1 of this study guide, some enterprises are designing and deploying their supply chains to obtain competitive advantage. Supply chains built around design concepts and manufacturing principles, such as build-to-order (BTO), continuous replenishment or integrated make-to-stock, can offer enterprises a significant source of competitive advantage. Other labels for different types of supply chain and the relationships that underpin them include:

◆　**Agile:** focused on fulfilling a wide range of fast-changing customer product need

◆　**Lean:** focused on the elimination of waste (which equates to cost) and inventory

◆　**Leagile:** focused on both customer needs and waste

◆　**Design:** focused on innovation

◆　**Clockspeed:** focused on time-based competition

◆　**Full service:** focused on an extended range of customer product and service needs.

The type of supply chain and the relationship that underpins it will depend on the basis upon which the enterprise chooses to compete. Thus, if the enterprise chooses to compete on cost, it may adopt a lean supply model. If it chooses to supply on customer retention and customisation, it may adopt an agile model. If it chooses to compete on time it might adopt a clockspeed model.

Of course, this is not to say that enterprises will employ one type of supply chain. Different product lines may require different types of supply chain and different types of relationship and some product lines may be based around more than one performance driver.

Increasingly, we can see that certain performance dimensions are 'order winners' and others are 'order qualifiers'. Order winners are dimensions of product and process performance which will lead to customer orders and reorders. In the 1980s quality was seen as an order winner. Order qualifiers are the minimum requirement for an organisation to gain a foothold in the market. The performance characteristics that allow organisations to offer order-winning or order-qualifying products change over time. Some commentators now say that quality is no longer an order winner. Customers now expect quality as a right, rather than as a need, and consequently it is now only an order qualifier.

Developing relationships for agility

Agile supply chain management grew out of the quick response and effective consumer response of supply chain management. It focuses on the customer. An important difference is that lean supply is associated with level scheduling, whereas agile supply means reserving capacity to cope with volatile demand. Whereas information transparency is desirable in a lean regime, it is obligatory for agility. Lean forecasting is algorithmic, but agile forecasting requires shared information on current demand captured as close to the marketplace as possible. Real-world supply chains are cyclical in character.

Within the agile supply chain, demand is managed using inventory strategies. The aim of the agile supply chain should be to carry inventory in as generic a form as possible, that is, standard semi-finished products awaiting final assembly or localisation. This is the concept of 'postponement', a vital element in any agile strategy. Postponement, or delayed configuration, is based on the principle of seeking to design products using common platforms, components or modules but where the final assembly or customisation does not take place until the final market destination and/or customer requirement is known.

The advantages of the strategy of postponement are several. Firstly, inventory can be held at a generic level so that there will be fewer stock-keeping variants and hence less inventory in total. Secondly, because the inventory is generic, its flexibility is greater, meaning that the same components, modules or platforms can be embodied in a variety of end products. Thirdly, forecasting is easier at the generic level than at the level of the finished item. This latter point is particularly relevant in global markets where local forecasts will be less accurate than a forecast for worldwide volume. Furthermore, the ability to customise products locally means that a higher level of variety may be offered at lower total cost, enabling strategies of mass-customisation.

Supplier characteristics for agile supply

Obviously, in all cases, supplier selection will depend on a range of factors and it is impossible to identify supplier characteristics that may be appropriate for a particular contract. However, some general characteristics of an agile supplier in a manufacturing supply chain may include:

◆ Flexible or cell-based manufacturing capacity

◆ Flexible training programmes in place

◆ JIT system in place

◆ Supplier understanding of trade-offs between set-ups and inventory

◆ EPL or Q.r methods of inventory planning

◆ Total productive maintenance programmes in place

◆ Multiple constraint synchronisation modelling in place

- ‘Single minute exchange of die’ (SMED) training and tooling

- Collaborative scheduling capacity

- Purchasing has a role in capacity allocation

- Marketability cost tracking.

Relationships for agile supply

Although we have looked at the main types of relationship, it is very difficult to determine the type of relationship required except on a case-by-case basis. Again, looking at some of the characteristics of this type of relationship, it may include:

- Supply base reduction

- Supplier proximity (global suppliers for global programmes)

- Information partnership both up and downstream using multiple information-sharing methods

- Process integration

- Joint buyer-supplier planning teams

- Joint problem-solving teams

- Joint strategy formulation.

Developing relationships for lean supply

Lean supply chain management focuses on the elimination of waste. Most definitions of waste rest upon the work of Shigeo Shingo, an engineer at Toyota. They are:

- **Overproduction waste:** make only what is needed now

- **Waiting waste:** eliminate bottlenecks and streamline processes

- **Transportation waste:** there is a demonstrable relationship between damage/deterioration and the number of materials handling operations. Can these be eliminated or reduced?

- **Processing waste:** does this product or part need to be made?

- **Inventory waste:** inventory hides problems. Can it be eliminated?

- **Movement waste:** first improve, then mechanise or automate

- **Defect waste:** accept no defects and make no defects.

Lean supply rests on the concept of supplier networks, where suppliers are part of a stable consortium. These networks are based on long-term relationships rather than competitive tendering (although the original sourcing is tender based).

Open book costing is an important element of these relationships. There is expectation that once the learning curve has been mounted and continuous improvement has taken hold, that costs and prices will reduce in subsequent years and that these savings will be shared. This is not necessarily a 'cosy' or a 'soft' relationship. Target costing creates tensions which, in some situations, has led to suppliers walking away from some major customers. Asset linkages are made where tooling is partly or fully funded by the OEM or first-tier supplier. Asset linkages can lead to problems because the supplier can face difficulties in persuading the customer to fund major overhauls which may be needed despite total productive maintenance programmes.

Demand is managed with the aim of smoothing production. Examples are quoted of production personnel being moved to sales in times of low demand. This is one of the major differences between 'lean' and 'agile manufacturing'.

Supplier characteristics for lean supply

Some years ago, the difference between 'pragmatic just-in-time' and 'romantic just-in-time' inventory management and manufacturing systems were made. Romantic JIT aims for zero inventory and therefore zero waste. Pragmatic JIT will work with minimum realistic inventory (MRI). In many ways suppliers for lean supply chains are romantic JIT suppliers and characteristics may include:

◆ Strong team emphasis

◆ JIT system in place

◆ Total quality management systems in place

◆ Waste reduction teams

◆ Electronic data interchange (EDI)

◆ Extensive forecasting and modelling capacity

◆ Order status tracking capability

◆ Vendor managed inventory

◆ Product development cost tracking.

Relationship strategy, policy and practice - Section 2c

Relationships for lean supply

For lean supply relationships, similar characteristics would be required to those required by agile supplier relationships, apart from the fact that information sharing is not required to be so multidimensional. Nonetheless, close working relationships are required to avoid the inflation of upstream orders to buffer uncertainty and prevent stock-outs. This amplification of demand uncertainty up the supply chain, known as the 'bullwhip effect', results in excess inventory and inefficiencies in the supply chain.

Developing relationships for design

The management of early supplier involvement has been shown to offer significant cost, time and quality advantages in the new product design process. Effective integration, once an organisation has decided to use suppliers in new product or process development, includes a number of issues:

◆   Careful supplier selection

◆   Co-location (physical or virtual) of supplier and buyer personnel

◆   Shared physical assets (information systems and manufacturing equipment)

◆   Formalised risk/reward sharing agreements

◆   Shared education and training programmes

◆   Direct cross-functional, inter-enterprise communication, project management and collaborative working systems

◆   Formal procedures for inducting suppliers

◆   Information partnerships – sharing of technical information and customer requirements on a continuing, as-needed basis

◆   Intellectual property agreements

◆   Supplier role definition – where are the cut-off points for supplier involvement?

Supplier characteristics for design supply

Choosing suppliers for early involvement in the design process or to act as elements of an integrated product design (IPD) team will clearly depend on expertise in the requisite design area. Specific issues may include:

◆ Shared CAD/CAM/VRML software

◆ Rapid product deployment experience

◆ Rapid prototyping capability

◆ Co-location of buyer and supplier personnel

◆ Creativity training

◆ FMEA capacity – the ability to test and analyse the likelihood of failure in a part or component, under given conditions

◆ Nature of R&D portfolio

◆ R&D strategy

◆ Integration between own production systems and R&D

◆ Modular planning and assembly cost tracking.

Relationships for design

A number of issues exist in terms of developing design relationships. Often, creativity and innovation lead to an individualistic culture within an organisation, and this can cause problems in cross-organisational working. In addition, there are issues with regard to the ownership of intellectual property within the relationship which need to be addressed. Characteristics of such relationships may include:

◆ Management of supplier integration into the new product/process development process

◆ Team building across functional and organisational boundaries

◆ Clear design briefings

◆ Effective project management

◆ Joint end-user/consumer research teams

◆ Gain-sharing agreements

◆ Technology licensing agreements.

Developing clockspeed relationships

Competitive advantage is a constantly moving target. In order to compete effectively, many businesses are choosing to compete on the basis of time. As a strategic weapon, many authors see time as the equivalent of money, productivity and quality. Managing time has enabled some enterprises to reduce their costs and also to offer broad product lines, cover more market segments and upgrade the technological sophistication of their products. These companies are time-based competitors.

Time-based competition (TBC) is defined as a strategy for the development of a sustainable competitive advantage, characterised by three major traits:

◆   First, it deals with only those lead time areas that are most important to the customer

◆   Second, these reductions in lead-time derive from the removal of waste from the processes involved

◆   Third, these lead-time reductions must be achieved through system analysis and attack of the underlying processes; they must not be product driven.

In such environments, TBC must be a strategy which achieves reductions in lead time through changes in the processes and structures used to design, manufacture and deliver products for a firm's customers.

It should be remembered, however that time-based competition will vary depending on the clockspeed within an industry sector. Clockspeed is the rate at which products and systems evolve within the value chain. One hypothesis suggests that a common characteristic of supply chains is the fact that the industry clockspeed a company faces increases the farther downstream it is located in the supply chain. Thus, in computer hardware industries, personal computer manufacturers experience faster clockspeeds (for example, shorter product life cycles) than semiconductor manufacturers, who, in turn, experience faster clockspeeds than the semiconductor equipment suppliers. Managing these differences means developing the right type of relationships.

Supplier characteristics for clockspeed supply

Again, clockspeed suppliers will share some of the same characteristics of lean and agile suppliers. In addition, there may be an increased emphasis on inventory issues. Characteristics may include:

◆ Geographic location or distribution hub location

◆ Line-side inventory holding

◆ Cross docking

◆ EDI/eMarkets

◆ Radio frequency identification (RFID) tracking systems

◆ Automated picking and kitting

◆ Process redesign and re-engineering

◆ Lead-time reduction programmes in place or completed

◆ Commitment to continuous improvement

◆ Product cycle time tracking

◆ Order configuration checking.

Developing relationships for clockspeed supply

In the same manner as with lean and agile supply, clockspeed supply requires the identification and synchronisation of processes across organisational boundaries. It may also require constant communication across the whole of the acquisition – logistics – manufacturing cycle.

Developing full service relationships

Full service supply has been described in some quarters as 'a myth'. Others believe that achieving full service supply is a realistic aim. A full service supplier would be an integrator or a provider of a complete range of services in all possible performance dimensions. These may include:

◆ Cost

◆ Delivery accuracy and lead-time reduction

◆ Quality as in reliability and consistency

◆ Customer service in all dimensions

◆ Flexibility and agility in terms of product line changes and mix

◆ Innovation as a cost reduction method and a customer order.

In addition, the full service supplier would also be positioned and skilled so as to be able to manage large elements of the overall supply chain. Full service suppliers would have in place technological, management and enterprise-wide systems and philosophies that would integrate processes throughout the supply chain.

At the time of writing, a number of enterprises had made claims to represent full service suppliers, but whether the actual management of all these supply performance drivers throughout the whole of the supply chain is achievable, is open to question. Like lean supply, full service supply may be a target that is never realised, although aiming for such targets is often beneficial and sometimes necessary.

ummary

An enterprise's requirement for appropriate commercial relationships arises from massive changes in the trading environment. Shifts in the way in which purchasing and supply contributes to the organisation mean that the management of the purchasing function is now much more complex. This complexity is reflected in the type of relational strategies that are employed. Relationships reflect the objectives of the enterprise, and these depend on the performance dimensions in which the enterprise chooses to compete. Some enterprises choose to compete on cost and quality, others choose to compete on mass customisation and still others on innovation or first-mover advantage. In some industries there has been an attempt to compete on combinations of different performance dimensions to meet differing customer needs.

Factors impacting upon relationships

The syllabus learning outcome for this subsection states that you will be able to:

◆ **Comment critically on the need for transparency in relationships.**

This subsection will cover:

◆ **Introduction**

◆ **The role of the purchasing professional within a commercial relationship**

◆ **Communication and relationships**

◆ **Factors within the relationship.**

Introduction

As we have already noted, individuals are important to commercial relationships. Enterprises do not have relationships; people do. Therefore there are obviously a number of issues with regard to the experience, skills and knowledge of the individuals involved. Many experts have noted that the role of the purchasing and supply professional is changing rapidly. These changes have taken place in response to factors such as:

◆ New technology
◆ Shifts in business and managerial practice
◆ Changes in customer and consumer sophistication
◆ Increasing competition.

As we have already seen, relationships are complex and can be difficult to work with. Part of this complexity arises because the factors that impact upon relationships are many and varied. This section has been written to consider the factors that impact upon relationships.

Broadly we can categorise these into five groups:

1. Individual factors, such as information-gathering skills, attitudes to risk or communication and political skills.

2. Relational factors, such as levels of trust, the psychological and legal contracting arrangements or the purchasing leverage.

3. Commercial factors.

4. Factors within the environment such as the regulatory background or the nature of the industry. We will look at these later in this section.

5. Factors within the enterprise, such as the degree of cohesion across functional boundaries, culture and the deployment of technology. We will look at these factors in section 3.

Before we consider these different sets of factors, it may be useful to consider the role of the purchasing professional within a relationship.

The role of the purchasing professional within a commercial relationship

Many authors have written about the role of the purchasing professional. Some have suggested that this role is to manage risk, others to ensure continuity of supply. Still others have suggested that it is to guarantee the five rights or to implement lean and agile supply programmes. Each role definition will depend on the experience of the writer and the circumstances described.

This study guide takes the view that the role of the purchasing professional is **to manage the behaviour of the supplier within the context of a commercial relationship**. This underpins all of the above, as it is impossible to achieve any of these roles without managing the supplier. Within a relationship it is often necessary for both parties to change. The faster, and more useful this change is, the better the relationship is likely to be.

However, for the purchasing professional the question remains: 'How do you get others to change their behaviour?' Traditionally, the purchaser achieved changes in supplier behaviour by using rewards in the form of contracts and punishments in the form of contract withdrawal. Nowadays, the purchaser requires a deeper understanding of how behaviour changes.

Changing supplier behaviour

Since antiquity, people have tried to understand how to change other people's behaviour. It has occupied the time and efforts of some of the best minds civilisation has produced. Frankly, no one has yet discovered the ultimate and final answer to the question. As a result, if you take the time to read widely in this area, you will be struck by the diversity and range of answers that social scientists have given to our question. How can we organise all these different ideas?

Changing attitudes

A starting point is to realise that we often cannot achieve behavioural change without changing attitudes. The creation of co-destiny or partnership relationships often requires a major shift in attitudes within both of the enterprises involved. It is also important to make sure that these new attitudes are used consistently. There is little point in changing attitudes unless these attitudes lead to a change in behaviour. There are two factors that impact upon the attitudes a supplier might adopt. These are:

1.   **Relevance** – is this attitude applicable?

2.   **Availability** – is this attitude operative?

If the attitude is both relevant and available, the target – in this case a supplier – is likely to use it. This is likely to lead to a change in behaviour, which remains consistent over time.

Understanding thinking

This ABC: **A**ttitude – **B**ehaviour – **C**onsistency model has one very practical implication. Mere attitude change is not sufficient to guarantee the desired behaviour change (which may range from agreeing target costing to implementing line-side stockholding). To change behaviour there is another real-world step to obtain the attitude-behaviour consistency sought. Practitioners must make sure that the attitude is both available and relevant in a given situation. When these two conditions apply, attitudinal and behavioural changes come about quite easily.

Another set of factors that apply to the way in which we adopt information, relate to the way in which we process or think about that information. Research seems to show that humans have two modes of thinking:

1. **Systematic thinking:** the systematic mode refers to a person who is thinking carefully and making an effort about thinking. Here thought processes are active, creative and alert.

2. **Heuristic thinking:** the heuristic mode, by contrast, is the other extreme. Here the person is not really thinking very carefully and instead is skimming along the surface of ideas. They are thinking enough to be aware of the situation, but they are not thinking carefully enough to catch flaws, errors and inconsistencies in the situation.

People are flexible in their thinking and can move back and forth between the two modes. Sometimes they are systematic and other times they are heuristic. The mode we use depends on situational and personality factors. For example, if the situation has strong personal relevance it is likely that the individual will use the systematic mode of thinking. If the situation has little relevance, he or she is more likely to use the heuristic mode of thinking.

People also have strong individual preferences for particular modes of thinking. Some people have a high need for cognition and typically think carefully about things most of the time. Other people have a low need for cognition and typically think as little as possible about a situation. The mode of thought will be driven by the situation and/or personal predispositions, but people can shift into the systematic mode when the situation warrants it.

When people are in the systematic mode, certain things will be very important and influential to them. These include facts, evidence, examples, reasoning and logic. These can be called 'arguments'. When people are in the heuristic mode, other things will be important. Because arguments (facts, evidence or reasoning) require a lot of cognitive effort and energy, the heuristic thinker won't use them very much. Instead, easier-to-process information will be employed. Things like the attractiveness, friendliness or expertise of the source will be more influential for the heuristic thinker. These things can be called 'cues'.

This suggests that there is no single factor (or list of factors) that will influence attitudinal and behavioural change. Depending upon the receiver's mode of thinking, some tactics will work and others won't.

activity 2

Think about the last major purchasing decision you made on behalf of your organisation. What factors influenced you in making this decision?

Now think about the last minor purchasing decision you made on behalf of your organisation. What factors influenced you?

Finally think about the last purchasing decision you made for yourself. What factors influenced you? Draw up a list of these factors and discuss them with colleagues or fellow students.

When people are thinking systematically, if they are influenced, it is more likely to stick precisely because they thought about it more carefully, fully and deeply. For heuristic thinkers, however, any influence is likely to be rather short lived, simply because they did not really think that much.

Interactional skills

Increasingly, the purchasing professional will rely on a number of 'tools' to achieve change within the relationship. These tools are designed to facilitate and, where employed properly, maintain behavioural change. The tools lie on a continuum, at one end of which lies power, in the middle lies influence and at the other end lies persuasion. All of these tools can be used to influence behaviour as part of a relationship. Purchasing professionals who can deploy all these tools effectively will be able to manage a much wider range of suppliers than those who can only deploy a limited number.

Power   **Influence**   **Persuasion**

An example of this might be where a purchasing professional needs to introduce lean or agile supply methods, including line-side replenishment within the supply base. Where the enterprise spends a significant amount with the supplier, this is often relatively easy. The supplier doesn't want to lose the order because it will have a significant impact on profitability, and will therefore comply. This is the use of coercive power or influence. Where the enterprise spends only a small amount with the supplier, and this is a small fraction of the supplier's total turnover, then the purchaser might need to use persuasion techniques.

Power, influence and persuasion are context specific. This means that we will use them differently in different situations. In addition to these tools we can also look briefly at two less context-specific tools that will impact on a relationship:

1. Communication.

2. Conflict handling.

In the following sections we will look at how power, influence and persuasion can be used to impact upon commercial relationships. In describing these processes we will talk about the source (the person or group this is using the power, influence or persuasion), and the target (the group or individual being controlled, influenced or persuaded).

Power in relationships

Defining power

In purchasing, people talk about leverage all the time. Leverage, or purchasing power, is a critical part of the toolbox of the purchasing professional. In the next section we will look at the way in which supplier tiering concentrates purchasing power through spend aggregation, and manages risk too. Power is, however, often misunderstood.

Many respected authors portray power as a negative force. In many cases it is seen as being the ability to control another party. In actual fact power is neutral. Power is the ability to expand and/or reduce the choices available to an individual or a group. Purchasers use power to reduce the choices available to a supplier by terminating a contract, but they also use power to expand a supplier's choices when awarding a contract.

Advantages and disadvantages of power

French and Raven, two sociologists, identified several types of power in the 1950s. These are:

♦ **Reward power:** the source's ability to provide target with rewards. This requires the source to carry out surveillance over the target to ensure that the desired behaviour is implemented

♦ **Coercive power:** the source's ability to punish target for non-compliance. Again this requires surveillance and may result in hostility from the target

♦ **Expert power:** source has superior knowledge in the domain in which they wish to exercise the power. The disadvantage is that the source must maintain their expert position

♦ **Referent power:** the target's desire to be similar to or identify with the source can mean that the type of reward available can be extended

♦ **Legitimate power:** the source, by virtue of role or position, has the right to tell the target what to do

- **Informational power:** the source's ability to control the information access of the target by withholding or providing information in such a way that the target is convinced. The disadvantage here is that it is very difficult to control all sources of information and, where reliable information is not available, people often make up their own in the form of rumours, which can result in undesirable behaviour

- **Alliances and networks:** this is an extended form of information power together with positional power

- **Access to and control of agendas:** another form of informational power

- **Control of meaning and symbols:** again, a form of informational power.

Using power

In order to employ power (or influence or persuasion) effectively, users often need to combine these strategies. We will look at the way in which strategies can be combined later in the section.

Influence in relationships

Defining influence

Power is often seen as negative. Influence, on the other hand, is much more respectable. For the purposes of this study guide we will define influence as the apparent ability to use power. Influence can, however, be much more. Social influence is seen in situations when people change their behaviour in the direction intended by one or more others. Influence moves from an influence source (the person intending to use influence) to an influence target (the person to whom it is directed). As well as a direct power source to influence, there is also indirect power whereby the source may use naturally occurring phenomena to use influence. Influence may be used to achieve a number of objectives including:

- **Compliance:** in response to requests

- **Obedience:** in response to orders

- **Conformity:** in order to adhere to norms or standards. Usually group towards individual

- **Commitment:** in response to the creation of a shared vision.

Using influence

As well as direct power, there is also a range of factors found within human beings that the source can take advantage of. Robert Cialdini, in his book *Influence, Science and Practice* identifies six major types of influence used by what he calls 'compliance professionals'. These are individuals whose main role is to achieve compliance from other people. Compliance professionals include vacuum cleaner salespeople, teachers, confidence tricksters and fund-raisers. These are people or groups who seek to achieve a change in people's behaviour in response to a number of simple techniques:

◆   Reciprocity

◆   Consistency/commitment

◆   Social proof

◆   Authority

◆   Liking

◆   Scarcity.

These methods appear to transcend occupation, region, personality and education. In other words, they work in many different situations.

Reciprocity
Cialdini identifies an 'iron rule of reciprocation'. This involves repaying in kind what another person has provided for us. If somebody does something nice for us, we feel we owe them the return of that kindness in some appropriate form. The source here is looking to create uninvited debts. In return for the debt incurred, the source seeks to manipulate us to reciprocate in a manner than reaps a net benefit to him or her. Reciprocal concession is the act of asking the target for something that could not reasonably be expected and then agreeing to take less. Again, the net gain goes to the source.

Commitment and consistency
It is normal to strive to be consistent. Once an individual has made a choice or taken a stand, he or she will encounter personal and interpersonal pressures to behave consistently with that commitment. Consistency is probably learned (as opposed to innate). Consistency is clearly a useful trait or characteristic. It means that individuals can rely on people to do the same things in the same sets of circumstances. Other people can therefore rely upon them, and begin to trust them. People strive to behave in ways that are consistent with their expressed values and principles; and similarly strive to avoid being perceived as inconsistent. The source here will seek to establish a consistent pattern of behaviour and then rely on this consistency to achieve their aims.

Social proof

Cialdini notes that if you are walking along the street and see a group of people looking up, it is a good bet that you will look up too. The fact that others engage in a particular behaviour constitutes a kind of 'social proof' that it is OK or appropriate. The principle of social proof says: 'The greater the number of people who do something, the greater the proof that it is correct.' There is a reciprocal dimension to this: 'If I do something and others follow me, it must be all right.' In the face of uncertainty, we invoke the principle: 'Convince and ye shall be convinced.'

Authority

We are likely to comply when we believe someone to be an authority. Authority can provide a shortcut to decision making. If we accept someone as an authority, and that person advocates certain behaviours, then we do not have to go through what might otherwise be a difficult decision-making process.

Liking

We are much more likely to comply with another when we like that person and/or perceive that he or she likes us. It is much easier to say 'no' to someone who is a stranger, or someone we don't like. The source here is in the business of constructing a world where they can quickly move from the role of stranger to one whom the target likes and can consider a friend. To do this the source may create similarities of background, beliefs and tastes or offer compliments (unsolicited rewards) to the target.

Scarcity

The scarcity principle states that if an item is available in limited quantities, or for a limited time, that knowledge psychologically increases its desirability. If there are not many left, we want them. If we can't have something, we want it. The closing-down sale or the time-limited special offer are classic examples of the use of the scarcity principle.

Persuasion

Defining persuasion

We looked at the way in which influence and power work. Now let's consider persuasion. As noted above, terms are often misleading but we can suggest that persuasion differs from power and influence because persuasion requires the creation of some area of agreement between the parties. Persuasion is co-created to a much greater degree than power and influence.

Persuasion in action

Persuasion is far more common than either power of influence. According to recent research, consumers are exposed to no less than 1,000 commercial messages every day. Whenever you look in your medicine cabinet, or your kitchen, or your organisation's stores, each item that you see is a war trophy, representing some company's victory over their competitors. For some reason, or maybe for no reason at all, they convinced you to trade your hard-earned money for their product. How did they do that, exactly?

These attempts to persuade people are key to social and commercial activity. Imagine if each attempt to persuade were replaced with coercion – the shop owner banning you from the shop and spreading nasty rumours about you if you didn't buy that T-shirt; your manager telling you that he wouldn't pay you this month because you hadn't worked hard enough; your friend telling you that if you didn't go out for a drink with him tonight, he would tell everybody what you'd said when you were drunk last week; the policeman simply shooting you in the back for doing 45mph in a 30mph zone.

Life and commercial activity would be impossible.

Persuasion, on the other hand, makes society work smoothly because successful persuasion makes coercion unnecessary. The ability to persuade, and to resist persuasion, is in many ways directly related to one's success in life – you would imagine that the topic should be taught in school. You'd think people would know their persuasion tactics as well as they know how to recite the alphabet. But how many people can recite ten principles of persuasion? How many can evaluate a situation and choose the right persuasive tool for the job at hand? Traditionally, purchasing and supply has never felt the need to persuade, because purchasing power has been enough to attain objectives. Within the old adversarial relationships there was no need to persuade, or indeed influence. Purchasing could coerce or reward instead.

In more complex, relationally based agreements, purchasing professionals need to learn a range of persuasive and influencing techniques. This is because the motivating effects of the contract are no longer as powerful as they were once. Purchasing professionals need to learn new ways of motivating suppliers within commercial relationships.

Using persuasion

Unlike influence and power, there is a much more extensive range of persuasion types which extend from education and advertising to more suspect methods such as propaganda and thought control.

Persuasion is perhaps most often seen in the field of advertising and marketing. Gaining people's attention and converting them into customers represents a large element of the research and expenditure on persuasion. There is, however, no reason why purchasing and supply functions should not make use of these tools and techniques to motivate and persuade suppliers of the benefits of a particular course of action.

Tactics of power, influence and persuasion

Different tactics and different combinations of tactics can be used at different times, depending on the objectives and the nature of the relationship.

Power tactics

Classically, the use of power tactics by the purchaser involve the use of reward (awarding a contract) and coercion (threatening to withdraw a contract). This is a salient example of power in action, and in many ways the act of buying has become a major symbol of power in our society with phrases such as 'the customer is king' demonstrating this power. Nonetheless, in an ongoing relationship, the use of power can be problematic as it may disempower suppliers. This can lead to resentment and later difficulties.

Let us consider the use of power with a supplier with whom an enterprise spends only a small amount, and with whom it is necessary to implement a vendor managed inventory. Power tactics here might include presenting information, facts or evidence to persuade the supplier that a vendor managed inventory is necessary (informational power).

It might be possible to mention the fact that others have complied (referent power). It might also be possible to mention the benefits for other customers (reward power). If this fails, the buyer might appeal to norms within the industry: 'it's the right thing to do' (legitimate power), and only then might he or she threaten or complain (coercive power).

Influence tactics

Many of the tactics used by people seeking to use power or influence are familiar to us. Often we use them all the time ourselves. However, transparency of tactics diminishes the likelihood of success. Often people will combine tactics to improve effectiveness and mask their real intentions.

Foot-in-the-door

Everyone is familiar with the foot-in-the-door (FITD) technique. This is a set of sequential requests whereby a small request to which nearly everyone will comply is followed by target request. Foot-in-the-door relies on the self-perception theory and the rule of consistency identified above. Self-perception theory says that people learn about their internal states (attitudes, beliefs or preferences) by observing their own behaviour. If they see themselves doing something, then they reason that they must like the thing.

Once the target has responded 'yes' to a small request, the person observes his or her behaviour and subconsciously thinks: 'If I'm doing this, it must mean that I have a favourable opinion about it.' This is followed rapidly by the second request and consistency kicks in. The person knows he or she should accept the second request because he or she is 'that' kind of person.

Rejection-then-retreat

Most people are also familiar with the rejection-then-retreat tactic, also known as the door-in-the-face method. This involves making a big initial request which nearly everyone will refuse, followed by target request. The explanation of rejection-then-retreat relies on reciprocity. By asking for something then giving it up, the source has created a sense that there have been concessions which elicit reciprocity in the target.

Both foot-in-the-door and rejection-then-retreat are often called the 'two step' by compliance researchers because they involve sequential questions. They both require advance planning. Sources must know where they are headed (the second request, the real target). Sources must know how they will get there (start high or start low?). Research also supports the fact that the target request must produce some common benefit; selfish appeals will not work. If you are using rejection-then-retreat, there can be no delay between requests. If you are using FITD, there can be no incentives for performance. If you implement the two-step properly, however, it could improve compliance effectiveness by 20%.

Low-balling or bait-and-switch

Another method that takes advantage of consistency is low-balling or bait-and-switch. Bait-and-switch techniques are illegal in many countries. They involve changing the 'rules' midstream. Sources may offer the target an excellent deal. This will induce the target to make a commitment. The source then changes the offer by decreasing the benefits or increasing the costs. Again, the source takes advantage of consistency/commitment because the target has already made a commitment, and will often follow through by accepting the lower offer.

Persuasion techniques

In the textbooks there is often an overlap between influence and persuasion techniques. For the purposes of this study guide we will treat them separately. Persuasion techniques include:

- ◆ **Association:** often communications are 'associated' with people or organisations that have high status, insinuating that if you follow a course of action or buy a product you will gain status too

- ◆ **Vividness:** people tend to identify items that stand out against a dull background. This is true whether this is a picture or a sentence. A few years ago, Benetton received lots of free publicity because of their use of a newly born baby in their adverts. This shocked people because the image was so vivid. Persuasion professionals can use long boring arguments with vivid information buried within them

- ◆ **Contrast:** sometimes items or ideas can be contrasted against others showing the preferred item or idea in a good light. Of course, the persuader chooses the item to contrast against

- **Credibility:** The persuader may use seemingly rational, and sometimes little-known, evidence to establish credibility, which shifts attention from the actual point

- **Distraction:** by introducing irrelevant arguments, the persuader may confuse the target and cause him or her to agree so as to avoid seeming or feeling stupid

- **Lengthy:** arguments may wear down the target

- **Framing:** the source of persuasion may 'frame' the argument in such a way as to guide the targets' choices. There may be no difference in taste from eating a segment of muscle tissue from a bull and a nice juicy steak, but the choice of words can guide response

- **Mere exposure:** some people are naturally prone to persuasion. Sometimes it is enough to put the product on a supermarket shelf or the idea in a newspaper

- **Behavioural modelling:** by showing an audience someone they respect, or someone they see as 'like them' carrying out an action or using a product, the persuader convinces the target of the intrinsic worth of the action or product

- **Multiple:** several arguments used together may again confuse a target and establish credibility

- **Narrative:** we all grow up with stories. Many of these stories represent potent vehicles for persuasion. Persuaders can use popular 'myths' about a range of factors to change people's view of a situation. Because they are familiar with the stories, people will use the narrative as a framework for thinking instead of thinking about the situation itself. These stories might be about success, the value of the individual, efficiency and pragmatism or a range of other appealing sentiments

- **Repetition:** broken record – saying the same thing over and over again in different ways is a communication technique used in assertiveness training. It also has a role to play in persuasion

- **Speed of delivery:** the rule seems to be to state weak arguments quickly and strong arguments slowly. By varying the pace of delivery, persuasion can be made more effective as speed controls both the type and nature of understanding.

In the last few subsections we have looked at a range of context-specific ways of changing attitudes and behaviour. In addition to the above, we also need to look at two other interaction skills: communication and conflict handling.

Communication and relationships

Everyone thinks that they communicate well. People receive very little feedback on their communicative skills and, like persuasion, it is not taught as a subject in primary school. People mostly develop their early communication skills in family groups, communicating with people that are familiar to them. This can cause problems later on because much of our most important communication within a commercial relationship is done with strangers – people from different groups and organisations who can often misinterpret our communication.

Everyone says that communication is important, and this is true. However, despite this, there is often only a limited view of what creates effective communication between different groups. This subsection will briefly look at some of the issues involved.

Defining communication

In order to improve communication effectiveness, it is necessary to agree a number of issues. These are:

1. **Communication uses symbols:** symbols are things that are used to represent something else, and are open to misinterpretations because they may be understood differently by different users – the word (symbol) quality might mean very different things to different suppliers.

2. **Communication is about creating a meaning:** we are often involved in meaningless conversations. Indeed some of you might believe that this communication is meaningless, but patience.

3. **Communication involves the transmission and interpreting of messages**.

4. **Communication takes place at different levels of awareness:** much communication is routine and we rely on existing patterns of behaviour when communicating in a routine way.

5. **Prediction of communication:** people that communicate predict the outcomes of their communication. In the same way that we like consistency, we also like our predictions to be accurate. People we know well are generally more predictable than strangers.

6. **Unintentional communication:** although we may intend to communicate in a particular way, we can communicate without intending to. Non-verbal behaviour, relative positions, clothing or gender can all be unintentional communication.

7. **Every message has a content dimension (what is said) and a relationship dimension (how it is said).**

8. **Structured communications:** communicators structure their communications in order to explain them. Sometimes people have differing explanations of the communication (a supplier may say that a delivery failed because of poorly organised cross-docking arrangements at your warehouse. Your warehouse manager may say that cross-docking didn't work because of delivery failures).

9. **Communication involves uncertainty:** every time we make a communication effort, we experience some uncertainty and therefore some anxiety. This may not be noticeable, but when it reaches high levels it interferes with communication effectiveness.

When people are really serious about improving their communication effectiveness, there are a number of areas of knowledge that they need to acquire and skills that they need to develop.

Communication knowledge

1. In terms of the knowledge people require to communicate effectively, perhaps the first item is a knowledge of their own motivation. Without understanding their needs in communicating, it is unlikely that communication will be successful.

2. The second item is knowledge of how to gather information. Good quality communication rests upon good quality information, and competent communicators use active and passive strategies to acquire information that will help them tailor their communication to the situation in which they find themselves. This involves gathering information through questioning, active listening and research.

3. The third item is that communicators need to understand that groups are different, and that these differences will impact on communication.

4. The fourth item is knowledge of likely alternative interpretations. Once the communicator understands how the communication could be interpreted, he or she is more attuned to the likelihood of misunderstandings which can be costly in a commercial relationship.

Communication skills

Skills for communication include the ability to think systematically, what Ellen Langer, an American psychologist and communications expert, calls 'mindfulness'. We have seen the differences between heuristic and systematic thinking when receiving messages, but we also need to use these when transmitting messages too. Skills also include the ability to tolerate ambiguity and uncertainty. Where there is a lot of uncertainty, and people do not tolerate this well, they tend to make judgements on first impressions. Although human information gathering about people tends to be quite accurate within their own groups, it may be inaccurate elsewhere, and this can also lead to costly mistakes. A third skill is the ability to empathise, or see the other person's point of view. This is a critical skill because it allows the communicator to understand the effects of his or her messages but it also improves predictive accuracy about what the person will do. This feeds into the fourth skill which is the ability to make accurate predictions and explanations. If the communicator can be accurate in this area, he or she can reduce uncertainty and therefore anxiety, reducing the possibility of misunderstandings.

Nonetheless, things can go wrong. When communication breaks down, we often find conflict. Conflict, and the way conflict is handled has a major impact on relationships.

Conflict in relationships

It is possible to describe a continuum with effective communication at one end and conflict at the other (see figure 8).

Figure 8: Communication breakdown

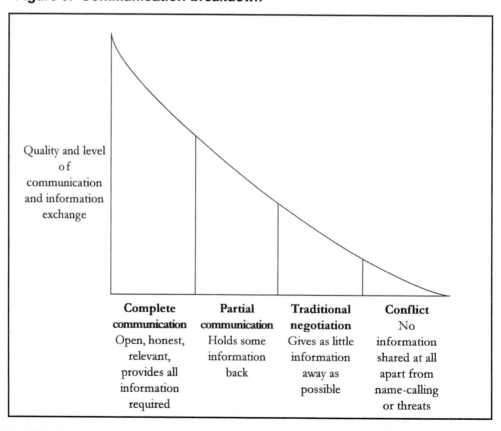

Complete communication	Partial communication	Traditional negotiation	Conflict
Open, honest, relevant, provides all information required	Holds some information back	Gives as little information away as possible	No information shared at all apart from name-calling or threats

The theory is that individuals and groups can find themselves moving along the continuum as their communication strategies fail to produce the intended effect. When communication breaks down completely, this results in conflict. It is important to understand the nature of conflict within a commercial relationship – because the effective management of conflict is vital in maintaining or restoring relationships.

Conflict is a situation where relationships have broken down. The determinants of our behaviour in conflict will often lead us to fight or flight when faced with difficult people or situations which are likely to lead to conflict. These primitive behaviours, attacking or running away, can be managed by taking a number of factors into consideration. The first of these is self-image or self-regard and regard for others.

Many of us are concerned about conflict and rarely deal with it comfortably. We see it as destructive and something to be avoided where possible. Kilmann and Thomas, working in 1975, identified a range of attitudes to conflict and potential conflict which depended on our regard for ourselves and our regard for others.

This model (figure 9) shows that if you have a low concern for your own and another party's needs or interests you will tend to use an avoiding style in conflict. People involved feel little motivation to confront or work to resolve the conflict because they have only low needs to satisfy.

Figure 9: Kilmann and Thomas conflict management styles

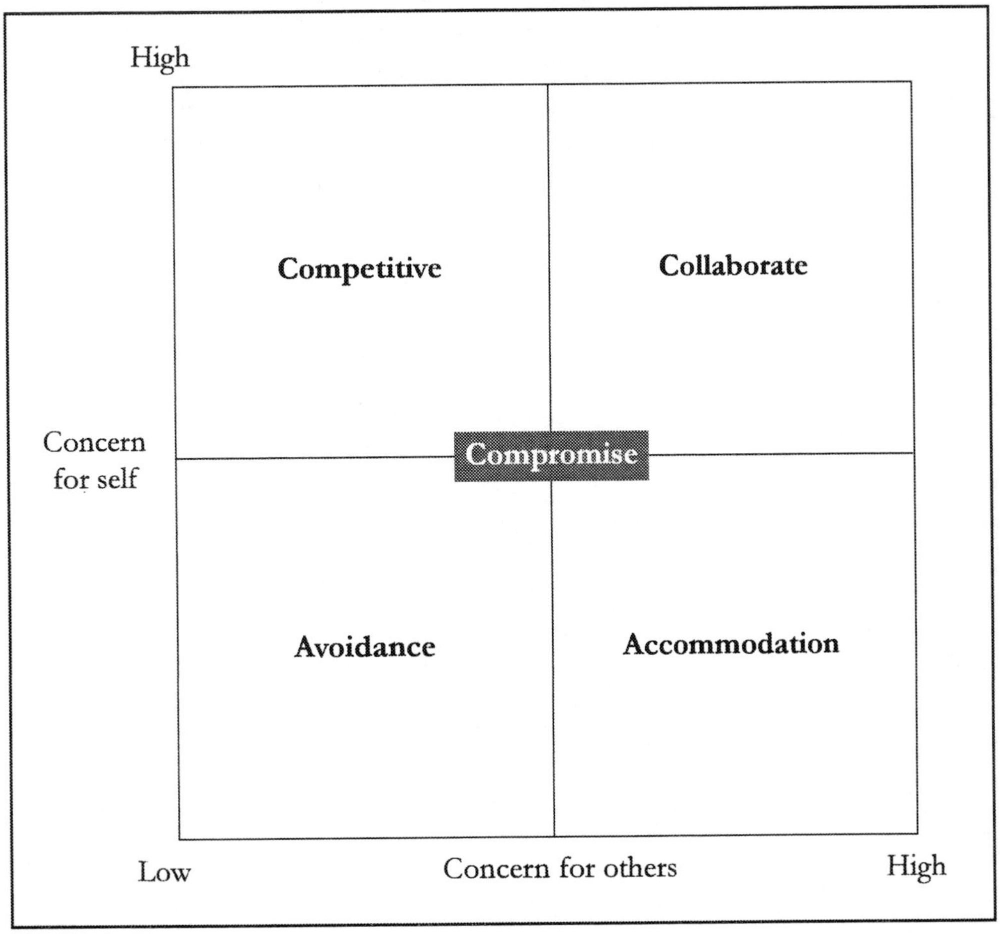

People who are not concerned about their own needs but are very concerned with the other person's will tend to show an accommodating style of conflict management. They will give in and sacrifice their own low needs. On the other hand, individuals who have a high concern for their own needs and a low concern for the other person's needs will demonstrate a competitive style.

People with high concern for their own needs and high concerns for the needs of others will tend to display a compromising style which splits the difference to gain a solution to the conflict. This style is often seen as the 'best' style to adopt, but it is the collaborative style which requires the most communicative skill. A collaborative approach will work to generate new solutions which are acceptable to both parties.

Kilmann and Thomas' work is useful but it is important to remember that there are factors which impact on this theory. The first is that no one will use just one style in a conflict situation. The second is that the nature of the relationship will effect the process. As you move towards a collaborative style you give messages that show a desire to improve the relationship. The last is that the parties' background and culture will effect their attitude to conflict. Some Far Eastern cultures are expected to avoid conflict at all costs. Consider all of these factors when you assess either your own conflict style or that of others.

Functions of conflict

Before we go on to look at some of the ways in which you can deal with conflict, let's try to analyse what it is that conflict does. It can be a constructive force. As a central part of everyone's life it helps people surface issues which they would not normally talk about. It can help bring people closer together. We've seen already, however, that many people find conflict difficult to handle and destructive. Conflict does not need to be destructive. The following offers a way of identifying the two types of conflict:

1.   Constructive conflict.

2.   Destructive conflict.

Constructive conflicts:

◆   Tend to be centred on interests rather than needs

◆   Tend to be open and dealt with openly

◆   Are capable of helping a relationship develop

◆   Focus on flexible methods for solving disputes

◆   Help both parties reach their objectives.

Destructive conflicts:

◆ Tend to be centred on people's needs rather than interests or issues of fact

◆ Focus on personalities not actions or behaviours: 'You are an awkward so and so' rather than: 'You've been awkward recently. What's been wrong?'

◆ Involve face-saving and preservation of power

◆ Attack relationships

◆ Concentrate on 'quick fix' and short-term solutions

◆ Tend to repeat themselves.

activity 3

Consider a conflict in which you have been involved. Would you characterise this as a constructive or destructive conflict?

What elements of the conflict led you to define it in that way?

What type of conflicts are mostly found in your workplace?

What type of conflict is found between your organisation and suppliers? Why is this?

Mapping conflict

Once you've identified the nature of the conflict, you might wish to consider the cause of the conflict. Conflict doesn't just happen; it develops through clearly identifiable stages. These stages are, however, often not identified by the parties that are involved in the conflict. These stages can be labelled as follows:

1. **No conflict:** the first stage is, of course, no conflict at all. This stage means that there are either no differences between the parties or else one or more of the parties are afraid for one reason or another to express a difference. This is a stage where parties may be avoiding conflict.

2. **Unexpressed conflict:** this stage occurs when one party feels that there is something wrong but will not or cannot express it. Many of us may have been in situations where we feel that there is something wrong with a relationship, but the other party refuses to identify the problem. The classic case is of the husband/wife relationship where the husband or wife asks what is wrong, only to be answered 'nothing'. Such unexpressed conflicts can turn into open conflict very quickly.

3. **Problem identification:** this stage will involve one or both parties identifying the issues which are, generally at this stage, interest issues which can be addressed easily. If issues are relational or emotional, however, it may be that the next stage of conflict is reached.

4. **Dispute:** the fourth stage is one where conflict has started to get out of hand. Parties will bring in issues that are not related to the problem. A party's needs not been met so he or she will escalate the conflict although there is a stage in which parties may try to involve others in the conflict, to try to obtain help.

5. **Help:** the fifth stage may involve other people either in an official or unofficial capacity. Individuals will appeal to a third party to attempt to resolve the conflict. Such a strategy can be dangerous for the third party, but generally their aim should be to get the parties talking again before the situation degenerates further into the penultimate stage.

6. **Flight or fight:** the sixth stage is one in which people tend to become very emotional and may allow the conflict to degenerate into physical or verbal aggression – hitting the other party or name-calling. The conflict is such that the parties involved no longer feel safe and will be forced to leave the relationship or attempt to destroy the other party or the relationship itself.

7. **The conflict cycle:** the final stage can demonstrate that conflict repeats itself. Once we get into stage 6 it is very difficult to emerge. People need to feel safe when they communicate, and effective communication helps them feel safe. Once safety is challenged, conflict can be perpetuated because we can't take the risk of talking to the other party. People in this position will often legitimise their position by talking about 'principles' or 'rights' as though the conflict is outside of themselves. Such conflicts may be impossible to handle.

Relationship strategy, policy and practice - Section 2d

Dealing with conflict

Once you understand the nature of conflict and the way it has come about, the next stage is to manage it. The next stage in managing conflict is to structure and analyse the underlying issues.

Structuring the issues

When conflict takes place, an individual's systematic thought can often be lost. Few, if any of us, stop to analyse the issues when a supplier lets us down for the third time in a row or the sales manager launches a major promotion without informing the purchasing department. Conflict here moves quickly through its stages, with no attempt to examine the issues. Nonetheless, if we want to manage conflict we have to consider the issues. This can be done by means of **DRIVE**:

D ata or factual issues relate to the facts about the problem. We may be in conflict because the April invoices have gone missing, which threatens our potential safety.

R elational issues reflect the nature of the relationship. The nature of conflict about the invoices will depend on the nature of the relationship. In a weak relationship, conflict is likely to be of a longer duration.

I nterest issues impact upon what needs the parties are trying to serve and what they are trying to achieve to meet those needs.

V alue issues involve individual sets of values which dictate attitudes. Issues here are about assumptions of what is 'right' or 'wrong'.

E motional issues are tied to the way in which a person's individual goals and needs are met. This set of issues includes concepts such as pride, dignity and fairness.

Managing conflict in commercial relationships

Once you've analysed and structured the issues in conflict, you can look at some of the tools that you can use to manage them. Remember that it helps to be as creative as possible in searching for solutions to overcome conflict. The narrower your search for information and solutions, the less successful your conflict management strategy is likely to be.

Enquiry

There are a number of broad strategies which may help you manage conflict. The first of these is enquiry. Once you have structured the issues, you may need to find out why the issues have led to conflict. Enquiry can involve:

◆ Checking by using your own words to paraphrase what the other person has said and to ask if they feel that you have understood

◆ Interpreting by offering your own understanding of the situation. 'I think that you are angry because... but you aren't saying so. Is that true?'

◆ Giving positive and negative feedback to show your own feelings about the person's behaviour before asking for their opinion. 'You've heard how I feel. Is there anything you want to say?' Feedback can include disclosure: 'I don't like to tell you this, but I am...'

Control

The second broad strategy is control. Control involves you in stepping back from the issues that are generating the conflict and creating your feelings. One way of communicating during a conflict is the 4R approach. Using this model you:

R eceive the other person's comments without interrupting. This shows that you are listening and value the other person's statement.

R epeat the other person's comments as objectively as possible. This can help the other person open up about the problem.

R equest the other person's proposed way of dealing with the problem. People who are unable to deal with conflict are often unable to offer solutions. Instead, they release tension and want to talk about the problem.

R eview the possible options.

Assertiveness

The final strategy is assertiveness. Assertiveness training became very popular in the late 1980s although there is little clinical evidence that suggests that it works. Nonetheless, assertion can be a useful way of communicating in the context of a good relationship. Assertiveness is about honestly disclosing your feelings in a way which is acceptable to the other person in the relationship.

Assertion techniques include 'broken record'. This involves you in repeating your statement using the same tone of voice and volume. 'I appreciate you are busy but...' and briefly stating what you need or want, your belief or opinion. Assertiveness is really only honesty or congruence in communication.

Whatever method you use, dealing with conflict or potential conflict involves you attempting to restore effective communication as soon as possible. Because conflict can involve emotional, value, interest and relational issues, our reaction is often dictated by our primitive behaviour patterns. Our initial reaction is to run away or turn and fight. In order to deal with these reactions we need to step outside the issues and to manage ourselves. Without managing our 'self' we are immediately discarding half of the resources within the relationship which we need to manage.

Conclusion

Relationships are impacted by the nature of the interactions of individuals and groups involved. There are some things that can be done to improve the quality of that interaction. These include having a wide array of tools and approaches including power, influence and persuasion. They also include communicating and handling conflict effectively. However, individual factors are by no means the only ones that impact upon relationships. We will now look at factors within relationships themselves.

Factors within the relationship

As we have said, relationships are complex. Part of the reason they are complex is because individual actions will clearly impact upon the relationship. In other cases, however, the quality of interaction is impacted on by factors within the relationship itself. Tracking, understanding and managing these factors is an important part of relationship success or failure. Broadly, when we think about relationships, we can consider two sets of factors:

◆　**Intrinsic factors:** that come from the relationship itself

◆　**Commercial factors:** that act upon the relationship.

Intrinsic factors

Differing needs

Perhaps the simplest approach to explaining why relationships fail is 'basic human needs'. These theories about the nature of conflict, conflict prevention and resolution within relationships have been endured as a major paradigm for more than half a century. In essence, the origin of this theoretical construction owes much to Maslow's 1954 work in which human motivation is based upon a 'hierarchy of needs', moving from basic physical requirements up to psychological requirements such as recognition, attainment and fulfilment. Different organisations have different needs. Failure to satisfy such needs leads to frustrations which, in turn, can result in aggression and, hence, conflict.

Power inequalities and asymmetries

Unequal power relationships have been seen by various writers as sources of frustration which engender conflict or at least threaten cooperation at various levels. Works on the relationship between unequal power and social conflict offer a good example. Disequilibria in power relationships have been used to explain the way in which inequalities can lead to conflict. In other words the need for recognition, self-fulfilment and self-actualisation is fundamental in one way or another for all human beings. The frustration that arises from the failure to empower or from the process of disempowering can lead to various types of conflict.

Intergroup and psychological dimensions

We have looked at some of the individual issues that impact on relationships. However, there are also a number of intergroup dimensions. Traditionally, interpersonal and psychological dimensions of intergroup relationships have been discussed in terms of cognitive psychology or concerns with images, perceptions, stereotyping and group processes. Broadly, the research seems to support the view that by being a group member you show a favourable bias towards your own group (or team, or organisation). This favourable bias is fine, except for the fact that groups also tend to show a negative bias towards other groups with whom they work, creating natural competition. An experiment in the 1950s looking at the creation of group identity led to such conflict between two artificially created groups that the experiment had to be stopped!

However, psychological and interpersonal studies are increasingly impacting upon relationship analysis in other ways. Growing attention is given to the issue of conflict cycles. This helps to explain ways in which conflicts are maintained over long periods of time.

Structural issues

The term 'structural' crosses over into various approaches to relationship analysis. Structure has also been used to describe the way in which internal processes can lead to conflict. Relationships can be affected by the rigidity of institutional perspectives and procedures. Institutions 'interpret' communications and 'feed back' from their external environment in terms of what will enhance their own survival, normally at the expense of others. Institutional survival means that those who are to survive in institutions by necessity must adopt such perspectives. While institutional perspectives, procedures and norms may not necessarily reflect human values, they inevitably mould overall behaviour.

Trust issues

Trust is often seen as a critical element in commercial relationships, but defining 'trust' is difficult. We all know what it is in practice, because we recognise that some suppliers can be trusted to do certain things, and others cannot. Trust can be defined as an expectation that others will do things such as:

◆　　Fulfil promises

◆　　Not try to take advantage

◆　　Behave consistently towards us.

We think of trust as generally being a good thing, because it enables us to work together effectively but, like power, trust is a neutral concept. Suppliers can be trusted to invariably fail delivery dates, which enables us to factor that failure into forward planning.

It has been said that there is no possibility for 'rational' individual behaviour in interdependent situations unless the conditions for mutual trust exist. Functionally, trust is a way of managing the coordination of tasks across organisational boundaries. In 'relationship' marketing, trust is seen as paramount in the successful management of the relationship between buyers and sellers.

Professor Mari Sako has made an attempt to define or classify trust as having three facets. Her definition rests heavily upon trust within contractual relationships. Indeed, she labels the first of her categories contractual trust which seems to be a belief that an entity, individual or organisation will fulfil its contractual obligations. The second she labels 'competence' trust and seems to involve a belief that an entity can fulfil its contractual obligations. The third she labels 'goodwill' trust and involves a belief that an entity can go beyond the fulfilment of its contractual obligations.

We can, however, draw upon a number of 'common sense' elements in identifying the components of trust:

Consistency

The first of these is consistency, or at worst predictability. In order for trust to exist we need to ensure that people will behave in the same or a predictable way over both time and different conditions. People that change in their behaviour towards us without sufficient reason over time or to meet different conditions are seen as 'capricious', 'inconsistent' or 'untrustworthy'. We tend to demand consistency before we can say that person is trustworthy.

Intention or motivation

The second is intention or motivation. Intention is a major component in 'successful' interpersonal relationships. Here trust seems to require an understanding of the motive of the part to be trusted. If the person here is well intentioned, we can see another element of trust.

Capacity

The third element of trust is capacity. Here the entity needs to demonstrate that not only is it willing, determined or committed to a certain course of action or pattern of behaviour, but also that it is able to behave in this way.

Visibility

The fourth element is visibility. Where an organisations intention or capacity cannot be easily perceived, there seem to be blocks to trust. Visibility, such as open book costing or process certification, reduces risk and therefore increases trust.

Group climate

In an earlier section of the study guide we looked at adversarial relationships. These 'traditional' relationships are often seen as bad in that they involve hostility, which is not altogether bad, but which often leads to inflexibility within the contract, and therefore high running costs when things go wrong.

The very existence of different groups and organisations can foster conflict and discrimination, sometimes hatred. We are especially likely to stereotype and discriminate against those from other groups, what we will call 'out-groups'. The very act of creating a team, for example, will create competition between that team and other teams. Sometimes this competition is useful; at other times it can be harmful, particularly if we need teams to be flexible and cooperate.

Within organisations, it is often difficult for individuals to see outside the 'walls' that define their view of the world. This leads to suspicion of individuals who do not see the world in this way, and who do not belong to their organisation. This suspicion is, of course, justified as other individuals feel exactly the same way. As the ancient Greeks labelled everyone who was not a Greek a 'barbarian', so individuals can label everyone who is not 'one of us' as 'one of them'. This is often particularly true of small suppliers.

In order to avoid these problems, it is often necessary to build bridges using effective communication techniques and by offering a superior and credible shared goal that breaks down the group climate.

Commercial factors

As well as the individual and relational issues that we have looked at, there are also a range of commercial factors that we need to take into consideration. Sometimes these factors will be within the control of one or both the parties within the relationship; at other times they will not. Nonetheless, it is important to recognise each of these factors when considering the commercial issues within the relationship. Factors here include:

- **Transaction value:** the amount of expenditure within the transaction as a proportion of overall customer spend/purchasing revenue

- **Transaction risk:** the likelihood that a supplier will fail in terms of price, quality, delivery, reliability, flexibility, innovation or service

- **Transaction contribution:** the degree to which the transaction contributes to the goals of the department, another department or the organisation

- **Transaction complexity:** the type, mix, range of contracts/activities/subprojects

- **Transaction volume:** the number of items

- **Transaction replicability:** the degree that other transactions can be substituted

- **Transaction predictability:** the impact of demand in terms of both quantity and type on both supplier and customer

- **Transaction longevity:** the length of time that the contract lasts or the likely number of repeat contracts

- **Transaction profile:** the trade-offs between price, quality, flexibility, innovation or service required by the contract

- **Transaction intensity:** the amount of time and other resource the management of the contract will entail.

It is very easy to think that a commercial relationship will rest only upon commercial factors. This is seldom true, and never true in partnership or co-destiny type relationships. Instead, relationships rest upon individual, relational and commercial factors. These factors will combine in different ways and to different degrees to impact upon the relationship between the parties.

The factors that impact upon relationships are complex in themselves. They depend in large part upon the role that the purchasing professional chooses to play. We can identify five sets of factors that will impact on relationships. So far we have considered three of those sets in detail. These are:

◆ Individual impact in terms of the skills employed

◆ Relationship impacts with regard to factors within the relationship itself

◆ Commercial impacts.

Summary

By considering how these factors might interact, it is possible to reach an understanding of the underlying issues and develop effective relationships, and understand the impact of these issues on relationships.

Self-assessment questions

SAQ 2.2

What are the six types of influence as identified by Robert Cialdini?

SAQ 2.3

What are the stages of conflict?

Relationships and supply chain policy

The syllabus learning outcomes for this subsection state that you will be able to:

◆ **Appraise appropriate sourcing policies from a relationship perspective**

◆ **Evaluate ethical, technological, legal, environmental and other relationship constraints and enablers.**

This subsection will cover:

◆ **Introduction**

◆ **Background**

◆ **Relationships and technology**

◆ **Relationships and the environment**

◆ **Relationships and regulation.**

Introduction

In the last subsection of the study guide we looked at individual, relational and commercial factors that might impact on relationships. This subsection considers some of the wider issues which might impact on relationships. Broadly these fall into four areas:

◆ Ethical issues

◆ Technological issues

◆ Environmental issues

◆ Regulatory issues.

Each of these areas may have a major impact on the nature of commercial relationships.

Background

At a strategic level, we have seen that the objectives of the enterprise will drive supply chains. For the purposes of supply chains policy we can suggest that supply chains can be divided into two types – the producer driven and the buyer driven. The former is characterised by high degrees of integration, and certain companies are able to exert control over backward and forward linkages within the chain. The latter is characterised by highly competitive and globally decentralised production units, with brand-name owners and retailers exerting substantial control over how, when and where manufacturing will take place and how much profit accrues at each stage of the chain.

In the past, enterprises have taken little interest in the behaviour of their suppliers beyond product price, specification, quality and availability. That has changed in recent years for a number of reasons ranging, from competitive advantage (for example, making sure that producers are responding to fashion signals from consumers) to legal liability (for example, EU food safety laws which require retailers to exhibit due diligence throughout the supply chain).

It is possible to identify a range of responses to these shifts. Ethical trading is a dimension of this expansion in corporate governance, requiring that marketers take responsibility for worker and human rights among their suppliers.

This is a significant change because, in the past, suppliers were only accountable to the state for upholding national laws. However, concern in the major consumer markets about labour and human right abuses began to pose a threat to an enterprise's own reputation, and it was no longer sufficient for them to say they had no responsibility for the behaviour of their suppliers. As yet, there are few legal requirements for enterprises to be responsible for supplier behaviour, but a mixture of consumer, media, lobbying organisation and investor pressure has led to a plethora of voluntary codes of labour/human rights practice claiming to measure company performance.

In the wider community we can also see a growing awareness of environmental issues, and the need for enterprises to follow sustainable policies. In some senses this is the application of business ethics and a growing need for increased accountability within corporate governance. Again, as with ethical behaviour, voluntary codes of practice exist, as do international standards – for example ISO 14031. Increasingly, however, governmental bodies in some countries are beginning to set enforceable legislation. This will also impact on commercial relationships.

Technology has perhaps been one of the most important drivers of business activity in the 20th century. The advent of desktop computers, the Internet, faxes and a range of manufacturing techniques has transformed industry and this has also effected the nature of commercial relationships.

There are also regulatory and legal impacts where states or transnational alliances, such as the European Union, have sought to preserve 'fairness' in competition, which means that certain bodies must demonstrate transparency in their sourcing and contract award procedures.

In considering all of these issues, we can set ethical and environmentally conscious procurement in the broader context of a fast-changing world, of increasing globalisation and the challenges of sustainability and social cohesion, where businesses will increasingly adopt socially responsible practices.

The reasons for this are that, for some commentators, business has become the most powerful institution on the planet. In such a view, business is replacing political parties, religious bodies, governments and other traditional organisations as the primary influence in people's lives. It has become the new driving force behind many forms of change and innovation due to superior financial clout and the way in which it touches on almost all aspects of people's daily lives.

Relationship strategy, policy and practice - Section 2e

Companies not only impact upon the lives of their employees, but also that of their stakeholders – their clients, suppliers, investors and the communities in which they operate. Often, they also impact regional, national and global politics, the environment (locally as well as internationally) and economics (the distribution of wealth between people and between countries). These effects can be both positive and negative.

According to some surveys, the public's view is increasingly that responsibility for addressing social issues lies with large companies, as well as the government. This has led to the growing importance of Corporate Social Responsibility (CSR). CSR involves a range of efforts to make companies look beyond short-term profit or 'product' and focus on their impact on people and the planet.

CSR is a very broad topic for debate, ranging from how companies treat their employees, to their involvement with the populations of less developed countries. It pertains to a number of current, hotly debated news items – sustainable development, global environmental degradation, massive company lay-offs, anti-globalisation demonstrations and, arguably, also terrorism. It is also a very timely discussion since governments, civil society and also many companies – multinational corporations in particular – have begun to reassess the responsibilities of businesses as citizens.

Since the debate is so broad, it is necessary to distinguish between a number of themes in CSR and the way it impacts on commercial relationships. These include:

◆ Responsibilities of companies towards their employees and, by implication, responsibility of employees towards their companies

◆ Responsibilities of companies towards other stakeholders (clients/customers, shareholders/investors, subcontractors and suppliers)

◆ Responsibilities of companies in respect to the political, natural and economic environment both locally and globally.

Although the question of commercial relationships, and the intelligent use of procurement strategies to promote corporate social responsibility is a thorny and difficult one, we can see that some organisations are developing CSR-based sourcing and procurement strategies. In public sector procurement CSR-based practice is an obvious way to encourage other organisations to use their supply chains, as well as promote best practice using market leverage.

When considering ethical and environmental issues, it is important for the procurement practitioner to consider CSR as a concept that can support an overall framework of practice which might reach from labour conditions within suppliers through to culturally specific business practices that may be unacceptable in western societies, such as 'facilitatory payments' or bribes.

We can see then that a wide and growing range of factors is continuing to act upon commercial relationships. Issues such as CSR will grow in importance, and procurement must be ready to meet the challenges they will bring.

Ethical issues in purchasing

Ethics are those issues which relate to moral or honourable matters in trading relationships. In talking about ethics it is possible to identify three core areas in which ethical issues may arise, which are:

1.   Responsibility to the profession or role of purchasing.

2.   Responsibility to the company or organisation in which the purchasing takes place.

3.   Responsibility to the wider community.

Each of these areas brings its own challenges. The subject of ethics in purchasing is a wide-reaching one.

Legal issues

Strictly speaking, ethical issues and legal issues are separate. There are clearly, however, issues that overlap, and legislation (both criminal and civil) applies to what might broadly be termed 'ethical matters'. In the field of company responsibility there is legislation affecting both the public and private sector with regard to ethics in supplier selection, false statements and engaging in external business activities. The Competition Act of 1999 places limits on awarding business in such a way as to create a cartel.

Other critical issues involve the duty of the directors in the management of risk. Recent reports have suggested that directors should become legally responsible for a much broader range of risk than the purely financial risk for which they are normally held responsible. This may include risks which arise due to fraud or malpractice, and we can expect that increasing emphasis will be placed on ethical behaviour.

In the field of ethical responsibility to the wider community we can see moves towards environmental conscious or 'green' purchasing. This may involve making sure that producers and resellers, as well as the buyers and users, act in an environmentally responsible manner in the purchase of products and services.

Why ethics are important

Ethical issues are perhaps more important than ever before, given the emphasis which many organisations and professionals put on managing relationships with suppliers. This increased emphasis on relationships means that many purchasing professionals are now in contact with their suppliers in a much less 'adversarial' manner than ever before. Supplier partnerships have expanded the grey area and blurred the lines on ethics.

Typically, purchasers face the threat of being influenced by personal relationships with suppliers. The rising importance of supplier relationships renders it critical for purchasing to focus objectively when making business decisions in spite of any subjective or emotional feelings the professional might have about a supplier.

As well as being faced with the problem of decision making in the shift to partnership, cooperative supply relationships may be giving rise to other threats as well. Closer relationships can give greater exposure to inside or confidential supplier information. The amount of work that often goes into selecting preferred suppliers can mean that purchasing staff are anxious to use these suppliers. This can lead to an increase in the frequency at which procurement professionals quote business that doesn't really exist, or disclose market bids to preferred suppliers.

Where ethics are important

Gifts

There are a number of areas where ethics are important. The first of these is in the area of gifts. These range from the apparently trivial, such as allowing buyers to consume meals with suppliers, through to the more serious issues, such as gifts. A recent study of ethics codes and policies showed that 71% allowed buyers to accept meals, whereas 7% discourage it and only 1% prohibit the practice. Business lunches were seen as more acceptable than dinners. Reciprocity seemed to count, as 63% allow meals as long as parties take turns treating (usually according to who was visiting whom).

Perhaps slightly more important is the degree to which suppliers should be allowed to bestow other social favours on buyers, and whether the buyer should accept them. These may include invitations to holiday parties, golf or other outings, and tickets to sporting events.

Even more important is the degree to which procurement personnel should accept gifts from suppliers, and the size and frequency of such gifts. Some organisations refuse to allow buyers to accept any gift. Some require that gifts bear corporate logos as proof of promotional intent. Some pool gifts and distribute them in raffles or other neutralising mechanisms. Frequently, outings and other miscellaneous forms of hospitality are allowed only if offered to all personnel in the customer company or supply management organisation. Others allow gifts below a certain financial limit. Still others allow a financial limit over time. The key issue here is to avoid both impropriety and the appearance of impropriety.

Loyalty

The second area is where a company may be open to the misuse of inside information. Engaging in outside business activities is clearly a problem in terms of establishing loyalty. Companies that share staff across functions may leave themselves open to allegations of mixed or misplaced loyalty. Many companies do prohibit their purchasing personnel from holding equity positions in supplier companies (with or without restrictions).

In addition we also need to consider the impact of sourcing policies on other organisations, particularly in low-wage economies. As we saw in the introduction to this section, voluntary codes exist with regard to the elimination of labour and human rights abuses such as child labour or unbreakable contracts of employment which can sometimes represent little more than 'slave labour'. As improved communication makes cases of this type more visible, purchasing and supply departments need to have procedures in place to avoid public censure.

Why ethics are sometimes disregarded

An awareness of the clear dangers in pursuing actions that will leave them open to allegations of malpractice is not always enough to steer purchasers away from trouble. Often ethical dilemmas involve complex issues. Choosing to give business to a company that you have done business with for 20 years, despite the fact that they do not offer the optimum performance, is hard. Setting suppliers against each other in competitive bidding situations is a tempting way of improving the situation for your company.

Many purchasing professionals would take the position that nothing will deter the truly unscrupulous. Many believe that you are an ethical person or you are not. Statements such as, 'We all know that the company's best interests come first, and we must all conduct ourselves as if we owned the company', are common.

One way of managing through these perceptions is to introduce an ethics policy or code of ethics. This in itself may not be enough. One common response is that, 'If an individual has questionable ethics, policy does not matter'. For others, though, the matter is not as simple. Some take the view that ethics policies are demoralising for those who do not cheat or take personal advantage.

Ethics policies

Ethics policies or codes of ethics should be designed and introduced with some care. Often such codes and policies are introduced and circulated without any understanding of the real issues that the buyer faces. Although purchasing professionals appear to favour strict, clear ethics policies, the real danger is to breach the code by accident, without realising that it is a violation of policy. This suggests that codes of ethics are often too vague. The opportunities for unethical behaviour, and the way in which unethical behaviour is interpreted, means that the buyer often needs more than a general statement of ethical standards.

In addition, poor enforcement of existing ethical guidelines and poor review can cause problems. Codes of ethics should be regularly reviewed to ensure that they meet the changing demand of the business environment.

Enforcement and review should also be carried out consistently across different functions. One criticism of policies and codes of ethics is that different standards apply to engineers, upper management and the company's own sales force, leading to a disregard of stated ethical guidelines.

In developing an ethics policy or a code of ethics, extensive consultation should take place to ensure that the code or policy is owned and committed to by staff that are asked to adhere to the code or policy.

To help purchasing staff understand the moral and potential legal implications of their actions, ethics policies should be supported by training and development actions. These actions need to be sensitively designed so as not to demonstrate an assumption of unethical attitude or behaviour among staff.

Managing ethics

Integrity is perhaps the most important element in business life, and also perhaps the most important component in business reputation. Reputation has a major impact on the way in which both customers and suppliers relate to the organisation in which you work. The transparency and consistency of the values that support day-to-day business operations will have an effect on the long-term success of that organisation. Although, talking about ethical behaviour can be difficult, the clarity of approach and action in the management of ethics is a prerequisite of success. Muddled communication leads to a muddled framework of understanding. This leads, in turn, to confusion in applying ethical standards. The rule for encouraging ethical behaviour in purchasing is to ensure that standards are both clear and clearly understood. Never assume in ethics.

Summary

There are three main areas in which ethical practice should be considered. Ethics in professional life, ethics in the workplace and ethics with regard to the wider community. Ethical behaviour in purchasing can range across a wide area of practice, from accepting gifts, through to managing competition between suppliers, to the impact of poor environmental purchasing policies on the customer, staff and people living in the area. Ethics is a difficult area for all staff and managers. For this reason, many companies avoid the problem altogether or pay lip service by implementing vague policies and codes of practice. This can lead to problems for the company as a whole and for the purchasing function in particular. With an effective ethics code or policy this can be avoided and, in turn, avoid misunderstandings among staff, suppliers and purchasers.

Ethical issues act as both a constraint and an enabler upon relationships. We will now consider another constraint and enabler-technology: the nature of technology and the effect this may have upon relationships within the supply chain.

Relationships and technology

Technological advances are, in many industries, reshaping the nature of relationships within the supply chain. These advances range from eProcurement systems through to powerful advanced planning and scheduling (APS) systems supported by complex mathematical algorithms that are beginning to make supply chain optimisation a reality.

The world of business seems to be changing at a phenomenal rate. One of the key elements in this change is the growth of so-called eCommerce, and the growing use of the World Wide Web and the Internet. More and more companies are discovering that the World Wide Web can have a profound impact on how they run their business. Open-platform-based technology that is both cheap and easy to install allows companies to use the Internet to open up new distribution channels, create online markets, increase revenues and boost the bottom line. In ways unimaginable just a few years ago, corporations are utilising Internet technology to set up electronic commerce businesses and successfully conduct trade over the Internet.

The impact of eCommerce

Broadly, it is possible to identify three main impacts for commercial relationships within this environment.

1. **Access:** the use of information technology to change the way in which employees can access the product or service base has implications for the purchaser. The changing nature of access means that sellers by-pass professional buyers, who have some of the information required, reaching the product or service user. This disintermediation process drives, and is driven by, products such as Internet-based catalogues and online auctions. Access strategies, what Bill Gates has called 'friction free capitalism', also include the ability to customise communication in an apparently interactive way with many potential users or buyers through the use of techniques such as dynamic hypertext mark-up language (DHTML), XML, Java-based languages and cookies.

2. **Choice:** the so-called 'death of distance' has increased the number of potential options as more and more companies with lower entry costs enter the marketplace. This provides the professional and non-professional buyer with a, sometimes vastly, increased choice framework. Intelligent agents or 'shopbots' that can source and compare different products and services in a range of different criteria are in development. These shopbots only compare products and services; they do not assess risk. Increased choice can contribute to increased risk. This in turn relates to the third impact.

3. **Control:** the use of information technology to manage the trade-off between organisational flexibility and empowerment and organisational expenditure has implications for the purchaser. Here purchasing or even smart cards can be linked to enterprise resource planning (ERP) systems and reduce the need for regulation by the purchasing department.

Relationship strategy, policy and practice - Section 2e

Using eCommerce

Access

Purchasing, in some senses, will benefit from B2B eCommerce. The reach of the Internet means that low prices will be much easier to find. Nonetheless, the best price may not have the impact it is hoped. In many cases, purchasing has driven costs back into the supply chain, and has either hidden these costs, as in the case of inventory, or caused the costs to 'break out' elsewhere in the organisation in a form of organisational cannibalism. This is due, to some degree, because of the difficulties in measuring costs in any useful way.

Choice

As we saw when we considered structural issues, electronic marketplaces and technology, such as reverse auctions, are having an impact on the nature of relationships between buyers and sellers. There is, however, a very real danger that a focus on price will lead to quality problems or that a focus on price and quality will drive out innovation. Using the Internet to collect information can lead to an improved impact.

Control

The fastest-growing market for optimisation technology is found in supply chain management (SCM), where intelligent algorithms supply the backbone for powerful advanced planning and scheduling (APS) applications, designed both as customer solutions and as a growing number of commercial packages. APS solutions allow enterprises to optimise their supply chains to reduce costs, improve product margins, lower inventories and increase manufacturing throughput.

While ERP and SCM systems are primarily involved in making key corporate data accessible in order to improve productivity, optimisation technology aims to address all of the business issues pertaining to supply chain design simultaneously. Optimisation begins with the development of a model in which each business issue is represented as a variable. The relationships between business issues are formulated as constraints, and the desired objective (such as maximising profitability) is imposed.

In general, long-term planning problems are solved using some variation of linear programming (LP), and operations research professionals are employed by many large companies to design in-house applications. LP is based on applied mathematics rather than computer technology.

The strategic business issues encountered in supply chain planning include:

◆   Number of manufacturing plants required

◆   Where they are located

◆   Which products they produce

◆   Number of distribution centres required

◆   Which products they stock and at what inventory levels

◆   Which customers the distribution centres serve

◆   Which suppliers are be selected.

Each of these issues is interrelated, with the answer to one affecting the response to another. LP is an effective technique for solving problems with linear constraints, frequently those with a longer time frame than are addressed in planning.

Short-term scheduling problems, such as those encountered in operations, are frequently addressed using a newer technique called constraint programming (CP). Scheduling helps with the question, 'How should I do it?' Some of the shorter-term scheduling problems most commonly addressed by CP include the best way to process orders in a production facility or the best sequence of stops on a delivery route.

Using the Internet, some enterprises are attempting to implement execution systems that give real time data for planning. A key capability for the most effective real-time execution system is quick feedback on customer orders, which is proving increasingly important for manufacturers that offer highly customisable products and just-in-time (JIT) production techniques. These execution systems feature available-to-promise (ATP) or capable-to-promise (CTP) capabilities. ATP determines whether a particular order can be met, based on current inventory and capacity. CTP takes optimisation a step further, checking factors like plant capacity and part orders to decide whether a new order can be inserted into the production schedule and still meet the requested date.

As eCommerce transforms the way business is conducted – with companies using the Internet to enter new markets, shrink supply chains, create value chains and meet the challenges of increased competition and global markets – optimisation will play a key role.

It should be noted, however, that technology is only one of the factors that impact upon relationships, and unless the purchasing practitioner gets the other elements right, costs and risks will be added to the relationship.

Relationships and the environment

It is a matter of increasing concern that the current path of economic development and population growth is threatening both the Earth's carrying capacity and people's capacity to cope. Global consumption expenditure, both private and public, has grown an average of 3% a year since 1970. This growth, however, is far from equal in all regions of the world. Rapid development in some countries happens at the expense of others in both present and future generations, thus deepening inequalities and social exclusion.

Purchasing has a major role to play in environmental issues and is also impacted by environmental issues. Increasingly, we see public and governmental pressure on organisations to implement so-called 'green procurement' policies. This can have a major impact on the purchasing decision and subsequently upon the relationship with the supplier.

'Green' procurement decisions imply consideration and choices of an extremely complex nature. Questions may include:

◆ How should a sustainable product be selected? Should this be done by considering the products' life cycle assessment or its environmental performance? Should the manufacturing process be an issue or the environmental management of the factory?

◆ What are the best solutions for the product's life cycle? In some cases being able to recycle a product is the best option, in others it is highly environmentally damaging.

Green products are generally produced in a manner that consumes less natural resources or uses them more sustainably, as with sustainable forestry. They may involve less energy in their manufacture and may consume less energy when being used, and they generally contain fewer hazardous or toxic materials.

Green products are also generally designed with the intention of reducing the amount of waste created. For example, they may contain recycled material or use less packaging, and the supplier may operate a 'take-back' programme.

Green procurement can also offer cost savings. In particular, buying 'green' usually involves products that are easily recycled, last longer or produce less waste. Money is therefore saved on waste disposal. In addition, green products generally require fewer resources to manufacture and operate, so savings can be made on energy, water, fuel and other natural resources.

Moreover, green products generally involve the use of fewer toxic or hazardous materials, reducing associated expenses such as permit fees, toxic materials, handling charges and staff training.

Organisations may require a green procurement programme as part of their environmental management systems, as certified under the EMAS and ISO 14001 regimes. In addition, new regulations increasingly require the adoption of green procurement practices. Organisations that practise green procurement will also be recognised as good corporate citizens. This will influence other organisations, and cause changes in markets, leading to increased availability of green products and falling prices.

Challenges to green procurement

Despite the advantages of green procurement, many organisations find that once they have developed a policy, the actual implementation of that policy can be difficult. This is because of a number of factors including:

Price
There is a perception that green products are more expensive than conventional alternatives. This may be true in some cases, particularly where development costs are reflected in the price; however, often there may be no significant difference. The real problem may simply be that products are being ordered in small quantities or are not available locally.

Sometimes a green product may have a higher up-front purchase price, but will cost less over its life cycle. For example, a non-toxic alternative to a toxic product will cost less to transport, store, handle and discard. It will require fewer permits, less training for staff and the consequences of an accident will be greatly reduced. Similarly, a product that uses less packaging and that is easily recyclable or reusable will carry a lower disposal cost.

Insufficient knowledge
Many organisations are unfamiliar with the concept of green procurement or with the options available to them. For an organisation to participate, it must have an understanding of concepts, vocabulary and terms.

Markets
Frequently, local distributors do not stock green products, or else they stock only small quantities. This can lead to delays in obtaining the product.

A lack of acceptable alternatives
Another barrier to green purchasing can simply be a lack of acceptable alternatives to the present product. For example, a few years ago in the furniture manufacturing industry, the use of water-based finishes as an alternative to solvent-based ones was impeded by the fact that water-based finishes presented technical difficulties which were costly to overcome, and they were of lower quality.

Guidance
It is important that guidance to suppliers is clear and integrates with local and national regulations. Suppliers may be asked to provide environmental specifications of the products they are offering. Purchasers, in the same way, should clearly define their needs and requirements.

Environmental issues can be expected to grow in importance.

Relationships and regulation

As we saw in the section on supplier assessment and selection, in some industries there are a number of rules which must be taken into account when embarking upon a commercial relationship. If you work in the public sector or former public sector bodies such as universities or utilities companies, you should be aware of the European procurement directives. These require that you observe certain safeguards. The legislation includes the General Agreement on Tariff and Trades which supports European directives preventing any public procurement body discriminating against a supplier from a member state on the grounds of location or ownership.

The European directive also supports a range of legislation in the UK including:

◆   The Public Supply Contracts Regulations 1995 (SI95/201)

◆   The Public Contracts Regulations 1991 (SI91/2180)

◆   The Public Services Contracts Regulations 1991 (SI91/2680)

◆   The Utilities Supply and Works Regulations 1992 (SI92/3279).

In the latter case, utilities companies are not only barred from discriminating against suppliers, but have to have a system in place to prove that this discrimination does not take place.

Within certain countries and certain industries there is a mandatory requirement to demonstrate good practice in procurement. For purchasers within these industries in countries operating within the legal jurisdiction of the European Community, and certain others bound by treaty, there are a number of obligations.

The industries

Industries effected by European Community procurement directives are as follows:

The Supplies Directive (93/36/EEC): relates to the delivery of goods. It includes purchase, lease, rental or hire purchase, with or without an option to buy.

The Works Directive (93/37/EEC): covers the execution and design of constructions or works corresponding to the requirements specified by the contracting authority.

The Services Directive (92/50/EEC): is defined very broadly and can include among others: studies, consultants' services, advertising services, transport services, maintenance and repair services, engineering services, financial services, computer services and legal services.

These three, supplies, works and services directives, were applicable to all EEC and EEA member states from 1 July 1994.

A separate directive (93/38/EEC) was issued, covering supply, works and services contracts awarded by utilities. These are defined as entities operating in the water, energy, transport and telecommunications sectors. The directive was a response to a number of considerations, and the definition given was not confined to a simple distinction between public and private tendering bodies. Instead, it treats certain tendering situations as identical, despite any differences of legal form that there may be between them. The activities falling within the scope of the directive belong in two categories:

1. Cases where a service is provided to the public via a technical network whose very existence restricts competition. The directive thus covers the provision or operation of networks which provide a service to the public in connection with the production, transport or distribution of drinking water, electricity, gas, heat, telecommunications, and railway, tramway and bus networks.

2. Cases where an entity exploits a geographical area for a particular purpose subject to a government concession or authorisation. Such purposes are:

    -   Exploring for, or extracting, oil, gas, coal or other solid fuels (except those specifically exempted by a member state with the agreement of the EC)

    -   The provision or airport, maritime or inland port or other terminal facilities to carriers by air, sea or inland waterway.

Contracts to which the directives apply are:

◆   Public supply and service contracts over a particular level in value

◆   Supply or service contracts over a particular level in value in the case of entities carrying on an activity in the transport, drinking water or energy sectors

◆   Supply or service contracts over a particular level in value in the case of entities carrying on an activity in the telecommunications sector

◆   In the case of public works contracts over five million euros.

Where a contract is subdivided into several lots, the total value of all the lots must be taken into account for the purpose of determining whether the threshold specified in the relevant directive is reached.

The obligations

In the United Kingdom, legal obligations on certain industries include:

- EC Treaty provisions which prohibit:
  - discrimination on grounds of nationality, either directly or indirectly
  - restrictions on the free movement of goods and services
  - restrictions on the freedom of establishment of service providers
  - measures of equivalent effect

- The EC procurement directives which:
  - reinforce the above Treaty provisions for contracts above a certain value
  - are based on principles of equal treatment, transparency and competitive procurement
  - establish a framework of rules to which procedures for the award of supplies, works and certain services contracts by public bodies and various utilities must be adapted

- The EC remedies directives which provide that, where the procurement directives apply:
  - suppliers harmed or at risk of harm from a breach of the EC rules (the directives, the regulations which implement them or any other relevant Community law, including the Treaty) are to have access to rapid and effective review systems with powers to grant interim and final remedies including powers to suspend the award procedure, to set aside decisions and/or to award damages
  - a corrective mechanism under which the European Commission can draw attention to alleged breaches and accelerate its consideration of infraction proceedings against the member state in the European Court of Justice (ECJ). In addition to powers to determine whether there has been a breach of Community law by the member state, the ECJ has powers to grant interim remedies or to order that the contract is not to be performed

- The UK regulations give effect to these provisions by:
  - providing mechanisms through which relevant suppliers can bring proceedings against the purchaser before the High Court in England and Wales, the High Court in Northern Ireland or the Court of Session in Scotland
  - providing for injunctive relief and/or damages, but with damages to be the only remedy if the contract has been entered into
  - imposing an obligation on purchasers to provide the information needed for the purpose of responses to the Commission. For purchasers other than departments, this obligation is enforceable by the courts on application by the department most closely concerned with the purchaser's activities.

- The European Economic Area Agreement and various European agreements under which purchasers have the same obligations towards suppliers from other European countries as they do to suppliers from other EU member states. The UK regulations identify the countries concerned and provide for the same remedies.

- The World Trade Organisation (formerly GATT) Government Procurement Agreement (GPA) under which obligations similar to those under the EC rules are enforceable by suppliers from other signatories to the GPA where it applies.

Common law in the European Commission Judiciary and UK courts

Community legislation was introduced to ensure that government contracts were open to all nationalities on equal terms and to make tendering procedures more transparent. To make it easier for resident and non-resident foreign firms to compete for public sector contracts, the Council issued directives to coordinate procurement procedures in all public sector procurement subject to the treaties. The aim of the directives is to coordinate national contract award procedures by introducing a minimum body of common rules for contracts above a given threshold.

The types of procedure

The directives provide three types of tendering procedure that can be used by relevant contracting organisations:

1. **Open procedure:** all interested suppliers, contractors or service providers may submit tenders.

2. **Restricted procedure:** only those suppliers, contractors or service providers invited by the contracting authority may submit tenders.

3. **Negotiated procedure:** the contracting authority consults suppliers, contractors or service providers of its choice and negotiates the terms of the contract with one or more of them.

For supplies, works and services contracts the contracting organisation has the choice between open and restricted procedures. They are both the general procedure. The negotiated procedure may be used only in justified cases and if the conditions required for its use are fulfilled. For utilities contracts they have a free choice between all three procedures, provided that a call for competition notice has been published in the official journal of the European Community.

It should be noted that in open and restricted procedures, negotiation with potential and actual bidders on fundamental aspects of contracts, including prices, is ruled out. Providing this is not discriminatory to the potential or actual bidders, discussions with such bidders may be held for the purpose of clarifying or supplementing:

- The content of their tenders

- The requirements of the contracting authorities.

The directives are aimed at making procedures more transparent in three main areas:

Prior information

The Public Works Directive requires contracting authorities to publish an indicative notice in the official journal before the launch of the award procedure. This notice should summarise the essential characteristics of the works' contracts which they intend to award and the estimated value of those more than five million euros. Directives on public supplies and services require contracting authorities to publish an indicative notice, as soon as possible after the beginning of their budgetary year, which sets out the total procurement by product area of a total estimated value, is equal to or greater than 750,000 euros which they foresee awarding during the subsequent 12 months. Such information should enable firms to be aware of the intentions of contracting authorities at a sufficiently early stage.

Publication of tender notices

Contracting authorities that wish to tender by open or restricted procedure, or by negotiated procedure with publication of a notice, must make known their intention by means of a notice. The normal minimum periods that contracting authorities must allow for receipt of tenders is not less than 52 days for an open procedure and not less than 40 days for a restricted procedure. This may be reduced to 36 and 26 days respectively, in the case of works or service contracts where an indicative notice has already been published. The normal delay for requests to participate in restricted procedures or negotiated procedures is 37 days (unless they qualify as urgent where the delay is reduced to 15 days). For utilities contracts, the delay must generally be at least 5 weeks and not less than 22 days.

Notification of a contract award notice

The supply works and services directives require contracting organisations to publish details in the official journal of how contracts have been awarded.

Summary

As well as being impacted upon by individual, relational and commercial factors, commercial relationships are impacted upon by ethical, environmental, technical and regulatory factors. All of these factors should be taken into account when considering the nature of the relationship you intend to develop. Because of the increasingly important nature of supply chain management, and the response of the general public to business behaviour, which might be considered irresponsible or unethical, these factors are likely to take on more importance in the future.

Self-assessment question

SAQ 2.4

Identify four common sense elements of trust.

 # saq responses

SAQ 2.1

Microsoft's 12 sources of risk are:

◆   Business partners
◆   Competitive
◆   Customer
◆   Distribution
◆   Financial
◆   Operations
◆   People
◆   Political
◆   Regulatory and legislative
◆   Reputational
◆   Strategic
◆   Technological.

SAQ 2.2

The six types of influence as identified by Robert Cialdini are:

◆   Reciprocity
◆   Consistency/commitment
◆   Social proof
◆   Authority
◆   Liking
◆   Scarcity.

SAQ 2.3

The stages of conflict are:

1.   **No conflict:** the first stage is, of course, no conflict at all. This stage means that there are either no differences between the parties or else one or more of the parties are afraid for one reason or another to express a difference. This is a stage where parties may be avoiding conflict.

2.   **Unexpressed conflict:** this stage occurs when one party feels that there is something wrong but will not or cannot express it. Many of us may have been in situations where we feel that there is something wrong with a relationship, but the other party refuses to identify the problem. The classic case is of the husband/wife relationship where the husband or wife asks what is wrong, only to be answered 'nothing'. Such unexpressed conflicts can turn into open conflict very quickly.

3. **Problem identification:** this stage will involve one or both parties identifying the issues which are, generally at this stage, interest issues which can be addressed easily. If issues are relational or emotional, however, it may be that the next stage of conflict is reached.

4. **Dispute:** the fourth stage is one where conflict has started to get out of hand. Parties will bring in issues that are not related to the problem. A party's needs has not been met so he or she will escalate the conflict although there is a stage in which parties may try to involve others in the conflict, to try to obtain help.

5. **Help:** the fifth stage may involve other people either in an official or unofficial capacity. Individuals will appeal to a third party to attempt to resolve the conflict. Such a strategy can be dangerous for the third party, but generally their aim should be to get the parties talking again before the situation degenerates further into the penultimate stage.

6. **Flight or fight:** the sixth stage is one in which people tend to become very emotional and may allow the conflict to degenerate into physical or verbal aggression – hitting the other party or name-calling. The conflict is such that the parties involved no longer feel safe and will be forced to leave the relationship or attempt to destroy the other party or the relationship itself.

7. **The conflict cycle:** the final stage can demonstrate that conflict repeats itself. Once we get into stage 6 it is very difficult to emerge. People need to feel safe when they communicate, and effective communication helps them feel safe. Once safety is challenged, conflict can be perpetuated because we can't take the risk of talking to the other party. People in this position will often legitimise their position by talking about 'principles' or 'rights' as though the conflict is outside of themselves. Such conflicts may be impossible to handle.

SAQ 2.4

◆ Consistency
◆ Intention or motivation
◆ Capacity
◆ Visibility.

examination questions

Exam 2.1

Identify and discuss three methods of working across functions within an organisation. Illustrate the discussion with examples of the advantages and drawbacks of each method.

Exam 2.2

The following two statements characterise two approaches to the management of commercial relationships. Analyse and discuss the statements, identifying which you feel is most accurate.

1. 'The management risk is the most important task of the purchasing and supply function.'

2. 'The management of supplier performance is the most important task of the purchasing and supply function.'

Exam 2.3

'It takes two to tango' – explain some of the factors impacting on change in relationships.

Exam 2.4

Identify and discuss the components of an integrated supplier development programme.

Exam 2.5

Purchasing consortia, supplier associations, supplier tiering and electronic marketplaces: consider the advantages and disadvantages of two of these from the viewpoint of:

1. The purchaser.
2. The supplier.

Exam 2.6

A major supplier has been supplying faulty goods for some time. It has become apparent that this is a problem with the tooling that the supplier has bought. Nonetheless, you have no alternative other than to terminate the contract. What steps could you take to minimise the impact on the relationship?

Exam 2.7

Explain the differences between a traditional contract, a relational contract and a long-term contract. What might be the benefits and drawbacks of each of these?

Exam 2.8

Describe some of the individual factors acting upon relationships.

Exam 2.9

How might you maximise the effectiveness of a vendor appraisal and selection programme? Illustrate with examples.

Exam 2.10

Describe some of the problems associated with service contracts. What steps might be taken to minimise these problems?

Exam 2.11

Discuss the similarities between the philosophies underpinning lean supply and total quality management.

Exam 2.12

Explain Kraljic's matrix, and discuss the relevance of this tool to the study of commercial relationships.

Exam 2.13

1.   Discuss the concept of the lean supply chain.

2.   Discuss the ways in which developing ideas in connection with eCommerce are impacting upon commercial relationships.

Relationship management

Objectives

When you have completed this section you will be able to:

◆ **Appraise the role of supplier associations, buying consortia, joint buying arrangements and other groupings in commercial relationships**

◆ **Appraise supply base tiering, and relationship implications of this practice**

◆ **Evaluate the role of the internal customer, including the concept of the intelligent customer**

◆ **Evaluate the potential and practicalities of supplier development from a relationship perspective. Recommend appropriate actions in relation to supplier development and upstream management.**

◆ **Explain the relationship life cycle**

◆ **Recommend appropriate approaches to the termination or suspension of relationships**

◆ **Evaluate the implications of relationship failure**

◆ **Comment critically on developing theory and practice in relation to relationship assessment and management.**

Section 3 comprises subsections:

a) **Structural issues**

b) **The role of the internal customer**

c) **The role of the supplier**

d) **Supplier development**

e) **The relationship life cycle**

f) **Relationship assessment**

g) **Management of supplier risk**

Structural issues

The syllabus learning outcomes for this subsection state that you will be able to:

◆ **Appraise the role of supplier associations, buying consortia, joint buying arrangements and other groupings in commercial relationships**

◆ **Appraise supply base tiering, and relationship implications of this practice.**

This subsection will cover:

◆ **Introduction**

◆ **Purchasing consortia and associations**

◆ **Supplier associations**

◆ **Supplier tiering**

◆ **eMarketplaces, virtual organisations, portals and other eStructures.**

Introduction

This section considers the way in which networks of organisations can be identified and how the structure of their relationships can be managed. In this subsection we will consider a range of issues including associations between buyers (purchasing consortia), associations between suppliers, and associations between buyers and suppliers in the form of eMarketplaces and vertical portals.

Purchasing consortia and associations

Consortia are groups of companies or organisations that come together to purchase goods and services so as to obtain a range of benefits.

These benefits may be price related or may involve extending knowledge, reducing administrative cost or improving the positioning of the purchasing function.

Consortia can range from the rudimentary form of organisation, where two or more companies come together to buy MRO goods, through to the complex form, where companies are involved in a research and development joint venture. As well as offering benefits, consortia can also involve drawbacks and costs. Consortia also involve costs in terms of management and organisation. Consortia and joint venture performance should be measured and monitored accurately. Many failures within joint ventures and consortia arise because of unclear objectives and poor monitoring mechanisms.

Why consortia?

Consortia can have several roles, depending on their level of autonomy and budget:

◆ In the first place, consortia can act as negotiating agents for the acquisition of goods and services. Here they can negotiate with a seller on behalf of a group of companies, creating a master or framework contract which sets the terms and conditions for subsequent purchases by companies from the seller

◆ Secondly, they can act to negotiate with a series of suppliers on behalf of a group of companies, creating a preferred supplier list. Individual companies can subsequently negotiate their own contracts within the framework created by the preferred seller list

◆ In the third case, they can purchase goods and services from one or more sellers for delivery to member companies, and then charge back the cost of the purchase (including a service charge, if applicable) to the companies. In this case, the consortium would pay the supplier a discounted amount, with the discount level depending on the discounts allowed to the companies receiving the benefit of the purchase

◆ Fourthly, consortia can purchase goods and services from one or more sellers for delivery to member companies, and pay for it all in some way that does not involve charging back the cost of the purchase to the companies. In this case the consortia is effectively acting as a third party buying organisation and should ensure that each company is not charged more than the appropriately discounted amount and receives its 'fair share' of the purchase discount.

Calculating consortia benefit

Clearly, in the case of most goods and services, the discount benefit is easy to work out. Companies will receive the discounted goods and the consortium will transparently pass through all discounts to the companies. There are, however, cases where the discount is less easy to assess.

In such cases the consortium should keep records or create an accounting system that documents the discount process. Discount rates and fees charged for purchases by consortia may be determined for each individual company if it is not unreasonably expensive to do so. In some cases this is easy. It is likely that a small consortia that centrally purchases, let us say, telecommunications products and services from one central budget, can safely apply an average discount to all purchases no matter which company is actually receiving the product or using the service.

However, in larger consortia, where the status of the individual member companies can significantly vary, simply passing on the same overall average discount to each company would not provide discounts equitably. This can be a source of conflict.

Relationship management - Section 3a

Although dividing up discrete objects or services between participating companies is relatively easy, the discount on some goods and services is much more difficult to calculate. For example, a consortium buying ten T-1 lines from a telephone carrier, each of which will be delivered to an individual company in a different area, will have no trouble specifying the recipient of each component of the purchase and dividing the pre-discount price by ten. Each company would then give the consortium an amount equal to the pre-discount price reduced by each company's own discount rate. The consortium would collect all the payments and pass them on to the seller. Or else, the consortium may have prepaid the seller the pre-discount price reduced by the overall average discount rate and then gets reimbursed by the participating companies.

It is much harder when services and products are inherently shared. Sometimes a T-1 line, a network server or a voice system is designed to serve more than one company. In this case some allocation system needs to be devised to divide up the pre-discount cost among the participating companies. For example, a network can be divided up by the number of attached workstations, with each company being charged its percentage of the total. Or a network can be divided by the number of user accounts, or by the number of staff using it, or perhaps by the number of users in the participating companies. Eventually, the consortium might want to use some kind of 'usage meter' to determine the load that each company makes on the shared resource. In any case, whatever method is used, it should be logical, defensible and backed up with clear documentation and explanation.

Consortium resources

Many people involved in the creation, development and management of purchasing consortia fail to recognise the costs involved in each of these activities. Rarely, if ever, is consortia activity cost free.

Most consortia need resources funding and staff to:

◆ Facilitate communication and coordination among consortium members

◆ Encourage staff development

◆ Pursue articulation agreements

◆ Develop policies

◆ Promote the programme to members.

In fact, research suggests that a lack of resources can be a significant barrier to the full implementation of consortium activity.

The allocation and use of resources is an issue for consortia. Questions here are whether consortia should have staff dedicated to consortium-wide activities and, if so, how many? In a recent survey of American consortia almost a third of the consortia reported operating without designated consortium staff. Three-quarters of consortium expenditures are for general administration, staff development and equipment. Staff time is most often taken up with coordination activities among consortium members. These can range from meetings preparing joint specifications to policy setting and development.

Non-price-related benefits

As noted already, there are a number of potential difficulties involved in employing consortia. Consortia purchasing is not necessarily the best option in terms of obtaining the best price by increasing purchasing leverage. There are, however, clearly good reasons for using consortia in some cases. There are also a range of other non-price-related benefits that can be obtained.

Technical knowledge and skill

Perhaps the first of these is when a company lacks in-house technical expertise for the products or services being purchased. Consortia procurement functions may be appropriate in circumstances where extremely technical knowledge is required or where knowledge of products or services is very limited.

For instance, in specialised purchases smaller companies may benefit from consortia purchasing if the company is taking on a new specialised product that requires extensive training and expertise to buy. Product and service examples here may include capital equipment, computers, telecommunications gear and services, fleet vehicles and electrical power.

Reduction in administration costs

The second example may be where purchased items are low in value and/or standardised and where purchases are repetitive. Consortia procurement here could offer benefits in standard, low-cost, high-volume parts, where there are few technical or quality issues: consortia purchasing for routine, everyday, high-maintenance items such as MRO and office supplies. Consortia buying could be extended to standard assembly components as well.

Strategic positioning

A third benefit might be in terms of strategic positioning of the purchasing function. The purchasing function may, for instance, be pursuing a goal of becoming less transaction oriented. In this case, consortia purchasing might be appropriate to reduce non-value-added work.

Measuring consortia performance

Consortia performance is about much more than just discount. In forming and managing a consortium it is often useful, or necessary, to develop a range of measures through which the effectiveness of purchasing consortia can be assessed. Such an assessment allows consortia members and staff to determine the optimal performance pattern for their consortia, and identify developmental paths for performance improvement.

Relationship management - Section 3a

It is possible to suggest that purchasing consortia carry out both core and non-core functions. The ratio of core to non-core functions will be determined by the overall strategic direction of the consortia. Some potential measure are given below:

Possible standards and metrics for consortia purchasing

Domain	Objective	Metrics
Management costs	Internal organisation of resources	Staff numbers Staff tasks FT/PT Staff training and development Budgets.
Information exchange		Number of meetings Meeting frequency Meeting attendance – numbers and grade Information products – type and nature Information systems – harmonisation and extent Procedures – degree of formalisation/consensus.
Service take-up	Positioning	Ratio of potential members/actual members Staff grade of members and attendees Ratio of non-pay spend employed in consortia/non-pay spend employed elsewhere Member expectations/satisfaction levels Feedback mechanisms for non-purchasing staff Nature of consortia staff tasks.
Education		Improvements in purchasing practice within consortia membership Improvements in key individual knowledge skills and attitudes.
Information	Management of supply	Completeness of information at every part of the purchasing cycle including contract management Number of contract errors Number of supplier failures (delivery/cost/quality/administration etc).
Management		Number of contract errors Number of supplier failures Dimensionality of supplier performance management Degree of supplier performance improvement Cost of management /degree of supplier performance improvement.

Disadvantages of consortia

Consortia procurement, although useful under certain circumstances, can involve a number of objections, particularly where the consortium takes on an independent, autonomous existence.

One concern is the issue of loyalty. In independent consortia, there may be concerns about the loyalty from employees as an incentive to obtain the best deals for the company. The difficulties in measuring consortia performance may lead to lack of ownership and lack of understanding of individual company processes, people and needs. For many companies, buying decisions need to stay with managers who have a personal stake in the success of their organisation.

Another concern may be the need for openness between different consortia members. Proper procurement requires the buyer to have extensive knowledge about his or her company's products or services. Third parties could lose, or never have, that extensive knowledge, leading to problems later.

A third concern is the management of risk within the consortium. The more companies involved in consortia purchasing, the more risk. Here the consortia can serve too many masters and become little more than a distributor. In such cases, unless a company can in some way guarantee enough business so the consortium looks after that company exclusively, there is no way to predict what will happen during critical supply periods when others are competing for the consortium's time and products.

Summary

Consortia purchasing can deliver a range of benefits including increased leverage with suppliers, reduced administrative costs and improved technical knowledge. There will be a trade-off in all consortia activity between the leverage obtained and the information given up by the members. This situation needs to be appropriately safeguarded. The form of consortium that you use, or take part in, can range from the rudimentary to the complex. Ensure that the form of consortium you employ is appropriate for the situation. The costs of consortia should also be considered. Consortia performance should be measured accurately and monitored accordingly.

Supplier associations

What are supplier associations?

Supplier associations are precisely what they say – groups of suppliers who form, or who are formed, together for a variety of reasons including mutual help and learning. The members of a supplier association may all supply one company, or are all from one region serving different customers, or may be tied to an industry. The associations are a method of introducing continuous improvement and business process improvement by transferring best practices from other members. They can also be used to gain competitive advantage and/or productivity improvements through cooperation. In Japan, supplier associations are known as Kyoryoku Kai or supplier circles.

Supplier associations can be very similar to purchasing consortia, but are often more clearly based around operations to gain cost, quality and delivery improvements. They may, of course, also collaborate on purchasing and marketing.

Advantages of supplier associations

Supplier associations are useful in that they naturally extend from the idea of partnership and longer-term contracts. In looking at traditional adversarial purchasing relationships, supplier performance improvement occurred naturally as suppliers competed for business. As longer term, relational contracts are used, there needs to be a way that competitiveness improves. Supplier associations are a method of developing suppliers without embarking on expensive supplier development programmes.

Peter Hines defines supplier associations as 'a mutually benefiting group of a company's most important subcontractors brought together on a regular basis for the purpose of coordination and cooperation as well as to assist all the members by benefiting from the type of development associated with large Japanese assemblers such as Kaizen, just in time, Kanban, U-cell production and the achievement of zero defects'.

The objectives according to Hines are to:

◆   Improve skills in JIT, TQM, SPC, VE/VA, CAD/CAM, flexibility and cost

◆   Produce a uniform supply system

◆   Facilitate the flow of information

◆   Keep suppliers in touch with market developments

◆   Enhance the reputation of the customer as a good business partner

◆   Help smaller suppliers lacking specialist trainers and facilities

◆   Increase the length of relations

◆   Share developmental benefits

◆   Provide an example to subcontractors as to how they should develop their own suppliers.

As well as being focused on operational issues, supplier associations can also be focused on strategic decisions, which may involve senior staff meeting across the association to set policy and long-term goals. Supplier associations can have a similar effect to supplier tiering in that they spread the cost of development across a number of organisations. The sharing of information which takes place can help improve the quality of collaboration and reduce costs.

Disadvantages of supplier associations

Supplier associations can be merely 'showcases' rather than achieving any real benefit. In Japan it is considered an honour to be asked to join a prestigious supplier association, as run by a major corporation. The use of supplier associations in the West is hampered by the fact that suppliers may not wish to share best practice in a competitive market.

In addition, supplier associations can be expensive to set up and run. In the United Kingdom a number of attempts have been made to set up an association, and only a limited number have succeeded.

Finally, there is an issue with regard to the nature of the industry and the relationship that has traditionally been in place. In tightly knit industrial sectors such as the automotive assembly industry, there are often networks of personal relationships which can facilitate the growth of associations. In other industries, these are less common.

Implementing supplier associations

There are a number of steps in forming a supplier association and deciding on an operating framework. Will the group be company sponsored, self-generated or sponsored by external facilitators? Will it be based around a company, a region or an industry? The company-sponsored variety may benefit from the parent company's expertise and resources. The regional variety often share resources such as training seminar costs and training materials, but may also share expertise by staff placements from other member companies for short periods. The regional type may be partially funded by the government and may have a full-time facilitator.

Joint projects, assistance in areas of expertise, development of common standards, training, courses, staff exchange or secondment, benchmarking, hiring of consultants or trainers, factory visits within the association, joint visits to outside companies or other associations are all common.

Supplier selection or the definition of membership parameters is important. Choosing who may join an association and who may not is also important. If the association is operationally focused, suppliers of common or catalogue parts may not be invited. Leverage is also a factor. Suppliers that are not dependent upon a parent for a significant (perhaps 25% or more) proportion of their business may not wish to take part.

A supplier association, like a purchasing consortium, will benefit from having its own set of rules and regulations. It may be run by a full-time member of staff from the parent company or, increasingly, by a full- or part-time coordinator from one of the companies. Support staff may be seconded for short periods, depending on projects and needs.

Often member companies pay a subscription fee. To set strategic direction, the association may have a steering group at director level, which perhaps meets annually. Some functional directors may meet quarterly. Engineers and front-line staff may meet more frequently or may form temporary full-time task groups to address particular problems.

Some associations consider social events to be important icebreakers. Within the association there may be a functional split by product category or by area of concern (cost, quality, delivery, production planning etc).

Summary

Supplier associations are groups of suppliers, generally brought together by an OEM or a first-tier supplier for the transfer of good practice, or to obtain benefits through group buying or shared operations. Supplier associations offer a number of benefits but they can be expensive and time-consuming to set up.

Supplier tiering

Introduction

A great deal has been written about supplier tiering. Broadly this is a practice whereby suppliers are consciously located in certain positions within the value or supply chain. Supplier tiering is often part of a supply base reduction strategy. For example, BP Exploration reduced its number of suppliers from 20,000 to 3,600, but it is also in many ways a risk management strategy too.

Advantages

In the component manufacturing industry, enterprises have been very alive to the changing world environment and also very alert in responding to new challenges. The number of suppliers is shrinking rapidly. Original equipment manufacturers (OEMs) increasingly prefer to deal with a very small number of first-tier suppliers. This offers a number of benefits including:

◆ Dramatic reductions in transaction costs including sourcing, negotiating and contracting

◆ Reduced cost and complexity in the management of inbound logistics

◆ Increased likelihood of supplier involvement in design, planning and after-sales support

◆ Selecting one supplier to coordinate the activities of several

◆ Reduced inventory costs and reduced inspection costs as these can be passed down to lower tiers.

Tiering also often takes place in industries where rapid product obsolescence is normal and new product launch costs are high. In this sense it is a risk-shifting strategy. OEMs, faced with rapid product changes are seeking to pass on investment/development risk, and can therefore trade off this risk against the scale advantage which can be given to a first-tier supplier. First-tier suppliers could also be supplying to OEM competitors and this may mean that costs and risk can be spread even further. A tiering strategy helps OEMs reduce the risk of very large investment, which becomes a liability later on.

This can be reflected in share prices and price earnings ratios. If you plot PE ratios on a scale, it is quite evident that many enterprises with low assets and high turnovers are supported by the market, and those with high assets and low turnover are not. The higher the asset turnover number, the higher the market capitalisation. In markets with very rapid product changes and product obsolescence, the OEMs cannot be stuck with the investment.

Disadvantages

There are also disadvantages to this strategy. The first of these is from the point of view of manufacturing control. Studies have shown that supply base reduction often only pushes suppliers into lower tiers where quality problems can be hidden until incorporated into the major sub-assembly, leading to product recalls. The second is from the viewpoint of risk, when first-tier suppliers can become much more difficult to deal with when they begin to trade with competitors at the same level as they trade with an OEM. As the proportion of an enterprise's spend reduces in relation to the overall turnover of the first-tier supplier, then the purchasing power of the OEM reduces and supplier compliance to change becomes more difficult to achieve.

eMarketplaces, virtual organisations, portals and other eStructures

Introduction

The so-called 'bursting of the dot-com bubble' has led to a shift in attitudes towards eCommerce among investors and the general public. For enterprises, the competitive forces of globalisation and technology are driving firms towards complex collaborations to achieve goals such as expanding into foreign markets, funding expensive innovation efforts and lowering production and other costs. Many enterprises are finding that supply chain initiatives which are complex and difficult to implement in the real world can become much easier in the virtual world. This section will consider how new technology impacts upon supply chain structures and commercial relationships.

Commercial relationships on the Internet

Trading using electronic communication over the Internet is a rapidly changing field. A good starting point in understanding this field is to understand the business models behind the technology. Business models, and the relationships that sustain them, have been one of the most discussed and least understood aspects of the Internet. There is a great deal of talk about how the web changes traditional business models and relationships. But there is little clear-cut evidence of exactly what this means.

In the most basic sense, a business model is the method of doing business by which a company can sustain itself, that is, generate revenue. This shows how an enterprise makes money by specifying where it is positioned in the value chain. Some models are quite simple. A company produces a good or service and sells it to customers. If all goes well, the revenues from sales exceeds the cost of operation and the company realises a profit.

Other models can develop different sources of revenue generation. Radio and television broadcasting is a good example. With all the talk about free business models on the web, it is easy to forget that in some countries radio, and later television, programming has been broadcast over the airwaves free to anyone with a receiver for much of the past century. The broadcaster is part of a complex network of distributors, content creators, advertisers (and their agencies) and listeners or viewers. Who makes money and how much is not always clear at the outset. Profitability depends on many competing factors.

eCommerce is giving rise to new kinds of business models and new types of commercial relationship. The Internet is also reinventing traditional models and placing these in a wider context. Auctions are a good example. One of the oldest business models, auctions have been widely used throughout the world to set prices for such items as agricultural commodities, financial instruments and unique items like fine art and antiquities. Companies like eBay have popularised the auction model and broadened its application on the web to a wide array of goods and services.

There are a wide range of models and relationships used on the web. They include:

- **Brokerage relationships:** brokers are market-makers – they bring buyers and sellers together and facilitate transactions. Those can be business-to-business (B2B), business-to-consumer (B2C) or consumer-to-consumer (C2C) markets. A broker makes its money by charging a fee for each transaction it enables

- **Advertising relationships:** the web advertising model is an extension of the traditional media broadcasting model. The broadcaster, in this case a website, provides content (usually, but not necessarily, for free) and services (like e-mail, chat and forums) mixed with advertising messages in the form of banner ads. The banner ads may be the major or sole source of revenue for the broadcaster

- **Infomediary relationships:** data about consumers and their buying habits are extremely valuable – especially when that information is carefully analysed and used to target marketing campaigns. Some firms are able to function as infomediaries by collecting and selling information to other businesses

- **Merchant relationships:** classic wholesalers and retailers of goods and services (increasingly referred to as 'eTailers'). Sales may be made based on list prices or through auction. In some cases, the goods and services may be unique to the web and not have a traditional 'bricks-and-mortar' storefront

- **Manufacturer-consumer relationships:** this model is predicated on the power of the web to allow manufacturers (companies that actually produce a product or service) to reach buyers directly and thereby compress the distribution channel (eliminate wholesalers and retailers). The manufacturer model can be based on efficiency (cost savings that may or may not be passed on to consumers), improved customer service and a better understanding of customer preferences

- **Affiliate relationships:** in contrast to the generalised portal, which seeks to drive a high volume of traffic to one site, the affiliate model provides purchase opportunities wherever people may be surfing. It does this by offering financial incentives (in the form of a percentage of revenue) to affiliated partner sites. The affiliates provide purchase-point click-through to the merchant. It is a pay-for-performance model – if an affiliate does not generate sales, it represents no cost to the merchant

- **Community relationships:** the community model is based on user loyalty (as opposed to high traffic volume). Users have a high investment in both time and emotion in the site. In some cases, users are regular contributors of content and/or money

- **Application service provider (ASP):** the utility model is a metered usage or pay-as-you-go approach. Its success may depend on the ability to charge by the byte, including micropayments (that is, those too small to pay by credit card due to processing fees).

Relationship management - Section 3a

Clearly, enterprises may use any or all of these models as part of a structural approach to the management of commercial relationships. We can, however, suggest that brokerage models, which include eMarketplaces, ASPs and infomediaries are most pertinent to our discussions here. Within the brokerage model, there are a number of approaches, some of which have a major impact on commercial relationships.

activity 4

If you have access to the Internet, try to find examples of each type of commercial relationship.

Brokerage models

Brokerage models can take a number of forms, such as:

◆ **Buy/sell fulfilment:** this can be an online financial brokerage, for example eTrade, where customers place buy and sell orders for transacting financial instruments. Also, travel agents fit into this category. In this the broker charges the buyer and/or seller a transaction fee. Some models work on volume and low overheads to deliver the best negotiated prices

◆ **Market exchange:** an increasingly common model in B2B markets. In the exchange model, the broker typically charges the seller a transaction fee based on the value of the sale. The pricing mechanism can be a simple offer/buy, offer/negotiated buy or an auction offer/bid approach

◆ **Business trading community or vertical web community:** a site that acts as an 'essential, comprehensive source of information and dialogue for a particular vertical market'. VerticalNet's communities contain product information in buyers' guides, supplier and product directories, daily industry news and articles, job listings and classifieds. In addition, VerticalNet's sites enable B2B exchanges of information, supplementing existing trade shows and trade association activities. For more information check out www.verticalnet.com

◆ **Buyer aggregator:** the process of bringing together individual purchasers from across the Internet to transact as a group so they can receive the same values traditionally afforded to organisations that purchase in volume. Sellers pay a small percentage of each sale on a per-transaction basis

◆ **Distributor:** a catalogue-based operation that connects a large number of product manufacturers with volume and retail buyers. B2B models are increasingly common. Brokers facilitate business transactions between franchised distributors and their trading partners. For buyers, it enables faster time to market and time to volume as well as reducing the cost of procurement. By providing the buyer with a means of retrieving quotes from preferred distributors – showing buyer-specific prices, lead time and recommended substitutions – transactions are more efficient. For distributors, it decreases the cost of sales by quoting, order processing, tracking order status and changes more quickly and with less labour

◆ **Virtual mall:** a site that hosts many online merchants. The mall typically charges set-up, monthly listing and/or transaction fees. The virtual mall model may be most effectively realised when combined with a generalised portal. Also, more sophisticated malls will provide automated transaction services and relationship marketing opportunities

◆ **Metamediary:** a business that brings buyers and online merchants together and provides transaction services such as financial settlement and quality assurance. It is a virtual mall, but one that will process the transaction, track orders and provide billing and collection services. The metamediary protects consumers by assuring satisfaction with merchants. The metamediary often charges a set-up fee and a fee per transaction

◆ **Auction broker:** a site that conducts auctions on behalf of sellers (individuals or merchants). The broker charges the seller a fee, which is typically scaled with the value of the transaction. The seller takes the highest bid(s) from the buyers above a minimum. Auctions can vary in terms of the offering and bidding rules

◆ **Reverseauction:** the 'name-your-price' business model, also called 'demand collection' and 'shopping by request'. The buyer makes a final (sometimes binding) bid for a specified good or service and the broker seeks fulfilment. In some models, the broker's fee is the spread between the bid and fulfilment price and may involve a processing charge. Frequently used in B2B exchanges

◆ **Classifieds:** a listing of items for sale or purchase. In the same way as newspaper classifieds, these are typically run by local news content providers. Price may or may not be specified. Listing charges are incurred regardless of whether a transaction occurs

◆ **Search agent:** an agent (an intelligent software agent or 'robot') used to search out the best price for a good or service specified by the buyer, or to locate information that is hard to find. An employment agency can act as a search agent broker, finding work for job-seekers or finding people to fill open positions listed by an employer

◆ **Bounty broker:** this often involves the offer of a reward (usually a significant monetary sum) for finding a person, thing, idea or other desired, but hard-to-find item. The broker may list items for a flat fee and a percent of the reward, if the item is successfully found

◆ **Transaction broker:** provides a third party mechanism for buyers and sellers to settle payment for a transaction.

This bewildering array of models and relationships is changing the way in which business is conducted in many industries. As well as these new and traditional types of relationship, there are also the marketplaces in which these relationships are maintained.

Relationship management - Section 3a

Vertical eMarkets and marketplace creators

eMarket exchanges and electronic trading communities tend to be focused on either vertical or horizontal markets. Vertical market trading communities tend to focus on one particular industry (steel, paper, electricity, paper or chemicals) and are usually supported by a number of major enterprises in that industry. There are hundreds of examples of vertical markets. The chemical industry, for example, developed a number of online marketplaces which ranged from simple online auctions to complex virtual distributorships that service entire continents.

Chemical markets have an advantage in that commodities for the most part adhere to well-accepted international standards in terms of labelling, quality and content, making online auctions easier.

Other vertical industry areas that have developed eMarketplaces include automotive, energy pulp and paper, high-tech manufacturing, publishing, metals, financial services, health care and many more. Many of these vertical eMarket trading communities are now being sponsored jointly and collaboratively by large and powerful industry leaders. Often, long-time competitors have become leaders in vertical electronic marketplaces.

The Covisint marketplace alliance between Ford, General Motors, Daimler-Chrysler and Renault-Nissan is probably the most famous example. This massively powerful collaboration allegedly involves 750,000 tier-three and tier-four suppliers, 50,000 tier-two suppliers and 1,500 tier-one suppliers, all tied to 14 vehicle manufacturers. Other marketplaces have been planned or opened in a range of sectors, some of which plan to offer collaborative design and planning and logistics services. For more information see **www.covisint.com**.

These enormously powerful industry coalitions are beginning to have a major impact on SCM strategy. As soon as suppliers reside on the database, and can update catalogues using file transfer protocols, price differences can be eliminated. As market leaders enrol second- and third-tier suppliers onto the marketplace, price transparency is increased and inventory management made easier.

---

activity 5

Consider what steps you might need to take in setting up an eMarket. How might you draft a request for proposals (RFP) or an invitation to tender (ITT) for such a product?

What might your organisation require? Prepare a rough draft, using bullet points for an RFP or ITT.

In many ways, these vertical industry eMarkets have an advantage over the horizontal or cross-industry trading exchanges in that the sponsors, as both buyers and (if manufacturers) sellers themselves, will tend to reap a huge benefit from the efficient supply chain management that can be implemented across the industry. In addition, vertical industry online exchanges are not driven by the need to make a profit in the way independent exchanges do.

Horizontal eMarkets

Horizontal eMarkets cut across the boundaries of industries and focus on broad categories of goods (office supplies, furniture, travel services, printing services) that are commonly purchased by many organisations. Horizontal eMarkets are often sponsored by eProcurement software groups or industry leaders. Horizontal exchanges have tended to develop in highly fragmented marketplaces, which are not dominated by a handful of key players, such as the printing industry.

There are a number of variations on this central theme, but basically all of these groups, whether known as trading hubs, exchanges or eMarkets, aim to create a single, industry- or product-line-focused portal, which will provide integration and, potentially, visibility throughout the whole supply chain. This will allow buyers and suppliers of every size, type and geographical location to transact all their business through a single source.

As noted above, each of these providers differs significantly in focus, size, level of service and market, and range from enormously powerful collaborations between automakers, to tiny eMarketplace hubs for buying speciality products, such as motorboat equipment or wine. All typically make their money by charging a 1% to 15% fee for each transaction, depending on volume and materials being sold.

Peer-to-peer markets

The World Wide Web is actually a centralised model. A single website is accessed by multiple users via a simple HTML (hypertext mark-up language) interface. This is ideal for publishing information to be read at a later time, but is less effective for real time interaction. The HTML interface is not as well suited to applications as a local user interface such as that employed by the Windows, Macintosh or Linux operating systems.

In addition, there have been problems in that a large proportion of Internet access is through low bandwidth and occasional access over dial-up links. The increase in cheaper, faster access is slowly improving and this is beginning to impact on business-to-business trading (B2B).

Overall, however, the picture is still confused. A particular industry might well be trying to support three independent markets, two large bricks-and-mortar (BAM) consortia and 10 private trading networks. For smaller suppliers and buyers, this means connecting to many different incompatible markets. For suppliers it means providing their catalogues in several different forms and makes integration for both sides a hard task. Many industries are still based around several overlapping hub-and-spoke models.

In the recent past, a series of applications have appeared that pass messages or data between Internet users directly, rather than routing them through a central hub or website. Generally there is a central index for searching (although even that can be distributed) but the information is passed directly. These networks have become known as peer-to-peer (P2P) networks.

The most famous P2P networks are ICQ, Napster, Gnutella and Groove. These systems typically have a Windows application for the user interface but use the Internet to connect peers together. Napster has been phenomenally successful, largely because it allows trading of free music but the underlying ideas can be used in electronic trading.

The idea is that some of the current problems in B2B could be avoided if standards were developed that allowed people to build P2P applications. Some organisations appear to be heading in this direction, but there is some distance to go. Most large commercial eMarket providers still require substantial installation ('a large footprint') on client sites. Instead, P2P offers the possibility of:

◆ A centralised index that knows where everyone is and what products/ services they provide

◆ An application on every user's site that is:
  - permanently connected to the Internet
  - able to take back-office information and publish it to the index
  - able to talk to other entities on other sites:
    – to get detailed product information
    – to negotiate trade
    – to collaborate on design specifications
    – to accept complete transactions

◆ Ability to post the transactions to the back office.

Other parties are attempting to create standards, which eMarketplaces can use to talk to each other and punch out, or offload requests that they can't handle locally. Although not strictly P2P, this may offer an interim step.

For this to happen, standards need to be accepted for the indexing approach and for the protocol between the users' clients. This may happen as a result of the success of a particular implementation, or it may require the standards to be independently developed so as to allow competing implementations to interoperate.

The future of eMarkets

Although obviously the trend is towards full integration, there are currently a number of differences (in buying parameters, product recognition codes payment systems, shipping and delivery techniques) that mean that purchasing through an eMarket is still not much more efficient than leafing through a paper catalogue and negotiating the price over the telephone.

One interesting issue with regard to the future of eMarketplaces is how the trend to software integration is mirrored by a similar trend in supply base rationalisation, which is one of the main tools of SCM. Companies such as IBM have significantly reduced the number of their MRO suppliers. In Europe, ten suppliers provide the company with three-quarters of all of its purchases in this field. As usually happens in supply base reduction, the number of suppliers may have remained the same as it was before consolidation, but IBM has used purchasing leverage to force the responsibility for negotiating and buying from thousands of suppliers down one level to a limited number of selected and trusted clearinghouse-type partners.

On the other hand, many SCM specialists assert that spot markets, auctions and many-to-many exchanges erode the trust relationship that is at the heart of strategic SCM. They argue that item price becomes the single most important criteria for trading with a particular seller, who may be one of thousands of suppliers, each one selling on multiple horizontal and vertical industry eMarkets. It is an unexpected strategic paradox that promises to divide SCM practice.

In looking to the future, there is little doubt that customer demand, legal barriers permitting, will soon force multiple and competing groups – eProcurement software vendors, ERP firms, market creators, auctions, exchanges, ASPs – towards consolidation. Customers are already demonstrating that they are increasingly looking for one or two organisations that can provide centralised sourcing and full service SCM for them.

---

activity 6

Compare the different types of electronic trading model and list the advantages and disadvantages of each.

Consider how such models might change in different industries. Discuss with colleagues or fellow students.

Relationship management - Section 3a

? self-assessment questions

SAQ 3.1

Outline the non-financial benefits of consortia and identify some of the measures that might reflect these.

SAQ 3.2

Identify four of the benefits and two of the disadvantages of supplier associations.

SAQ 3.3

Identify five types of brokerage relationship which might support an electronic marketplace.

The role of the internal customer

The syllabus learning outcomes for this subsection state that you will be able to:

◆ **Evaluate the role of the internal customer, including the concept of the intelligent customer.**

This subsection will cover:

◆ **Introduction**

◆ **Purchasing roles**

◆ **Developing an internal customer focus.**

Introduction

As we saw in Section 1 of the study guide, purchasing activity is integral to the whole of the organisation and, therefore, requires that relationships within the organisation support the adequate management of external commercial relationships. We looked in that section at some of the approaches and tools for the management of internal relationships. This subsection looks at one common approach to the management of internal relationships, the internal marketing of purchasing.

Purchasing roles

When we go on to look into public sector procurement, we will consider some of the potential roles of purchasing within the organisation in more detail. One critical underpinning role is that of the marketing of purchasing, and this requires the development of a marketing orientation within the purchasing function.

Marketing theory emphasises the importance of developing a customer orientation within an organisation. This concept is often supported by the need to develop a market orientation. Employees should be encouraged to not only focus on the needs of the end customer but also to recognise other employees as internal customers.

The idea of the internal customer came to the fore in the total quality management literature, where an internal customer orientation was pursued, primarily for efficiency and cost-related objectives. Within the field of quality, the concept of 'next operation as customer' has often made a major contribution to quality programme implementation.

The notion of an internal customer suggests that every employee is both a supplier and a customer to other employees within the organisation. An internal customer orientation is considered part of the organisational culture that guides the attitudes and behaviours of organisational members to deliver quality to other employees. Internal customer orientation, in this context, is considered the organisation culture that most effectively creates the behaviours needed for the creation of superior value for internal customers.

Advantages

Developing a customer orientation within the purchasing function is also a means of impacting the quality of the firm and its outputs. This is especially important for organisations operating in service environments themselves since they cannot easily differentiate their services. Increasingly, service organisations need to recognise that as the intangibility of the service offering increases, there is greater need to pay attention to the details of service delivery.

Given the intangibility of services, the management of organisations operating in service industries has a more limited span of control over the services being provided. This means that an internal marketing philosophy can often help the whole organisation operate as one. This means that an overall customer orientation can help employees recognise that, as the external customer's only contact with the firm's offerings, they become both the firm and its service within the customer's perception.

Adopting a customer focus offers staff the opportunity to develop skills in customer service. In this sense 'practice makes perfect': staff who practise serving internal customers develop competences that can be transferred to the external customer.

Disadvantages

Although the internal customer idea is, on first appearance, very appealing, a number of arguments have been advanced, which suggest that internal customer focus might have disadvantages. Indeed, some authors have suggested that an internal customer orientation could lead to poor organisational performance. These authors have argued that an increased focus on the internal customer will divert attention from the external customer, leading to organisational marketing myopia, resulting in the organisation losing touch with its external customers.

Developing an internal customer focus

Developing an internal customer focus can be a challenging task. To successfully integrate an internal customer philosophy into the organisational culture, those responsible must show how organisational success depends on the degree to which core groups of employees subscribe to and share a common set of beliefs and values. These common beliefs and values must be supported by the organisation's activities. The integrative elements of such a vision include positioning of the service concept, redesign of internal business processes, customer service training and the management of customer expectations. Integrating these, and other elements, should lead to the development of shared goals and values.

Senior management has the responsibility of integrating the management philosophy of internal marketing into the overall culture of the organisation. Most organisational culture literature treats integration as a top-down phenomenon with a critical role being played by senior managers in overseeing the diffusion of cultural norms in the firm. Making a cultural change is more difficult and takes longer to implement than simply changing a strategy. In spite of the level of difficulty, this change is necessary for the development of a new and more customer-oriented organisational culture. Cultures are, however:

♦   Holistic

♦   Historically determined

♦   Socially constructed

♦   Soft

♦   Difficult to change.

The diffusion of culture 'norms' or ways of behaving, such as service orientation, can be supported by managers and staff considering – and treating – employees as 'quasi-customers'. This treatment of employees as customers can serve as a mechanism to enhance and develop the level of communication that takes place, supporting participation at every level of the organisation.

This communication can ensure that purchasing staff, and others, understand the way in which the service provided actually interacts with the supplier and how the quality of that service impacts on the external customer.

This interaction informs management of the potential rewards of an internal marketing philosophy through such measures as customer satisfaction and profitability. While research focusing on the link between internal marketing and overall performance are beyond the scope of this work, enhanced customer satisfaction, increased revenue and increased profitability are viable consequences to a customer-oriented service firm.

Summary

Internal marketing and focus on the internal customer can be successfully incorporated into the organisational culture of an organisation. For this to take place, senior management must lead the way in instilling the values and beliefs that an 'internal customer' exists at every level of the organisation.

This communication of the belief that customers exist both inside and outside the organisation can help in establishing values and norms that all employees can share. These behavioural norms can contribute to changes in the organisational culture. Internal marketing, with its focus on managerial implementation via marketing activities, such as product and service promotion, customer expectation management, segmentation and demand management, can help the organisation develop an internal customer-centred philosophy as part of the organisational culture.

The role of the supplier

This subsection will cover:

◆ **Introduction**

◆ **The concept of role**

◆ **Developing roles**

◆ **The environment.**

Introduction

We have already seen in this study guide the drivers that are pushing changes in commercial relationships. These drivers have clearly changed over time. In some industries, notably automotive and construction, customer pressure on performance engendered a growing understanding of the nature of organisational networks. As these networks of organisations began to appear, the customer organisation tended to keep the suppliers at arm's length. The buyer had the controlling hand in setting up supplier contracts and was constantly on the lookout for price reductions or cheaper sources. The stressful economic climate of the 1970s led to increasingly adversarial relationships between the buyer and supplier. Competition continued to increase, and the adversarial relationships were shown not to work effectively in complex industries and uncertain environments.

The Japanese were doing things differently, and the early 1990s saw many studies attempting to understand these differences. But after years of adversarial relationships and aggressive business practices, many organisations have struggled to build partnership-style relationships and have found it very difficult to adopt a truly collaborative approach, despite beginning to understand the benefits of such a strategy.

Other factors that impact on relationships are the role of the parties involved in the relationship, the nature of the transaction process itself and the task environment in which the relationship takes place. In some ways, commercial relationships are the easiest element to manage, as changes in role can be much more difficult to achieve. Although we might use the word 'role' casually to describe a set of behaviours, the concept of role is much more complicated.

Figure 10: Partnership-style relationships

Task environment	Role
Transactional process	Relationship

The concept of role

Erwin Goffman (1959), an eminent sociologist, brought the word role into current scientific thinking when he suggested that social life could be perceived as a drama, during which the expressiveness of an individual can be seen as performance. Goffman uses the term 'performance' to refer to all the activities of an individual that occur during a period marked by her/his continuous presence before a particular set of observers and that have some influence on the said observers/audience.

This idea of 'role' is a very powerful one, and indeed can lead to other, less desirable constructs or concepts. These include the idea of stereotyping where a supplier may be considered to have certain characteristics, such as greed, obstructive behaviour or untrustworthiness, simply because they are a supplier. It is, therefore, important to remember that roles can be flexible and that people within an organisation can take on multiple roles.

This is seen within some approaches to the role of the supplier in new product development. In the past, suppliers weren't involved early in the process. The activities of the product development process were carried out in series, and suppliers were only involved towards the end of the process. This meant that in a manufacturing industry, a typical product could involve many stages, and many different stakeholders. Such a product might be 'born' in the marketing department, and then go through conceptual design, engineering design and failure mode effect analysis, testing, detailed design, manufacturing engineering, process planning, tooling, NC programming, production planning, purchasing, machining, assembly, testing, packaging, and even installation and maintenance in some cases.

Often, supplier involvement would be limited to manufacturing some of the parts. They wouldn't be involved at the design stage, and often their work only started when they received the released design documentation. Usually, they would raise good questions about some aspect of the design. The resulting change process wasted time, led to the introduction of new problems, and often resulted in the product getting to market late.

As well as having an impact on performance, this approach didn't take advantage of supplier knowledge and experience. Despite being a world-class producer of a particular component, suppliers might not be consulted on initial specifications and design, and instead be expected to produce to a plan developed by individuals with much less experience.

In addition, traditional roles often meant that suppliers were only brought into the process to compete against each other on pricing. As a result, the company finished up working with a large number of suppliers, and even with different suppliers on similar products.

Often the product development process needs to be reorganised to get products to market faster, reduce the cost of product development and to make sure the product provides customer satisfaction – leading to repeat buying behaviour. There are many possible approaches to reorganisation; many of them will increase the reliance on suppliers and enhance and develop supplier roles.

However, as some manufacturers learned to involve suppliers in the product development process and were attempting to introduce them in the new product programme as early as possible, there were both practitioners and academics who saw this as too high risk an approach. Instead they suggested that, due to the subjective and iterative nature of the design process, the degree of confidential information that may be generated, and the inability to measure and monitor technical capability, early supplier involvement would only lead to opportunistic behaviour and, ultimately, competitive disadvantage.

This balance of risk and performance is, of course, at the heart of the purchasing task.

Developing roles

In many industries, however, organisations do engage in a certain level of collaboration with their first-tier suppliers. Companies that focus on upstream product specification and design activities, where they can best use their resources, will want to outsource downstream activities where they are not cost-effective (for example, in detailed drafting) or are less competent than specialised organisations (for example, in parts manufacture), so suppliers will have a greater role to play in these areas.

In some literature, 'partnership' is seen as a preferred role for suppliers. Here we might see the roles as involving a range of factors that might include:

1. Cost management in the same way that QS 9000 defines such a role for suppliers to large automotive assemblers.
2. Innovative suggestions.
3. Longer-term planning and early supplier involvement in product or service design.
4. Sharing of information, including cost information and transparency, facilitating planning.

However, roles, like relationships, are subject to change, and we often need a more dynamic model that explains how these change. In order to identify how a supplier can, and should, act to maximize the value creation for the customer, it is often useful to consider learning processes between the buyer and supplier. This may involve looking at the link between a supplier's offerings and learning processes and a customer's various learning processes, some of which were considered in section 1 of this study guide.

When we consider roles, however, it is also essential to consider the environment of the industry in which the role is being practised.

The environment

As we have already seen, the management of relationships is complex and difficult. Many factors impact upon relationships, and these factors often also impact upon role. In fast-changing, volatile trading environments, the role of the supplier may involve setting up (and breaking off) new partnerships fairly quickly.

Market fluctuations, and therefore roles and relationships, can be driven by rapidly changing customer preferences, rather than supplier strategy. In many industries, better-informed customers are becoming less loyal and more demanding about what they buy. The effects of market volatility is both worsened and helped by information and communications technology, which allows organisations to make use of information embedded within enterprise systems, as a key factor in business relationships.

It is, therefore important, to take the environment into account, and achieve the right balance of control and risk management in developing suppliers into new roles. We cannot force partnership or transactional roles and relationships where such roles and relationships are not matched with the environment in which the business operates.

Summary

Supplier roles, in many industries and markets, have changed considerably over the past two decades. These changes can be seen in many areas. One of these is quality, where the receiving inspection process used places much of the cost and responsibility on the purchaser. This responsibility has largely shifted to suppliers, requiring them to provide evidence of product quality, often through reporting of process stability and capability. Elsewhere, the involvement of suppliers in new product development has become critical in many industries.

It should be noted though, that shifts in roles, and relationships, must be sensitive to changes in the nature of the trading and operating environment, and to changes in the nature of the transaction processes used.

Supplier development

The syllabus learning outcome for this subsection states that you will be able to:

◆   Evaluate the potential and practicalities of supplier development from a relationship perspective. Recommend appropriate actions in relation to supplier development and upstream management.

This subsection will cover:

◆   **Introduction**

◆   **What is supplier development?**

◆   **Using supplier development.**

Introduction

In the previous parts of this study guide we have looked at how to identify relationships, select appropriate frameworks and consider some of the structural aspects of those relationships. Once we have actually embarked on these relationships, the next step is to maintain them. Broadly defined, this might be called the process of supplier development.

What is supplier development?

As with so much else in the field of supply chain management, supplier development means different things to different people. Some people refer to competitive tendering as 'supplier development' as it helps the supplier develop tendering skills. For other buyers, supplier development may consist of statistical process control workshops.

For the purposes of this section we can suggest that supplier development consists of a range of activities integrated into a relatively seamless whole to ensure effective supply chain management. These activities may include:

◆ Sourcing strategy

◆ Vendor assessment (surveys, site visits)

◆ Supplier rating and qualification

◆ Supplier award programmes

◆ Use of new technology (for example, computer-supported collaborative working, advanced planning and scheduling)

◆ Cross- or multi-disciplinary team working

◆ Supply base reduction

◆ Joint supplier problem-solving team

◆ Supplier development 1 (Kaizen teams)

◆ Supplier development 2 (redesign of internal processes)

◆ Electronic data interchange

◆ Supplier associations (Kyoryoku Kai)

◆ Longer-term contracts

◆ Partnership (win-win negotiation, partnering agreements)

◆ Lean supply (JIT, for example)

◆ Standards development

◆ Supplier tiering

◆ Cost analysis methods (VA, ABC, WLC, TCO)

◆ Cost management (VE, gain sharing, inventory management and re-engineering).

As can be seen, many of these processes refer to the manufacturing sector. This is because much supplier development work grew from quality control and assurance problems experienced in that sector. This is not to say that the principles of supplier development cannot also be applied in service industries. The use of process redesign across organisational boundaries can also be useful to service enterprises, as can the use of contracting strategies.

Relationship management - Section 3d

Using supplier development

Because of the different meanings of supplier development, this subsection will consider an integrated framework of suppler development, which includes seven elements. This is not to say that all these elements need to be in place in every case, but this framework demonstrates how the elements of a supplier development strategy interlock. These elements are:

1. Sourcing strategy.

2. Analysis strategy.

3. Communication strategy.

4. Infrastructure strategy.

5. Motivation strategy.

6. Standards strategy.

7. Development strategy.

Each of these elements is described on the following pages in detail with the objectives of the strategy, a description of the processes used and some of the pitfalls.

1. Sourcing strategy for supplier development

Objectives

The objectives of a sourcing strategy should be in keeping with the philosophy of the extended enterprise, which is to ensure that suppliers have the capacity and capability to match systems and policies with the enterprise's current and changing needs. This, as we shall see, may be mitigated by ethical and environmental considerations.

Processes

Many organisations that are global in scope base sourcing policy upon raw materials and labour costs. This can be mitigated by the need for technical innovation. Enterprises that work in technically sophisticated markets may need to consider a range of issues when sourcing. Environmental pressure groups, ethical issues, plant and distribution hub locations all contribute to make sourcing decisions politically as well as price sensitive.

In addition, an emphasis on early supplier involvement in the design process and supplier innovation will impact on sourcing decisions, as will the need to ensure continuity of supply. This can also have an effect on sourcing policies as an enterprise may prefer, in some cases, supply assurance over part price. In some industries, the majority of an enterprise's suppliers will be situated in areas contiguous with their plants.

Supply base reduction or rationalisation also has an impact on sourcing. Suppliers may be brought into an extended enterprise to act as first-tier supply team leaders. An enterprise may assign a particular supplier to act as team leader for particular platform groups.

Potential pitfalls

As we have seen, in reducing supplier numbers and increasing the complexity of sub-operations, enormous savings can be created and the risk of obsolescent stock-holding reduced. However, it is also necessary to achieve a balance between autonomy as an enterprise and dependency on the supply base. This involves the strategic use of the make-or-buy decision. In some cases, this balance can be exceeded, and enterprises can become too dependent on some suppliers. This can also have an impact on labour relations.

In addition, this closeness can also cause problems for suppliers. Examples exist where closeness between an enterprise and supplier has an impact on the supplier's relationship with other customers. One of these relates to a supplier refusing an audit from another major customer because they felt that the audit was designed to uncover process improvements developed jointly by themselves and a major customer.

2. Analysis strategy for supplier development

Objectives

Supplier development is expensive. This means that it is important to target efforts carefully. There is little point in carrying out supplier development with a first-tier supplier if the problems lie in the second or even third tier. This means using an analysis strategy to identify the capabilities and competences of different suppliers within different supply categories or platform groupings. These capacity profiles can be used to match suppliers to particular projects and issues within the product development and manufacturing process.

Processes

It can require considerable effort to identify suppliers in both first and lower tiers. This, in the case of manufacturing enterprises, may be carried out on a platform-specific basis. 'Platform' in this case refers to a specific group of manufacturing processes carried out to produce a particular product.

One way of analysing data is to develop supplier capability profiles. These profiles can be used to identify suppliers with complementary skills and capacity to carry out specific projects.

As well as looking at individual suppliers, analysis also needs to look at the relationships between suppliers. In this way an understanding of the complexity of the supply chain becomes clear and the supplier development task can be broken down into manageable chunks. A manager within one large automotive supplier stated, 'In the old days we didn't even know where the bolts came from!' Mapping out the chains can help identify significant opportunities for cost reduction. One automotive assembler discovered, for instance, that even a simple-looking item like a roller lifter – a £30 engine part – required 35 separate suppliers.

Analysis enables purchasing and supply to identify opportunities for cost savings and innovation by eliminating gaps and overlaps within the extended enterprise and enabling better distribution of work tasks across business processes. Examples of improved task distribution here are:

◆ The aggregation of operations within one supplier that had previously been carried out in twelve separate suppliers.

◆ The strategic use of vendor managed inventory within one supplier, who fed other key suppliers from stock.

Carrying out an analysis might involve a range of actions including supply chain mapping and business process analysis workshops.

When the American automotive company Chrysler carried out the task of mapping the supply chain the vice president of procurement and supply met with 200 suppliers from the lower tiers of the Robert Bosch supply chain and asked, 'How many people in this room supply Chrysler?' Perhaps ten of the first-tier suppliers raised their hands and the VP said, 'Wrong! You **all** supply Chrysler!' Making suppliers aware of their contribution to the overall business is often a major step in the communication process.

Potential pitfalls

The cost of mapping supply chains and identifying cost reduction and aggregation opportunities can be high. The scale of the task has also had some effect on the credibility of the process within an enterprise as a whole. Establishing cost management opportunities often shows how much more opportunity there is, but also how difficult it is to reach these opportunities. This means that budgets for analysis of supplier development can be difficult to find.

3. Communication strategy for supplier development

Objectives

Communication is perhaps perceived as the major tool in supplier development. Communication is the way in which trust can be developed, information acquired and shared and business opportunities identified. The objectives of a communication strategy may be to create seamless relationships across an extended enterprise, which will involve and motivate suppliers to identify opportunities for improvement.

Processes

There are a number of elements within any communication strategy which contribute to its overall effectiveness. Perhaps the most important of these is to introduce and maintain a strong, unambiguous message that both staff and suppliers within an extended enterprise can understand and then subscribe to. In many organisations this message has been about price or total quality. Increasingly, we can see organisations turning to the fulfilment of customer needs as a message. Some enterprises in technically complex sectors, such as aircraft assembly or semiconductor manufacture, may flag innovation as a way of avoiding future costs. The quality and credibility of the message is a key factor in supplier development.

Once the key message has been designed, it needs to be supported by an internal programme of education and training. Effective internal communication is supported by extensive use of cross-functional teams (CFTs). These may, in turn, be supported by trained facilitators to help avoid some of the problems CFTs face in their initial stages. This is also assisted by the use of a range of information and communication technologies.

Communication for the purposes of supplier development means that everyone needs to hear the same message and buy in to the same key objectives. Everyone needs to work to manage costs, improve quality, ensure delivery, improve customer satisfaction or capitalise on existing technological advances. One critical element of communication is also about the future. This may involve committing to existing suppliers when developing a new technology or process.

Message effectiveness can be improved by ensuring that it is repeated by the buying enterprise, and also by other enterprises and trade associations. In this sense, communication is marketing. Multiple communication channels increase message credibility and effectiveness where messages from one customer may be ignored. One way in which external communication infrastructure can be developed is through supplier conferences. Conference areas may be dedicated to specific issues: cross-platform issues or strategic issues.

The purpose of these conferences is to improve the business relationship with the suppliers through a bi-directional communication channel and provide recognition for their efforts and work in achieving preferred supplier status (if supplier awards and tiering are used). Strategic conferences may address the accomplishments of suppliers as a group and recognise their achievements through a supplier certification process. Platform-specific conferences may look at suppliers for a given programme and discuss current platform plans and future marketing strategies with the specific suppliers.

In addition to the conferences, transactional and relational communication can take place using a variety of EDI and intranet/extranet functions. Communication also takes place through supplier development programmes and supplier award programmes. These are explained in more detail on the following pages.

4. Infrastructure strategy for supplier development

Objectives

In order to communicate effectively, there is a need for a simple, powerful and consistent message that can be easily communicated, and also for a range of tools that will support that message. We can identify two types of communication, which rely on different tools. These are:

♦ **Relational communication:** which may require frequent face-to-face communication supported by phone/e-mail, for example

♦ **Transactional communication:** which may involve EDI, electronic procurement systems, for example.

This involves developing a broad-based information and communication technology (ICT) infrastructure that will enable the message to be transmitted both internally and externally. This can involve heavy expenditure on both EDI technologies and communication technologies, such as dedicated extranets and eMarketplaces.

Processes

Communication tools need to extend along the chain, but also through the enterprise itself. Where enterprise resource planning (ERP) systems are employed, these may assist in lateral intra-enterprise communication, but within large enterprises this still requires a great deal of investment.

Some enterprises are historically fragmented. One organisation that the author has worked with had 43 plants employing over 200 different types of information and communication system. Interoperability was limited, to say the least, as plant could not 'talk' to plant and, even within plants, functions could not exchange information effectively. In such environments, an enterprise might look at a 15% to 20% annual increase in capacity with extensive data mining and data warehousing taking place to support activities.

This is not, however, to suggest that even with ERP implementation there is always a total enterprise-wide information infrastructure in place. Again, a lack of strategic planning can mean that more than one corporate intranet exists and that ERP fails to include some functions.

Potential pitfalls

Although comprehensive information infrastructure may be in place, this does not necessarily mean that information is used to its fullest extent. Information can still too often be filed rather than being used, and the very complexity of the information systems used means that there is little cross-referencing between different information systems. In addition, information is not introduced systematically into an overall risk management framework.

5. Motivation strategy for supplier development

When employing supplier development programmes, the common assumption is that suppliers that need developing will be grateful for development activity. This is often far from true. More often than not, supplier development programmes need to include a motivational element. There are often two key components of a motivation strategy which are:

1.   Gain sharing.

2.   Supplier award programmes.

Gain-sharing

A good example of gain sharing is Chrysler's SCORE programme. This was established as long ago as 1989, offering a challenge to Chrysler suppliers to continuously seek out and identify opportunities to lower costs in the vehicle manufacturing process. In the first ten years of the programme, SCORE has achieved $3.7 billion in cost savings.

During SCORE's first years, cost reduction ideas came in at a rate of more than 100 a week and Chrysler has considered approximately 25,000 supplier-submitted proposals since the programme was introduced. In the first years of the programme's introduction, complaints were received from suppliers with regard to the timescale from idea submission to implementation. This led to the average processing time for proposals dropping from 199 days in 1987 to 89 days in 1993.

The ideas can be quite small. One supplier, Sure-Flow Plastics & Engineering, reduced the thickness of the splash shield (a sheet of plastic that covers the wheel well) on the 1995 minivan, for a relatively tiny saving of $72,500. But in aggregate, SCORE has been a huge success. Of the $1.2 billion in cost savings achieved through SCORE, Chrysler recognised $325 million in direct savings in 1997. The company estimates that suppliers have received a similar windfall from the programme.

Relationship management - Section 3d

Gain-sharing programmes are used in a number of industries. They enable the pursuit of quality, efficiency and affordability without eroding suppliers' profit margins.

Supplier award programmes

Award programmes are common in a number of industries. Generally such programmes offer a number of award levels. Awards should, in order to work, be linked to targets or processes in a specific area. Awards should also not be easy to obtain.

Award ceremonies should be managed carefully. One automotive assembler informed the managing director of a key supplier that his firm was being downgraded from gold to bronze status at a public award ceremony that was later reported in the *Financial Times*. Unfortunately, the managing director had received no advance warning of this downgrading, because the enterprise had only informed the supplier's production engineers. This led to a major dispute and strained relations for several months.

The benefits of award ceremonies are to demonstrate how key suppliers, both within the extended enterprise and outside it, are all given the opportunity to demonstrate that they are willing to work with the buying enterprise. The superordinate goal of the awards is to show how an enterprise and its suppliers can work together to try to change the way business is done. This seems to be seen by suppliers as the most exciting, rewarding and at the same time, the most challenging part of building and perfecting an extended enterprise.

Awards may be given in a number of categories including:

◆ Cost reduction

◆ Customer support

◆ Delivery

◆ Price

◆ Quality

◆ Technology

◆ Warranty.

Potential pitfalls

Potential pitfalls for motivation are about failing to maintain the vision and energy within the process and suppliers beginning to see the system's awards as 'just another event'.

6. Standards strategy for supplier development

Objectives

One of the main problems in supplier development is effective communication. We have seen that communication at a strategic level needs to be clear and powerful. However, communication at an operational or tactical level also needs to be effective. One of the ways of improving communication effectiveness across organisational boundaries is to use process-based standards. Cross-company standards are obviously more powerful than company-specific standards. Standards are used to give suppliers a clear and unambiguous message with regard to minimum standards of quality performance.

Processes

Process certification has, to some degree, lost some of the faith that it engendered in the mid-1980s. At that time, many OEMs saw ISO 9000 as the only certification standard needed, and indeed this is still true in some areas of the Pacific Rim. QS-9000 is sometimes seen as being identical to ISO 9000. However, QS-9000 adds clauses to many of the ISO 9000 elements. The QS standards can be used in a number of ways.

In some areas, QS-9000 was can be used as a process certification methodology, whereby supplier processes are mapped by the supplier and certified by external agencies. This does not, however, remove the need for the audit of process. Despite the fact that audit is a shared function, process audit is an expensive procedure and Ovenden are currently looking at ways in which these costs can be reduced.

In other areas QS-9000 designed to provide a framework for guidance. The programme provides a clear and relatively unambiguous (see below) message for suppliers about the type of processes required within the supply base.

What is QS-9000?

QS-9000 is the name given to the quality system requirements of the automotive industry which were developed by Chrysler, Ford, General Motors and major truck manufacturers and issued in late 1994. QS-9000 replaces such quality system requirements as Ford Q-101, Chrysler's *Supplier Quality Assurance Manual*, GM's NAO *Targets for Excellence* and the truck manufacturer's quality system manuals. The aim of QS-9000 was to eliminate demand variance and waste associated with redundant systems.

Proof of conformance to QS-9000 is certification/registration by an accredited third party such as underwriters' laboratories (ULs) or the American Bureau of Shipping (ABS). Companies that register under QS-9000 are considered to have higher standards and better quality products. QS-9000 is mandatory for suppliers in some industries.

Why QS-9000?

Ostensibly, QS-9000 has been designed to help suppliers stay ahead of their competition. It will do this by filling gaps in the business and quality systems that can cause problems. QS-9000 is designed to eliminate redundant and unnecessary work practices. QS-9000 tells current and potential customers that the product has consistent quality and is manufactured under controlled conditions. This system is globally accepted as proof of quality in the automotive industry and is also a major customer requirement.

How QS-9000 differs from ISO 9000

QS-9000 is sometimes seen as being identical to ISO 9000, but this is not true. Even though each element of ISO 9000 is an element of QS-9000, QS-9000 adds clauses to the majority of the ISO 9000 elements. For example, QS-9000 adds requirements for a business plan, tracking customer satisfaction and bench-marking to element 4.1 of ISO 9000 management responsibility. QS-9000 also uses sector-specific requirements. The following requirements are not based on ISO 9000:

◆ Production-part approval process

◆ The requirements for gaining approval from the customer to run a new or altered part or process

◆ Continuous improvement

◆ Automotive suppliers are required to have systems in place to ensure that organised, measurable improvement activities take place for a variety of business aspects

◆ Manufacturing capabilities

◆ Requirements for planning and effectiveness for equipment, facilities and processes

◆ Requirements for mistake proofing and tooling management.

Associate responsibilities

In order to become QS-9000 certified, a supplier must first prepare staff. Each employee will have responsibilities under QS-9000. Once time studies, machine and operator layout and production rates have been set by the industrial engineer, then some of these responsibilities include:

◆ Performing all work in compliance with all documented procedures and work instructions that may apply

◆ Having access to all procedures and/or work instructions that are applicable to the job

- Knowing the supplier's QS-9000 quality policy statement

- Cooperating with internal and external auditors

- Attending and completing all required training sessions

- Attending all meetings that are applicable to your job function (management reviews, problem-solving meetings)

- Respecting the document control and quality record procedures

- Complying with corrective actions

- Completing all forms, logs and other records which are called for by your procedures and work instructions in a consistent, timely manner

- Notifying appropriate personnel of non-conformances which could cause a quality problem or finding during an audit.

QS-9000 audits

When the employees are prepared for their responsibilities they are randomly audited by two types of auditors:

1. **Internal auditors:** a team of people who are employed by the supplier.

2. **External auditors:** a customer representative of the QS-9000 certification auditor.

The auditor's questions may include:

- How do you do your job?

- Do you have work instructions or a procedure?

The auditor might then ask specific questions concerning the procedure.

Examples include:

- Are you familiar with the company quality policy?

- Can you tell me what it is?

- What does it mean to you?

The auditor may also ask to see any forms or records. Audits are normally scheduled and the supplier will be notified. Therefore each supplier will have time to prepare, and they will usually have a practice audit so that everyone is prepared. However, the supplier should always be prepared for an audit by having their procedures and quality policy statement ready.

Procedures should not be followed only when there is an audit. The purpose of the QS-9000 system is to consistently produce a quality product. If procedures are followed only at the time of the audit, the suppliers will not be comfortable or knowledgeable with them when the auditors come through. Therefore, receiving certification becomes much more unlikely. More importantly, the goal of consistent production of a quality product will more than likely have been defeated.

The most important thing to stress with regard to QS-9000 and certification is that it is not a productivity or even a quality comparison with other suppliers. It is simply a check to see if you, as a department or company, are doing what you said you have been doing every time you produce a part or product.

QS-9000 quality statement

The QS-9000 quality statement tells of a supplier's objectives for quality and commitment to quality, and is relevant to company goals and customer needs and expectations. The quality statement will be given to all suppliers in the form of a laminated card that they must keep with them at all times. The quality statement should be posted in all areas of the facility. Though it is not necessary for each supplier to memorise the quality policy statement, they should be able to read it from the card or wall and say what it means to them. All management personnel must know the quality policy statement.

QS-9000 was developed to ensure customer satisfaction, beginning with conformance to fundamental quality requirements and utilising such concepts as continuous improvement, defect prevention and the reduction of variation and waste in the supply chain. QS-9000 is an expansion or adaptation of ISO 9000 that is more comprehensive and more applicable to the automobile industry and its suppliers.

It is possible to use other standards to guide suppliers, improve the quality of communication and reduce the possibility of misunderstandings. There are, however, real dangers in misusing standards.

Potential pitfalls

Some problems exist with standard-based strategies. These include cost and the speed and accuracy of updates. The release of later editions of QS-9000 has not been accepted complacently. Some suppliers have noted that a lot of little changes, taken collectively, add up to a big change. Others noted requirements that add little or no value to processes or products, rather than relying on the discretion of the people who understand the process best.

The alignment of process improvement and cost reduction can be hard to achieve. Within the automotive industry, customers may demand anywhere from 5% to 15% yearly cost reductions. Suppliers believe that QS-9000 merely asks them to fulfil more requirements, with less money, resources and time.

Changing quality systems can be costly and confusing, and changes to the standard have unsettled some suppliers. For instance, the third edition of the standard requires a supplier to perform dock audits of products in finished inventory, which some suppliers resent, because they feel that by the time a product reaches the shipping dock, other quality checks within the system should already have ensured that it was acceptable.

For QS-9000 users, the changes were being made because so many companies were just receiving SPC information and warrants from suppliers, and failing to act on them. They were never reviewing them to see whether those things actually met the specification.

Auditors speak of countless audits where the actual certificate of compliance or certificate of analysis failed when checked against the spec and the actual component or ingredients. Many auditors speak of companies where the SPC from their contractors showed out-of-control conditions and out-of-spec readings, but where no evaluation or corrective action has been taken. For customers, new editions of QS-9000 offered an opportunity to challenge the supplier base to start looking seriously at subcontractor control.

7. Development strategy for supplier development

Objectives

The combination of sourcing, analysis, standards, communication and motivational strategies can all be integrated into a relatively seamless whole to ensure that the supply base is managed effectively. There is, however, a clear need to ensure that the system is not only managed but improved. Although this improvement process is an integral part of the strategies mentioned above (innovation in SCORE, reviews of QS-9000 standards and targets in supplier awards), the whole can be supported by a process of Kaizen or continuous improvement.

Processes

Kaizen teams can be used with key suppliers to identify cost savings and potential performance improvements. These include:

◆   **Kaizen:** continuous, incremental improvement in an activity to create more value with less waste

◆   **The identification of Muda or waste:**   or an activity that consumes resources but creates no value

◆   **The use of process maps or spaghetti charts:** a map of the path taken by a product as it travels through production – so-called because the product's route typically looks like a plate of spaghetti

◆ **The implementation of standard work plans:** a precise set of work instructions specifying cycle time, task time, work sequence and minimum inventory needed.

Kaizen has its origins in the Toyota Production System. This lean manufacturing philosophy, originated at Toyota Motor Co by Taiichi Ohno after World War II, has spun off a wealth of quality tools and techniques. Among these are just-in-time delivery schedules, Poka-Yoke (mistake-proof) production processes and kaizen.

In theory, Kaizen should be carried out over a short time period, typically five days. The first day is devoted to team training. The second day, employees gather data about a problem and brainstorm solutions (the second night may be spent physically changing the work environment if it seems necessary after the brainstorming session). On the third and fourth days, employees test the solution, make adjustments and document each change as it is made. On the fifth day, the Kaizen team presents its solution.

This five-day 'blitz' is designed to overcome resistance to change by moving faster than it would be possible for the company's bureaucracy to step in and stop progress. Kaizen improvements take place quickly, before vested interests can convince the change agents in a company that they don't need to be done. Even the physical changes, such as moving machinery, happen quickly. The idea is not to debate which of two ideas is the best one – choose one quickly and implement it.

This is how a company is expected to make continuous incremental improvements. Also, because Kaizen teams have no capital budgets they are forced to make changes that don't cost money. Instead they draw on practical experience and creativity.

Kaizen training generally consists of three phases.

1. The first phase stresses the need to improve operations to remain competitive. In every kaizen, there's a concrete result: eliminating steps in the process, eliminating unnecessary work or reducing the staffing level. The solution might involve using less manufacturing floor space for your equipment and staff. There are many, many small ways in which you reduce waste or become more effective as a result of a Kaizen team's work.

2. The second phase of the training process addresses Kaizen philosophy and methodology, showing how they fit into a plant's production cycle or processes. Data is gathered on the current situation through time observation, counting inventory, measuring square footage of the floor space and creating a spaghetti diagram, which follows the steps of the process all over the factory and outside to the customer and the supplier.

   Then brainstorming may come up with a new layout for the equipment or process or with a method to reduce the inventory that allows flow to continue but reduces the amount of inventory that is in process. Kaizen treats any point in the manufacturing process where goals are not being met or there is room for improvement as a potential problem to be solved.

3.   The third phase of Kaizen teaches teams analytical data collection and problem-solving techniques, including training in working as a team, creating agendas, keeping minutes, handling action items and focusing on the team mission. Teams are taught skills such as brainstorming; making checklists, diagrams and surveys; and creating histograms, Pareto charts, run charts and statistical process control charts.

Diagnostic methods

Although building teams and teaching them problem-solving skills is important to kaizen, getting input from every employee is what makes Kaizen work. Kaizen philosophy asserts that every employee, regardless of education or experience, has valuable suggestions to contribute.

For example, new employees are frequently most aware of processes that are difficult, confusing or poorly documented. Diverse life experiences can also shed new light on a problem. For Kaizen teams, respecting every employee's potential contribution to the improvement process is kaizen's greatest strength. For instance, staff from different cultural backgrounds may bring a broad range of experience to develop innovative ways of dealing with difficulties.

Potential pitfalls

Although a key element in the overall strategy, Kaizen has had its drawbacks. These are caused by two main factors:

1.   The first is the speed of implementation and the top-down corporate effort and commitment needed for this management technique. Keeping up with new procedures can be difficult when changes are made so quickly. QS or ISO certification can conflict with kaizen, so managers and staff both have to make sure that standard operating procedures accurately reflect operations. This means ensuring good follow up on the paperwork side of kaizen. Often Kaizen teams create energetic 'quick fixes', which are not sustainable in the longer term. This can often mean that the team revisits the supplier several times.

2.   The second is that, in many cases, Kaizen teams are identifying deep-rooted problems and are staying well beyond the 'five-day limit'. Many Kaizen problem-solving projects are put on a 30-day or even 60-day schedule instead of completed during a short-term Kaizen event. This dramatically increases costs.

Kaizen is often easy in theory and hard in practice. Enterprises can underestimate the amount of time and effort it takes. For instance, team formation and training take time, which can temporarily disrupt the production process. Productivity may also take a dip while Kaizen-driven changes are being made. Short-term slowing may discourage a company from pursuing longer-term goals.

Kaizen often fails because it is given only lip service by supplier managers, owners and staff. The supplier must support a culture open to employee-driven, rather than manager-driven, change. Proponents of Kaizen state that in our current culture, executives and managers are supposed to know the answers, but with Kaizen, executives and managers need to know the right questions. Many suppliers, particularly smaller businesses, are not receptive to this type of approach.

One of the keys to gaining worker support for the Kaizen concept is one of its central ideas: that no workers be laid off as a result of the process improvements. Theoretically, within the Kaizen approach, displaced workers get a better job as a result. For instance, if a three-person operation is reduced to two people, the most experienced worker may leave the operation and become part of the resource team. He or she would go from being a line worker to working on team projects like instituting more plant-floor improvements, plus working on the 30-day list the Kaizen team leaves behind. These principles have not always been followed by Kaizen teams or by managers after the team has left. This has also had an impact on the longer-term effectiveness of the strategy.

Summary

As can be seen, supplier development is much more than an emphasis on quality of production and the sharing of information. It involves a wide ranger of activities that need to be integrated into a cohesive whole to ensure robustness and effectiveness. Where activities are integrated, they will support each other, and the overall effect will be much greater than if single activities were used in isolation. Different combinations of strategies will work in different industries and for different enterprises. Choosing the right combination of strategies is the critical challenge faced by the purchasing and supply function. Although the scale of the example given above is large, the principles are applicable in all cases.

Self-assessment question

SAQ 3.4

Identify some of the factors that might impact upon customer-supplier relationships.

.

The relationship life cycle

The syllabus learning outcomes for this subsection state that you will be able to:

◆   **Explain the relationship life cycle**

◆   **Recommend appropriate approaches to the termination or suspension of relationships.**

This subsection will cover:

◆   **Introduction**

◆   **The product life cycle**

◆   **The customer life cycle**

◆   **The procurement life cycle**

◆   **The relationship life cycle**

◆   **Relationship violation and termination**

◆   **Contract renewal.**

Introduction

Companies operate in dynamic changing environments. There have been a number of attempts to explain these environments in terms of a life cycle approach. Broadly, we can identify four life cycle approaches:

◆   The product life cycle

◆   The customer life cycle

◆   The procurement life cycle

◆   The relationship life cycle.

The product life cycle

The 1970s were noted for management theories focused on product life cycles. Companies were organised around how products were conceived, designed, tested, developed, approved, manufactured, sold and distributed. The theory was turned into practice and companies finally had a handle on how products come and go in the marketplace.

As a product moves in the product life cycle from launch to growth, market maturity and possibly to eventual decline, there are important implications for the purchasing and supply function.

Development and entry stages

Operations flexibility is at a premium. The product may be made in low volumes. Its design features are still being fined-tuned and there are still market uncertainties. In the early 1980s personal computer standards were still unresolved. Product design and volumes were unpredictable.

Cash flow is negative. Development costs at the point that the first product is sold or first-customer-served costs are at their height as the launch itself demands marketing and promotional expenditure. This continues until the product is established and even then promotion is a normal cost of sale. Sales revenues must catch up. This is the classical breakeven point concern.

Late growth and maturity

The product and market are stable. The aim is market share and cash generation with operations achieving consistent, high-quality, low-cost output. Predictability is more important than flexibility. Investment in operational improvements aims to lower costs. Products moving into decline may attract design changes which will require operations to implement. For a car, there may be a trim or body shell upgrade but the changes may be just skin deep. Improvement is the constant call as the firm strives to keep its existing products from entering terminal decline.

The customer life cycle

The product focus was, however, weak in that it ignored the fact that customers made up the market. By taking the customer into account during the 1980s and 1990s, focus shifted to the customer life cycle.

There are two levels of customer life cycle. The first of these is the focus on the transaction. In this model, the marketers pay attention to five discrete steps along the buying continuum which are:

1.   **Reach:** claim someone's attention.

2.   **Acquisition:** bring that person into your sphere of influence.

3.   **Conversion:** turn that person into a paying customer.

4.   **Retention:** keep that person as a customer.

5.   **Loyalty:** turn that person into a company advocate.

Ideally, a prospect is led through all those steps and kept satisfied enough to repeat the steps when called for the next purchase. In reality, however, 'fallout' can occur at each step along the way.

Because buyers can abandon a solution or be diverted to another one at so many points in the buying life cycle, marketers who pay close attention to behaviours at and between each step will learn just where their marketing efforts are most vulnerable to attack from competitors or, worse, inertia.

The second level of focus within this model is that instead of looking at a customer as a series of 'one-off' orders, sellers were encouraged to define strategy as the overall long-term series of events that comprise the entire set of transactions that a given buyer will effect. This led to models such as 'customer lifetime value' (CLTV).

Customer lifetime value is a simple and powerful concept, which can be defined as the expected value of profit to a business derived from customer relationships from the current time to some future point in time. The primary result of this shift in focus was a shift in the order-taking process such that subsequent customer contact was driven by the hope that the same buyer would return to the seller for more business.

Both the product and customer life cycle models have proven to be one-directional in that the 'customer is king' and therefore the seller has little or no part in understanding the customer's customer and their needs. In other words, the customer life cycle never really moved beyond the simple aggregation of the value of all orders received over the lifetime of the buyer or seller in that relationship.

The procurement life cycle

Definitions of the procurement life cycle vary. For some authors it involves a number of stages which may include:

1. Identification of potential sources.

2. Market analysis.

3. Needs analysis.

4. Request for information.

5. Supplier screening/pre-qualification.

6. Request for proposals/tender issue.

7. Tender assessment/supplier selection.

8. Contract negotiation.

9. Contract drafting.

10. Contract award.

11. Contract monitoring.

12. Product review and continuous improvement.

13. Management of variation.

14. Contract termination.

15. Disposal.

Relationships will be very different at each stage of this cycle, as will the respective levels of effort involved from both the buyer and the supplier. Traditionally, the role of the purchasing and supply function was much more closely involved with the early stages of this cycle, and the supplier took over in the later stages. More recently, in many organisations and enterprises, the purchasing and supply function has become more closely involved in later stages of the process.

In addition, the integrated nature of supply chain management means that purchasing and supply functions should be increasingly accountable to a range of functions across the enterprise, and the days of buying a good or a service and then forgetting about it once the contract was signed are rapidly disappearing.

The relationship life cycle

In addressing the question of a relationship life cycle, there are a number of issues that the purchasing and supply function needs to face. As noted already, relationships are difficult to assess in any objective way. Although it is true that relationships change over time, the reasons that they change are often difficult to understand, and the way in which individual relationships change is almost impossible to predict.

Factors causing changes in relationships

Knowing what causes relationships to change is important to both buyers and sellers. In the field of social psychology there are four groups of explanations as to why this happens in relationships between individuals. These are:

1.   Relational theories.

2.   Behavioural theories.

3.   Social exchange theories.

4.   Conflict theories.

It may be useful to briefly consider each of these.

Relational theories

According to relational theories, people develop models of what a relationship should be and transfer those models into their everyday activities. These models lead to different styles of behaviour within a relationship including:

◆   **Secure:** where individuals find it easy to get close to others

◆   **Avoidant:** where individuals experience difficulty in getting close to others

◆   **Ambivalent:** where people do not think that their relationships are as close as they might like.

Some surveys seem to demonstrate that over 45% of individuals have avoidant or ambivalent behavioural patterns. By identifying traits or predispositions towards a behaviour, relational theory helps explain why people often go through the same patterns within their relationships. In commercial terms this may explain why some organisations find partnering difficult. It nonetheless fails to explain why people who are secure about relationships still go through relationship break-up.

Behavioural theories

According to behavioural theory, people learn from interactions with their partners, whether they are in a good relationship or not. So behaviours such as openness and honesty would lead people to believe that they are in a good relationship. Behaviours such as concealment and dishonesty would lead them to believe the opposite. This view rests upon the way in which relationships are perceived and assessed. People are generally very accurate when it comes to person perception, but these perceptions are normally incomplete. Individuals rarely look at the total picture; more often they look unconsciously at a range of factors such as dependability or liking. In commercial relationships, perceptions may be around technical capability ('Can the factory deliver to this specification?'), but may ignore relational capability ('Will we be informed throughout the design build process?'). Behavioural theories offer a simple way of explaining why relationships change (people change and their partners become unhappy), but they don't explain why these changes take place.

Social exchange theories

Social exchange theories are based on a market model of relationships where individuals involved make decisions about their relationships, based on the costs and benefits involved. The outcome of a relationship, using this approach, rests upon the player's perception of the benefits and cost. These costs and benefits may be financial or they may be much broader. Individuals expect to receive benefits that are commensurate with their costs and a profit according to the investment they make in the relationship. Individuals also weigh the alternatives available to them. They may stay in a relationship with little benefit, where the alternative has even less benefit. One of these theories also suggests that the benefits and costs attached to a relationship need to be seen as fair by the people involved. Social exchange theories are reflected in some degree by the relational contracts we will consider later in this study guide.

Conflict theories

Conflict theories fall into two groups. The first are crisis theories, which deal with external circumstances that act upon the relationship. In a commercial relationship these circumstances may range from a market collapse, to persistent quality problems from a third-tier supplier. There is a range of mitigating factors that can help relationships manage through a crisis including the network of support available. The second group is theories about the way in which conflict is handled within a relationship. As we have already seen, all relationships are prone to experiencing conflict.

Albert Hirschmann suggested that people react to conflict by using one of four styles:

1. **Exit:** this may include behaviour such as ending a contract, thinking about ending a contract, changing the nature of a contract, threatening to end a contract or actively sabotaging a contact.

2. **Voice:** this may include discussing contractual problems, compromising, seeking mediation before problems escalate, suggesting solutions, asking the partner what is wrong and trying to change either oneself or the partner.

3. **Loyalty:** this may be waiting and hoping things will improve, supporting the partner in the hope that things will change and continuing to have faith in the relationship.

4. **Neglect:** this may include ignoring the partners request's for change, criticising the partner for things unrelated to the problem, chronically complaining without offering a solution.

We looked in section 2 at conflict-handling as one of the factors that impacts upon relationships. These behaviours can be mapped on to a conflict-handling grid.

Figure 11: Conflict-handling grid

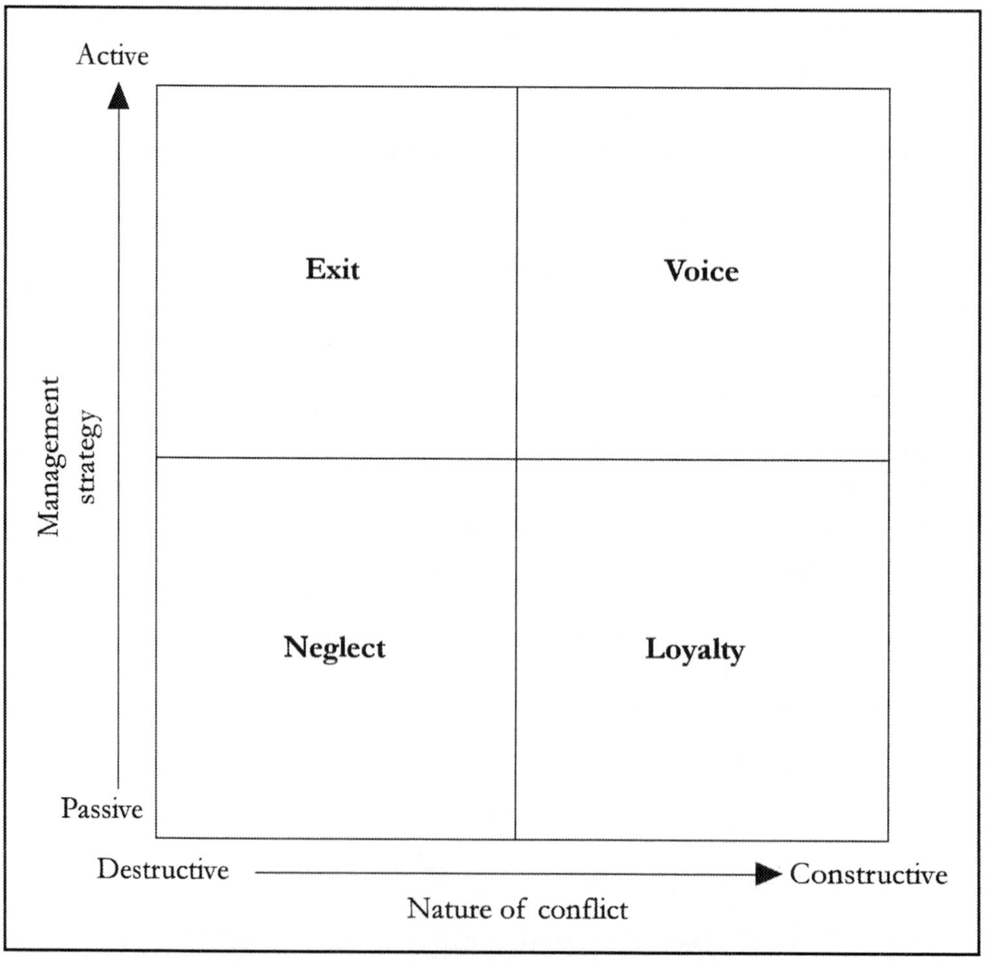

Relationships may move through these quadrants depending on a range of factors and the individual's ability to manage the conflict.

Nature of relationship life cycles

Because relationships are complex, interactive processes, it is difficult to describe a life cycle common to all commercial relationships. Parties to a relationship become acquainted, work more closely together, recede and approach in an ongoing fluctuation of states. During this time, they will consciously and unconsciously assess the state of the relationship. As we saw at the beginning of section 1, there may be many decision makers involved in this assessment, and production may have a very different idea to purchasing about the state of the relationship. This means that any attempt to break relationships into stages in time is likely to be misleading. By and large all we can say is that some relationships go through a process of growth maturity and decline in the same way that products do. However, it is important to recognise that not all relationships do, and that the rates at which they change vary widely from relationship to relationship.

One way in which relationships may change is in the degree of integration that takes place within them. Integration may include the integration of tools and systems such as information systems and ordering systems. It may also include the degree to which people within the respective organisations or enterprises 'think alike' as a result of shared experience and shared attitudes.

This change will be influenced by a range of factors including:

- **Perceived needs:** do both parties have a common understanding of the needs within the relationship and are these communicated effectively?

- **Comparison processes:** how the supplier compares to other suppliers

- **Conscious selection processes:** around price, quality, innovation, for example

- **Unconscious selection processes:** around personal liking, trust, for example

- **Interactional skills:** such as communication or conflict management

- **Objectives:** how much autonomy do the parties want to preserve? Is the goal a superordinate one?

- **Cultural blueprints:** what a relationship should be like

- **Public or private commitment:** the degree to which the contract is known outside the relationship

- **The way in which the relationship is maintained:** using bidirectional openness, communication, role and task clarity, for example

- **The way in which the relationship is ended:** is any warning or feedback given?

Employing the relationship life cycle

We have seen how the product and customer life cycle operate. Using the product life cycle approach, an enterprise launches a product priced at £200.00. Let's say that the technology of the product typically implies a product life cycle of five good years with little or no maintenance and then rapidly decreasing utility. After ten years it is assumed that the unit is useless. The seller optimises the deal around the individual transaction.

The customer life cycle approach extends this time line and, providing customer service is demonstrated throughout the life cycle of the product (free or discounted maintenance, for example), then the buyer might come back to the same seller to get a replacement. Therefore, the seller is not considering a single transaction, but a series of transactions, which might generate £1,000 over the duration of the buyer/seller relationship.

By looking at the relational life cycle, the skilled purchasing and supply professional can help the enterprise manage the flow of goods, services and information, so as to optimise the resources within the relationship. This can result in effective communication, which can help the buyer and seller work jointly to better understand the customers' customer needs so that they can both serve them better than another competing value chain.

This can lead to both repeat business and new business. It can open new market segments, new locations or geographies and new industries. Such arrangements are rare, but can offer significant competitive advantage in value chain management.

Relationship violation and termination

It is important to remember that the environment in which contracts are used is changing. We can suggest that contracts rely on the perceptions of the parties involved. In a legal sense, companies, and some other organisational forms, are considered to be legal entities. In other words, companies can contract themselves, and the contract will be legally enforceable on the company as a whole. This means that regardless of the changes in personnel or management, the company still has to enforce the contract.

Of course, this is where many contract problems stem from. Although the contract is with the whole organisation, some parts of the organisation may not be 'involved' in the contract. This means that a tool operator who is not interested on a particular day could make a mistake and cause a problem for the customer, which costs millions in reputational and legal damages and equal amounts in legal fees.

The traditional answer to this problem was self-interest and self-protection, and a number of methods were deployed to ensure that this answer worked. These included supervisory management and payment by results at an individual worker level. Later, persistent problems led to the introduction of total quality management, which emphasised the involvement of the whole of the workforce in the task. How well this works over time is unclear.

Relationship management - Section 3e

In this sense, contracts can only ever be partial. One of the tasks of the purchasing professional is to embed the contract in the whole of the organisation, and we have already looked at some of the ways in which this can be done. However, the problem still remains within a commercial relationship. How do we handle contract violation and termination?

There are a number of fundamental issues with regard to contract violation and termination including:

◆ In some senses, it is impossible to separate out the legal or transactional elements of the contract, and the relational element. Every contract has a relational element

◆ Contract violation is commonplace. Individuals and groups break contracts all the time

◆ Violated contracts will lead to some sort of adverse reaction by the injured party

◆ Relationships can survive the breaking of a transactional contract.

Types of violation

Individuals and groups tend to consciously or unconsciously classify violations into types, depending on the capability and motivation of the party violating the contract. These are:

1. If the party is willing but incapable because of external factors such as a landslide destroying a supplier's plant.

2. If the party is capable but unwilling because circumstances have changed – another customer has ordered goods at a more advantageous price, for example.

3. If the party is capable and willing but violates the contract because of divergent interpretations. Both parties misunderstood the meaning of the contract.

4. If the party is incapable because they have perhaps lost key staff or because they were incorrectly selected. They may also be unwilling because the contractor has treated them poorly.

This classification will also tend to look at the reasons behind the motivation of the violating party. If they are motivated by opportunism, it can be considered a more serious breach than if they had been negligent. All of these classifications tend to take place in a framework of what is fair or just.

Figure 12: Kilmann and Thomas conflict management styles

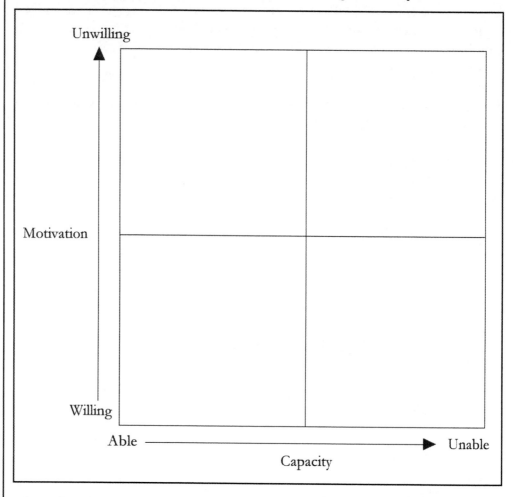

As well as classifying the type of violation, parties in a relationship tend to also classify the impact of the violation. Typically, classification tends to rest on:

♦   The size of the loss caused by the violation

♦   The type and nature of remedies offered

♦   The credibility of the explanations of the reasons for the violation

♦   The strength or value of the relationship.

In handling contract violations, it is often too easy to shout and scream at the person perceived as being responsible. As we saw in section 2, when we looked at conflict management, this does not help manage the violation effectively, and can add to a climate whereby more violations are likely to take place. It should be noted that individuals monitor each other's behaviour, and that the frequency of monitoring increases in relationships which are considered untrustworthy or untrusting. The more monitoring goes on, the more likely we are to see problems and the worse the situation can become.

Just as in the transactional/legal contact, there also need to be procedures within the relational contract for managing violations, and these procedures need to be seen as fair by both parties.

Examples of such procedures might include:

♦ Giving the violating party an opportunity to explain the violation

♦ Being open to this explanation

♦ Looking for evidence

♦ Offering an opportunity to remedy the violation

♦ Ensuring that the remedy is fair (supplier penalties for stopping production such as a £5,000 payment for every half-hour the line is stopped may not be seen as fair)

♦ Building stages into the process to slow down escalation.

This type of informal procedure can help avoid termination of the contract, or the type of neglect behaviours which we looked at in the exit-voice-loyalty-neglect cycle. In some cases, however, the contract will require termination. This may be initiated for a number of reasons. These may be ongoing problems with the relationship, shifts in market conditions or technology or simply termination due to the end of a product life cycle.

Whatever the reason for termination, there are a number of considerations that can be taken into account where the aim is to preserve the relationship.

Successful terminations tend to:

♦ Be well structured with proper procedures

♦ Have valid, well-articulated reasons

♦ Be clearly communicated

♦ Involve accurate, balanced feedback

♦ Be prepared for by both parties

♦ Involve acknowledgement of the work within the existing contract

♦ Frame the contract/relationship in terms of long-term objectives

♦ Leave the door open for renewal or replacement of the old contract with a new one.

Contract renewal

As we will see in section 4 of the study guide, relational contracting may require a series of contracts between the buyer and the supplier. Often, purchasing staff think only of the immediate contract, but it can be useful to think of the second or third contract you intend to award in a particular area. In addition, contracts, as we have seen, do fail. In these cases it is important to recognise the fact that a new supplier will need to be found. In such cases renewal is more like re-award.

What is contract renewal?

Contract renewal is the process of re-awarding some aspect of a current contract with one or more suppliers in a similar or different arrangement. The options are:

◆ To retain the scope of the existing contract

◆ To split the scope of the existing contract

◆ To broaden the scope of the existing contract

◆ To eliminate the requirement for the contract.

The process of contract renewal is important because it:

◆ Provides the buyer with an opportunity to gain leverage, extracting better value and service than might otherwise have been obtained

◆ Provides an opportunity and an incentive for suppliers to become more innovative in their solutions. New offerings can be given a chance to compete and the incumbent will need to produce more imaginative solutions to the challenges faced to stand a chance of winning

◆ Allows for greater flexibility to comply with strategic and tactical objectives as the contract can be re-scoped to accommodate changing business needs

◆ Helps the buyer re-evaluate needs. Lack of time and focus pressures mean that buyers rely on the maxim, 'If it ain't broke, don't fix it'. Contracts that do not badly underperform are often just extended on similar terms. This can be problematic if competitors are obtaining better terms through contract renewal.

Objectives

The objective of any contract renewal is to generate the best deal to meet current and future requirements. Planning the new contract may involve the development of a new business case which answers questions such as:

◆ Which elements delivered under the old contract are still required?

◆ What will be the impact of a shift in these goods or key performance indicators?

◆ What will be the impact of a supplier change on the enterprise, other suppliers and the current supplier?

◆ How can this impact best be managed?

◆ Are there new requirements?

◆ How can new requirements best be delivered?

The key decision to be addressed is the scope of the new contract or contracts. Cascading from this decision will be the nature of the new contract or contracts – what kind of relationship is required with a provider, including its length and funding arrangements.

Implementation

As noted earlier, the work involved in planning and awarding a new contract is often a deterrent to contract renewal. Focus therefore tends to be on the specification development process, the sourcing decision and the bidding and negotiation stages. It is, however, important to think like a chess player – several moves ahead – and consider the current needs of the enterprise and the likely future needs.

Current and future needs

Identifying and evaluating current and future sourcing options might include decisions on how to optimise:

◆ Current supply for which there will be a future need

◆ The make-or-buy/provide-or-buy decision about supply for which there will be a future need

◆ Supply for which there will be only a limited future need

◆ The effect of new technologies, business models and regulation on existing supply arrangements and future needs.

Past performance

The next issue to consider is the past performance of the contract. What scope is there for improvement? Factors to consider may include:

◆ Contract flexibility

◆ Range of products and/or services

◆ Customer satisfaction

◆ Intelligent customer capability and rating

◆ Innovation

◆ Total performance.

Contract handover

Handover of the contract from one supplier to another can require careful management. The handover process should be driven by the need to ensure business continuity. This is especially important if the handover is made mid-contract or mid-project.

Timing of renewal

Obviously, if a contract is failing, you may have time to prepare for renewal. Issues that may impact on timing are business stability, organisational readiness and the current state of the market. This must be considered as far as possible before terminating and renewing the contract.

Summary

There are a number of life cycle models available which offer a framework to approach transactions (buying and selling) and also a number of approaches, which help explain changes in relationships. These changes sometimes take place at different rates between partners and in different circumstances so these models do not really help us predict the way in which relationships will progress or regress. In considering contracts it is important to recognise that violations of contract are fairly common and that relationships can survive contract violations. It is also important to recognise that relationships will often terminate at some point. Managing this termination effectively is likely to maintain the relationship. Before termination occurs, the purchasing and supply department should think about contract renewal and how this can best be implemented.

self-assessment question

SAQ 3.5

What are the likely characteristics of a successful contract termination?

Relationship assessment

The syllabus learning outcomes for this subsection state that you will be able to:

◆ **Comment critically on developing theory and practice in relation to relationship assessment and management.**

This subsection will cover:

◆ **Introduction**

◆ **Setting relationship objectives**

◆ **Relationship maps or models**

◆ **Assessing process-model correspondence**

◆ **Closing the gap.**

Introduction

In section 2 of this study guide we looked at supplier selection. As we saw, the purposes of supplier selection are many and varied. Once a supplier has been selected, however, there is still a monitoring requirement to assess the degree to which the relationship between a supplier and a buyer are facilitating the interests and outcomes of both enterprises involved in the relationship.

This monitoring role is a critical one. We have seen that relationships consist of a set of processes, some of which are difficult to understand and manage. Any part of managing within a relationship must involve assessing how the relationship is working. Before we go on to look at assessing relationships, we can briefly look at the control cycle, which sets out four elements that need to be in place for any process, or set of processes, to be controlled.

Figure 13: The control cycle

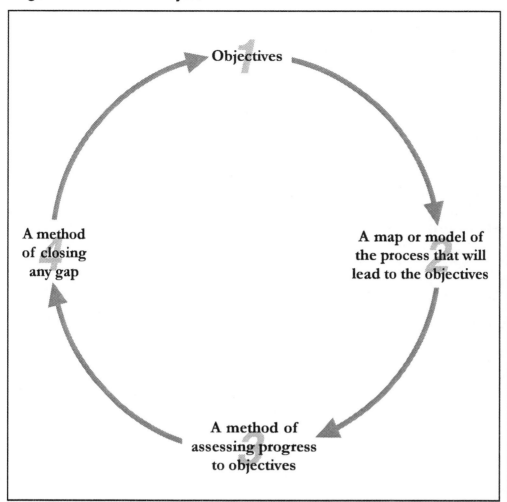

In order for any process to be controlled there needs to be four elements in place. If any of these elements are missing, the process will not be controlled.

These four elements are:

1. Objectives need to be in place because, without objectives, control is meaningless.

2. A 'map' or 'model' of the process being controlled in order to show how objectives will be reached.

3. A method of assessing how the process corresponds with the model.

4. A method of closing the gap between the model and the process.

These elements are in place in all control systems from shower taps to accounting systems. They can also be put in place within relationships, depending on the objectives, model, process assessment and gap-closing mechanisms chosen.

Setting relationship objectives

When setting objectives for the relationship, there are a number of approaches that can be taken. Objectives can be set:

◆ Unilaterally by the buyer or the supplier

◆ Jointly by both the buyer and the supplier

◆ Openly with no hidden objectives

◆ Covertly with many hidden objectives.

Figure 14: Objective setting

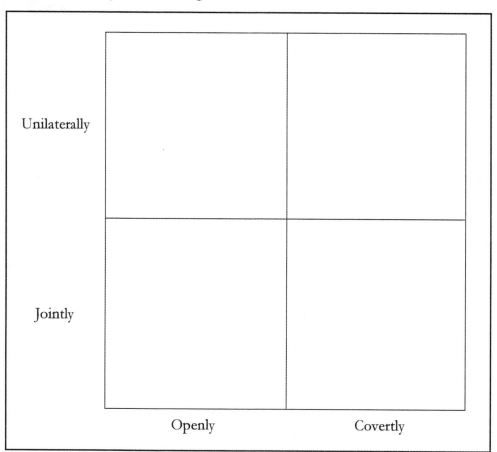

The method of choosing objectives will impact on the nature of the relationship. This is not to say that the joint, open quadrant will always be correct, only that if an enterprise is seeking a partnering arrangement, that selecting objectives in the unilateral/covert quadrant will not necessarily help.

There are a number of ways in which joint, open objectives can be defined and set. These may include supplier workshops in which objectives can be defined and negotiated, or this may be carried out using survey methods and techniques.

Relationship management - Section 3f

Some common objectives for a relationship involve the generic outcomes, which may include:

- Cost
- Delivery
- Quality as reliability
- Quality as consistency

- Flexibility/agility
- Level of service
- Innovation.

A method called 'importance performance analysis' can be used to determine the choice of relationship objectives. This might involve purchasers and suppliers working together to plot the importance of the objective and its likely performance as seen in figure 15 below.

Figure 15: Objective and likely performance graph

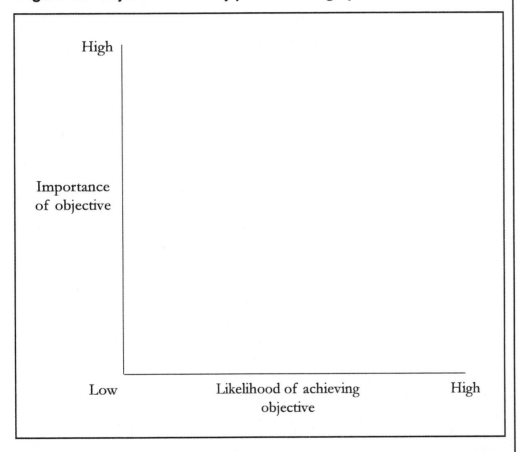

By selecting objectives on the basis of the importance to the respective parties within the relationship, and the contribution that the objectives are likely to make, both buyers and suppliers are likely to reach agreement about the overall objectives in a timely manner.

Relationship maps or models

Once objectives and metrics are decided, the next step is to develop the relationship map or model. There are a number of relationship models. Everyone should be familiar with the supplier positioning model whereby purchasing and relational strategies can be decided according to the degree of risk and expenditure involved.

Another view of the positioning matrix was developed at the University of Bath, whereby relationships were positioned according to the strategic or tactical contribution that the supplier makes and the nature of the economic relationship. This gives four forms of supply relationship:

1. **Traditional relationships:** where the adversarial approach is still key and purchasing power is used to achieve lower prices in a competitive market.

2. **Stress relationships:** describe even more adversarial relationships where buyers drive suppliers to the wall by demanding lower prices and increasing product complexity.

3. **Resolved relationships:** have hidden some of the problems faced in the first two forms and may involve the introduction of SPC training, TQM methods and some supplier or customer involvement in solving joint problems.

4. **Partnership relationships:** as we have seen, are characterised by information/risk/reward sharing, the setting of joint goals and openness in dispute avoidance and resolution.

Models such as the supplier positioning matrix or the above relationship positioning model are interesting but less than useful in the real world when we are involved in managing relationships. There are many more variables than spend value, or length of relationship. In section 2 of this study guide we looked at some of the factors that impact on the relationship.

If we consider a range of models, there are a number of common factors which impact upon the nature of the relationship (see table opposite). It is important to remember, when considering these factors that information with regard to their impact is often difficult to obtain. Transaction value may be an important factor but value is perceived and depends on the overall market share which an organisation's purchase represents compared to the market share achieved by the supplier.

This means that customer and supplier perceptions may differ. In addition, circumstances may change, leading to changes in these factors. Also some of these changes may be beyond the control of the purchasing and supply function, and when considering the contribution of these factors it is important to consider the degree to which these factors will vary over the course of the relationship.

Factors impacting on relationships	Customer perception	Supplier perception	Variability
Transaction value – the amount of expenditure within the transaction as a proportion of overall customer spend/ purchasing revenue	Low – High	Low – High	Low – High
Transaction risk – the likelihood that a supplier will fail in terms of price, quality, delivery, reliability, flexibility, innovation, service etc.	Low – High	Low – High	Low – High
Transaction contribution – the degree to which the transaction contributes to the goals of the department, another department or the organisation	Low – High	Low – High	Low – High
Transaction complexity – the type, mix, range of contracts, activities and sub-projects	Low – High	Low – High	Low – High
Transaction volume – the number of items	Low – High	Low – High	Low – High
Transaction replicability – the degree to which other transactions can be substituted	Low – High	Low – High	Low – High
Transaction predictability – the impact of demand in terms of both quantity and type on both supplier and customer	Low – High	Low – High	Low – High
Transaction longevity – the length of time that the contract lasts or the likely number of repeat contracts	Low – High	Low – High	Low – High
Transaction profile – the trade-offs between price, quality, flexibility, innovation and service required by the contract	Low – High	Low – High	Low – High
Transaction intensity – the amount of time and other resource the management of the contract will entail	Low – High	Low – High	Low – High

It is possible to then plot these factors onto a graph. When plotting these estimates, it should be remembered that there is a relationship with some of the factors and by considering the different graph shapes, purchasing professionals can obtain an idea of the way in which different levels of value, volume, intensity etc impact upon relationships in their own industry.

Figure 16: Graph of factors impacting on relationships

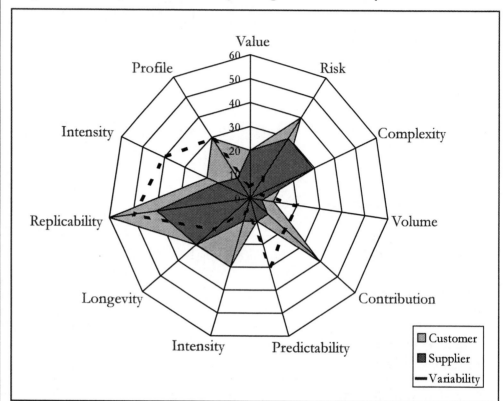

Assessing process-model correspondence

In understanding how the process and the model correspond we are forced to rely on metrics. Without reliable and agreed measures it will be impossible to measure how people reach these objectives. Just as an accountant needs figures to assess the performance of an enterprise, so a purchaser and supplier need figures to assess the performance of the relationship.

Selecting metrics is often challenging. Reasons for this include:

1. **The effort involved in measuring:** although some enterprises may carry out inbound quality inspection, delivery accuracy assessment etc, many do not. In addition, in multi-site, multinational enterprises, consistent measurement does not take place within organisations. Inventory recording practices often vary within Europe and are even more different from continent to continent. This means that data is often simply unavailable or the way in which it is interpreted is different. This is changing under the influence of advanced planning, scheduling and supply chain optimisation tools, but many enterprises in non-manufacturing sectors do not see the need to expend this effort.

Relationship management - Section 3f

2. **The use to which measures are put:** suppliers are often concerned about the fact that broader measures may be used as a way of leveraging price (cost). This means that they may be reluctant to measure. In addition assessment data is rarely used to improve joint performance. Instead, the measuring party uses it to suggest improvements in the other party. This can lead to conflict.

3. **Measure variations over time:** relationship needs will change over time, as will relationships. Measurement changes need to be recorded, validated and communicated.

4. **The perceived need for measurement:** buyer-supplier relationships do not take place in isolation. When entering into any relationship we look at our prospective partners' other relationships. The assumption is that if a supplier can supply a number of other buyers, the supplier will also be able to supply us. In this sense we trust other people's judgement, although this does not necessarily offer the optimum solution.

Nonetheless, the metrics chosen will have a major impact on the relationship. Relationship assessment can be validated against the same criteria that are used in vendor assessment. Common metrics for relationship assessment might include:

◆ Price against target or against market assessment

◆ Rejected parts per thousands/tens of thousands/hundreds of thousands delivered

◆ Scrap and rework costs

◆ Number of deliveries arriving within an agreed time window

◆ Order lead times

◆ Administration costs

◆ Levels of service expressed in terms of accessibility, courtesy, competence, for example

◆ Number of innovative suggestions per time period

◆ Range of stock-keeping units (SKUs)

◆ Mix of SKUs.

These outcome metrics can also be supported by process metrics. In many industries, customers have implemented target costing across the board. In the oil and gas industry, for instance, some customers have advised their suppliers that they require 15% cuts across the board on prices within a set period of time. The problem with this strategy is that the buyer has no idea of the cost structure within the supplier. Suppliers do not use activity based costing, and there is therefore no way of knowing how cost reductions of this scale will impact upon product quality. In hostile environments, such as drilling in the North Sea, such cost reductions can have a major health and safety implication.

The logic for using process metrics is that the buyer can see the impact of changes in price, delivery, for example, on quality or innovation. By understanding the relationship between supplier processes and the outcomes the buyer needs, it is possible to obtain a finer degree of understanding about the relationship, and use the right approaches to influence the relationship in useful ways.

Closing the gap

Closing the gap between the expected and desired state and the actual state relies on the use of strategies and tactics which range from contract management, through to supplier development and interpersonal skills. We have looked at these in section 2 of this study guide when we looked at factors that impact upon relationships, and also earlier in this section when we considered supplier development.

 # Summary

Relationships are difficult to assess and manage but it is possible to employ a framework which will help us work within them more effectively. This involves working with suppliers to develop objectives for the relationship and to develop a model that can be used to assess relationship progress. This will also involve defining metrics for the relationship so that relationship progress or failure can be measured and corrective action taken. In some cases, however, relationship assessment may be insufficient. External factors may impact on the relationship in such a way as to cause failure. This requires a risk management strategy.

Management of supplier risk

The syllabus learning outcomes for this subsection state that you will be able to:

◆   **Evaluate the implications of relationship failure.**

This subsection will cover:

◆   **Introduction**

◆   **Risk reduction**

◆   **Managing risk**

◆   **Crisis management.**

Introduction

Risk management is based on being able to distinguish between an event that is truly random and an event that is the result of cause and effect. The demand for risk management and risk management professionals has risen dramatically over the past quarter-century. These experts specialise in assessing and quantifying the risks involved in numerous activities and are employed by insurance companies, financial companies, environmental companies and national governments.

Humans have been attempting to understand and manage risk for centuries, but a formal approach to risk management began in the 1970s when the understanding of risk was brought into the modern age. The 'polar bear strategy' of author John F Ross points to a mini-revolution beginning in the 1970s that brought the understanding of risk into the modern age. This revolution was linked to the emergence of the new science of risk analysis, which in turn arose from a critical accumulation of data in health and safety and the introduction of high-speed computers.

The polar bear strategy refers to an old joke about an engineer and a purchaser walking along an ice floe in the Arctic when they see a polar bear running towards them. The purchaser immediately begins to strap on snowshoes but the engineer says, 'Don't be stupid. You can't outrun a polar bear. They can move at thirty miles an hour over ice!'. The purchaser looks up at the engineer and says, 'I don't have to outrun the polar bear. I only have to outrun you!' Risk, in this case, is clearly comparative and not absolute.

In section 2 we looked at risk assessment and the tools that we can use to assess risk and improve the quality of our decision making. This section looks at risk management strategies. Of course, contracting, which we shall look at in the next section, is a risk remediation strategy and we have looked earlier at supplier assessment, relationship assessment and supplier development, all of which are methods of assessing and managing risk.

Risk reduction

Contracting is a risky business and there is no way of eliminating all the risk involved. Although it may be possible to eliminate the risk of quality failures by using Kaizen and lean supply methods, other risks such as lack of innovation may be introduced. This might be because suppliers become so lean that they have no spare resource for research and development.

Risk professionals know that they cannot eliminate risk, but by analysing costs, benefits and methods of risk reduction and mitigation, they can help enterprises and other bodies make informed decisions about risk. Increasingly, risk management rests upon the use of sophisticated analytical techniques for making sense of this information.

Ross writes: 'It's a revolution that affects each and every one of us. In essence, we as individuals can use these new intellectual tools and perspectives to become our own best risk analysts.'

The management of risk is a key challenge for supply management. Assessing risk accurately is a critical task for the purchasing and supply function. Approaches to risk can include:

◆ **Assessment:** to identify the nature of the risk within the supply base – is it a delivery risk, quality risk or a cost risk? Risk assessment requires that the supply chain be viewed as an end-to-end process and will often require extensive mapping exercises, as well as assessment

◆ **Reduction:** where organisational spend is a high proportion of a supplier's total turnover. Some manufacturing groups in the Far East will not contract with a supplier unless their spend is over 80% of the supplier's total turnover, creating high levels of dependency. This tactic is clearly not available to many purchasers

◆ **Avoidance:** one way of avoiding risk is to ensure that purchasing always works with the same suppliers that it has worked with in the past. A drawback here is the fact that existing suppliers may not let us down, but they may not give us the best possible performance either

◆ **Management:** this is the use of contractual and relational tactics to ensure that risk is balanced with potential performance. The management of risk depends on the acquisition of good quality information which can be used to predict how often risks are likely to occur and what might cause them. This is how insurance companies operate by collating risk data and using sophisticated analytical techniques to forecast, with degrees of confidence, the likelihood of those risks occurring in particular time periods and geographical location or within certain demographic groups. Purchasing can also collate data with regard to supplier performance and use similar techniques to forecast supplier failure

Relationship management - Section 3g

- ◆ **Allocation:** much of the design and development of contracts is about the allocation of risk to different parties, but it can help to remember that sometimes risk needs to be allocated internally as well as across organisational boundaries.

Once sources and degrees of risk are known, it is possible to propose and implement strategies to reduce risk. It is generally true to say that preventing the occurrence of risk is more effective than dealing with risk once it has occurred.

Managing risk

If risk analysis shows a high risk (valuable and vulnerable), then prevention activities are recommended. For example, a hacker attack on a company's website is easy to attempt and can have a considerable negative impact on the company's reputation and ability to do business. So risk management strategies would put prevention strategies in place such as upgraded firewalls and other security features which would make it harder for the attackers.

On the other hand, if value is high but vulnerability is low, then insurance and back-up activities are recommended. For example, the loss of a key supplier would have a high impact but low probability of occurrence so back-up procedures such as contingency contracts for secondary suppliers are required. In addition, trade disruption insurance might be obtained which, although time limited, would give the enterprise sufficient time to reconfigure the supply chain.

Risk management also includes balancing costs versus benefits for any reduction of risk. Simply put, the cost of risk management measures to reduce the threat should not exceed the value of what is being protected. For example, purchasing managers must be able to justify the cost of security measures, both financial costs and user inconvenience, in light of the expected frequency of risks and the anticipated loss resulting from a risk occurring. So, extensive assessment can be justified to protect a high value contract, but a more limited assessment may be required in a contract which had a lower impact on an enterprise's core activities, remembering the fact that it can be difficult to assess core and non-core activities.

The more serious the risk involved, the more the factors should be broken down and analysed into their individual sub-parts. By breaking down the risk factors into the smallest possible components, we are able to isolate key events and/or determinants and seek to determine how to best manage them. In order to do so, the purchaser must estimate the probability that one of these events that expose us to risk could occur. If the probability of incurring a loss is high, we may decide to avoid it altogether, avoid part of it, develop a contingency plan to deal with it and/or budget funds to deal with its occurrence.

However, when the unforeseen occurs, we need to put contingency or crisis plans in place to minimise the effect of the damage on the enterprise's key operations.

Crisis management

In the previous sections we have considered how to manage and mitigate risk. We will now consider the legal issues that surround risk and how contracts may help manage this risk. Sometimes, however, it is impossible to analyse risks. The 11 September 2002 attack on the World Trade Center is a good case in point. Although information may have been available to security agencies, it is unclear to what degree that information could be shared or how accurate the information was. The attack was an unforeseeable risk.

The 11 September attack affected supply chains in a number of ways. Manufacturers that used the web to regulate incoming parts and keep inventories to a minimum were thrust into chaos that day when parts didn't come and assembly lines were brought to a halt.

Lean inventories, which had been a source of competitive advantage, quickly became a handicap following the terrorist attacks in New York and Washington, which grounded air traffic and slowed or stopped cross-border commerce. These delivery failures shut down many assembly lines and cost some large original equipment manufacturers £8,000 per minute. This was a risk that enterprises had never had to factor into their supply chain planning before.

In an increasingly global economy, purchasers face trade-offs between cost and risk. Suppliers' factories may be damaged by earthquakes, their logistic channels may be destroyed by mudslides and their credit be attacked by financial terrorism.

In the event of such risks, it is vital that the enterprise develops and maintains a disaster recovery or business continuity plan.

According to one model of dealing with crisis there are three levels of activity. These are:

◆ **Primary prevention:** activities designed to prevent a crisis from occurring

◆ **Secondary prevention:** steps taken in the immediate aftermath of the crisis to minimise the effects

◆ **Tertiary prevention:** provides long-term follow-up to those most affected.

We have looked as risk assessment and some methods for preventing crisis. In the secondary prevention stage, the objective is to minimise the harm (financial, reputational or other) which occurs.

A contingency plan needs to be developed by a team representing all functional areas of the enterprise, and this team should include suppliers wherever feasible. If the enterprise is a large, complex business, this may involve the establishment of a formal project team, which should have senior management approval and support.

Perhaps the first contingency planning task is to prepare a comprehensive list of the potentially serious incidents that could affect the normal operations of the business. This risk register should include as many incidents as possible, no matter how remote the likelihood of their occurrence. Generating such a list requires cross-functional teams and a series of brainstorming sessions, which may be iterative in the same way as scenario planning workshops are used in developing strategy.

Again, each occurrence should be assigned a probability rating. Each occurrence should also be rated for potential impact severity level. From this information, it will become much easier to frame the plan in the context of the real needs of the enterprise. Once the assessment stage has been completed, the structure of the plan can be established. The plan will contain a range of processes designed to move the organisation from its disrupted status to normal operations.

The first important process would deal with the immediate aftermath of the disaster. This might involve emergency services or other specialists who are trained to deal with extreme situations. It might also involve communication strategies for reassuring staff, shareholders and family members. The next process would be to identify which operations should be resumed and in what order. Such a plan will hold detailed task sets, and should identify key individuals and their key responsibilities in the event of an occurrence.

Once a plan has been developed it should be tested rigorously. The testing process itself must be properly planned and carried out. It should be remembered that individuals often find crisis difficult to deal with, and the way to overcome the problems that stem from this is to make sure that testing is rigorous, regular and carried out by the individuals responsible in the event of an occurrence. Test procedures should be documented and the results recorded. This also gives feedback, which can be used for fine-tuning.

It is necessary for contingency arrangements to be communicated effectively to all staff and that they are aware of their own duties and responsibilities. Equally, it is important to audit both the plan itself, and the contingency and back-up arrangements supporting it.

Contingency planning must always be kept up to date and applicable to current business circumstances. This means that changes to key business processes should be reflected within the plan. A risk manager can be assigned responsibility for ensuring that the plan is maintained and updated regularly. This individual can also, therefore, ensure that information concerning changes to the business process is properly communicated.

Longer-term effects of crisis management can range from personal trauma experienced by staff through to the need to re-calibrate forecasting models. Plans may need to allow for counselling of staff or families, and this may include financial, location and other assistance to help individuals come to terms with crisis.

In other cases, many industries' supply chain applications rely on demand forecasts developed over time by collating data from ERP, sales and historical reporting tools. In the face of disruptions, companies may have to discard old forecasts and re-calibrate their applications without knowing when demand will rebound.

summary

Purchasing, as an important part of the supply chain team, may also have a role in crisis management. Unforeseen crises can have a major impact on the operation of supply chains, particularly those operating with lean inventories. Effective crisis management requires preventative action, followed by action to minimise the immediate impact of the crisis and subsequent longer-term plans to restore operations.

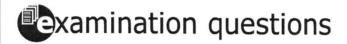examination questions

Exam 3.1

As part of its sourcing and relationship strategy a company may decide to outsource some of its requirements. Explain what this means and discuss the possible beneficial and negative implications of outsourcing.

Exam 3.2

Explain the particular role of a first-tier supplier.

Exam 3.3

Describe the basic philosophy of total quality management and its implications for purchasing.

 # saq responses

SAQ 3.1

Benefits include:
- Technical knowledge and skill
- Reduction in administration costs
- Strategic positioning.

Measures include:
- Ratio of potential members/actual members
- Staff grade of members and attendees
- Ratio of non-pay spend employed in consortia/non-pay spend employed elsewhere
- Member expectations/satisfaction levels
- Feedback mechanisms for non-purchasing staff
- Nature of consortia staff tasks
- Improvements in purchasing practice within consortia membership
- Improvements in key individual knowledge skills and attitudes.

SAQ 3.2

Advantages of consortia membership can be wide-ranging and include:
- Improved leverage
- Enhanced standardisation and, therefore, cost reduction
- The development of product and technical knowledge across different sectors and organisations
- Reductions in administrative costs
- Strategic positioning within a marketplace.

Disadvantages may include:
- Increased risk
- Loss of focus on the needs of the individual organisation
- Difficulties in sharing information across consortia membership.

SAQ 3.3

Types of brokerage relationship which might support an electronic marketplace are:

- **Buy/sell fulfilment:** this can be an online financial brokerage, for example eTrade, where customers place buy and sell orders for transacting financial instruments. Also, travel agents fit into this category. In this the broker charges the buyer and/or seller a transaction fee. Some models work on volume and low overheads to deliver the best negotiated prices

- **Market exchange:** an increasingly common model in B2B markets. In the exchange model, the broker typically charges the seller a transaction fee based on the value of the sale. The pricing mechanism can be a simple offer/buy, offer/negotiated buy or an auction offer/bid approach

- **Business trading community or vertical web community:** a site that acts as an 'essential, comprehensive source of information and dialogue for a particular vertical market'. VerticalNet's communities contain product information in buyers' guides, supplier and product directories, daily industry news and articles, job listings and classifieds. In addition, VerticalNet's sites enable B2B exchanges of information, supplementing existing trade shows and trade association activities. For more information check out www.verticalnet.com

- **Buyer aggregator:** the process of bringing together individual purchasers from across the Internet to transact as a group so they can receive the same values traditionally afforded to organisations that purchase in volume. Sellers pay a small percentage of each sale on a per-transaction basis

- **Distributor:** a catalogue-based operation that connects a large number of product manufacturers with volume and retail buyers. B2B models are increasingly common. Brokers facilitate business transactions between franchised distributors and their trading partners. For buyers, it enables faster time to market and time to volume as well as reducing the cost of procurement. By providing the buyer with a means of retrieving quotes from preferred distributors – showing buyer-specific prices, lead time and recommended substitutions – transactions are more efficient.

  For distributors, it decreases the cost of sales by performing the quoting, order processing, tracking order status and changes more quickly and with less labour

- **Virtual mall:** a site that hosts many online merchants. The mall typically charges set up, monthly listing and/or transaction fees. The virtual mall model may be most effectively realised when combined with a generalised portal. Also, more sophisticated malls will provide automated transaction services and relationship marketing opportunities

- **Metamediary:** a business that brings buyers and online merchants together and provides transaction services such as financial settlement and quality assurance. It is a virtual mall, but one that will process the transaction, track orders and provide billing and collection services. The metamediary protects consumers by assuring satisfaction with merchants. The metamediary often charges a set-up fee and a fee per transaction

◆ **Auction broker:** a site that conducts auctions on behalf of sellers (individuals or merchants). The broker charges the seller a fee, which is typically scaled with the value of the transaction. The seller takes the highest bid(s) from the buyers above a minimum. Auctions can vary in terms of the offering and bidding rules

◆ **Reverse-auction:** the 'name-your-price' business model, also called 'demand collection' and 'shopping by request'. The buyer makes a final (sometimes binding) bid for a specified good or service and the broker seeks fulfilment. In some models, the broker's fee is the spread between the bid and fulfilment price and may involve a processing charge. Frequently used in B2B exchanges

◆ **Classifieds:** a listing of items for sale or purchase. In the same way as newspaper classifieds, these are typically run by local news content providers. Price may or may not be specified. Listing charges are incurred regardless of whether a transaction occurs

◆ **Search agent:** an agent (an intelligent software agent or 'robot') used to search out the best price for a good or service specified by the buyer, or to locate information that is hard to find. An employment agency can act as a search agent broker, finding work for job-seekers or finding people to fill open positions listed by an employer

◆ **Bounty broker:** this often involves the offer of a reward (usually a significant monetary sum) for finding a person, thing, idea or other desired, but hard-to-find item. The broker may list items for a flat fee and a percent of the reward, if the item is successfully found

◆ **Transaction broker:** provides a third-party mechanism for buyers and sellers to settle payment for a transaction

SAQ 3.4

Some of the factors that might impact upon customer-supplier relationships are:

◆ **Transaction risk:** the likelihood that a supplier will fail in terms of price, quality, delivery, reliability, flexibility, innovation or service

◆ **Transaction contribution:** the degree to which the transaction contributes to the goals of the department, another department or the organisation

◆ **Transaction complexity:** the type, mix, range of contracts/activities/ sub-projects

◆ **Transaction volume:** the number of items

◆ **Transaction replicability:** the degree to which other transactions can be substituted

- **Transaction predictability:** the impact of demand in terms of both quantity and type on both supplier and customer

- **Transaction longevity:** the length of time that the contract lasts or the likely number of repeat contracts

- **Transaction profile:** the trade-offs between price, quality, flexibility, innovation or service required by the contract

- **Transaction intensity:** the amount of time and other resource the management of the contract will entail.

SAQ 3.5

Terminations should be:

- Be well structured with proper procedures
- Have valid, well-articulated reasons
- Be clearly communicated
- Involve accurate, balanced feedback
- Be prepared for by both parties
- Involve acknowledgement of the work within the existing contract
- Frame the contract/relationship in terms of long-term objectives
- Leave the door open for renewal or replacement of the old contract with a new one.

Contracting and relationships

 Objectives

When you have completed this section you will be able to:

◆ **Evaluate the role and value of contracts in relationships**

◆ **Propose alternatives to contracts where appropriate**

◆ **Determine appropriate approaches to the management of contracts, including payment methods**

◆ **Explain and demonstrate the use of clauses employed for incentivisation purposes**

◆ **Propose appropriate clauses employed for the purpose of accommodating changing costs**

◆ **Evaluate the use of leasing or hiring arrangements as an alternative to buying**

◆ **Access the relationship issues particularly relevant where relationships are concerned with service provision**

Section 4 comprises subsections:

a) **The role of contracts**

b) **Relationship aspects of contracts**

c) **Relationships in the service context**

d) **Relationships in connection with hire or lease contracts**

Introduction

Contracts play an important part in relationships, and relationships affect the way in which contracts are created and enforced. This section will consider some of the ways in which this occurs and the idea of the contract as a multilayered document, with different layers addressing different elements of the relationship.

The role of contracts

The syllabus learning outcomes for this subsection state that you will be able to:

◆   Evaluate the role and value of contracts in relationships

◆   Propose alternatives to contracts where appropriate

◆   Determine appropriate approaches to the management of contracts, including payment methods

◆   Explain and demonstrate the use of clauses employed for incentivisation purposes.

This subsection will cover:

◆   **Introduction**

◆   **Factors in selecting contract types**

◆   **Types of contract.**

Introduction

Over the course of earlier sections within this study guide, we have seen that the selection and management of commercial relationships rests upon a range of factors. These range from developing and understanding the nature of customer supplier relationships, through to the management of interpersonal issues, such as communication and influencing skills within those relationships.

This section of the guide has been written to explore the way in which contracts can be used in the management of relationships. Broadly we can suggest that a commercial relationship consists of two elements. The first of these is the management of supplier performance, and we have seen how tools, such as supplier development, relationship positioning and assessment broadly, though not exclusively, support performance management. The second element is the management of risk, and we have considered how to assess and plan for risk. In this section we will suggest that different contract types can be used in the management of risk. Broadly, we can see a range of needs within the contracting process.

It is possible to say that all contracting is a balance between risk, flexibility and control. It is also possible to say that relational contracting requires a better balance between these elements in order that the contract and the relationship work together to both ensure performance and to maintain the relationship needed. In addition, we can see a shift in perspective with regards to focus in contracts. The traditional form of contract placed an emphasis on mitigation – putting things right after they have gone wrong. This traditional contract often attempted to punish breach severely in order to prevent breach occurring.

Of course, breach of contract can occur for a variety of reasons, some of which are beyond the control of the supplier or the purchaser. This means that, more recently, we can see an increasing emphasis on prevention within commercial relationships, avoiding problems before they occur or managing problems as they occur. There is still, however, a tension in the use of contracts to support commercial relationships.

Increasingly this means that purchasers and suppliers need to choose the right type of contract.

Factors in selecting contract types

There are many factors that the purchaser might wish to consider when selecting and negotiating the contract type. They include the following:

- **Price competition:** normally, effective price competition results in realistic pricing and a fixed price contract is ordinarily in the buyer's interest, but this might be offset against other factors

- **Price analysis:** price analysis, with or without competition, may provide a basis for selecting the contract type. The degree to which price analysis can provide a realistic pricing standard should be carefully considered

- **Cost analysis:** in the absence of effective price competition and if price analysis is not sufficient, the cost estimates of the supplier and the purchaser may provide the basis for negotiating contract pricing arrangements. It is essential that the uncertainties involved in performance, and their possible impact upon costs, be identified and evaluated so that a contract type can be negotiated that places a reasonable degree of cost responsibility upon the contractor

- **Type and complexity of the requirement:** complex requirements, particularly those which are unique to the situation, may result in greater risk assumption by the purchaser. This may be true in the case of complex research and development contracting projects, when performance uncertainties or the likelihood of changes make it difficult to estimate performance costs in advance. This may shift to a fixed price contract once development is completed

- **Urgency of the requirement:** if urgency is a primary factor, the purchasing organisation may choose to assume a greater proportion of risk, or it may offer incentives to ensure timely contract performance

- **Period of performance or length of production run:** in times of economic uncertainty, contracts extending over a relatively long period may require economic price adjustment clauses

- **The supplier's technical capability and financial position or market situation:** the relevant positions of the contracting parties, with regard to technical leadership, financial situation and the number of potential suppliers in the marketplace, will make a difference to the type of contract chosen

- **The adequacy of the supplier's accounting system:** there is little point in using cost-plus-type contracts where it is difficult or impossible to identify cost data. Before agreeing on a contract type, other than firm fixed price, the purchaser should always ensure that the contractor's accounting system will permit timely and accurate development of necessary cost data in the form required by the proposed contract type. This factor may be critical when the contract type requires price revision, while performance is in progress, or when a cost-reimbursement contract is being considered and all current or past experience with the contractor has been on a fixed price basis

- **Concurrent contracts:** if performance under the proposed contract involves concurrent operations under other contracts, the impact of those contracts, including their pricing arrangements, should be considered

- **The extent and nature of proposed subcontracting:** if the contractor proposes extensive subcontracting, a contract type reflecting the actual risks to the prime contractor should be selected

- **Contracting history:** risk often decreases as the requirement is repetitively acquired. Also, product descriptions, or descriptions of services to be performed, can be defined more clearly.

Types of contract

Once the purchaser has considered the factors that will impact on the contract, then he or she will need to decide on the type of contract that they wish to propose.

A number of contract types exist. At one end of the contractual spectrum is the 'firm fixed price contract', under which the contractor is fully responsible for performance costs and enjoys (or suffers) resulting profits (or losses). At the other end of the spectrum is the 'cost plus fixed fee' contract, in which allowable and allocable costs are reimbursed and the negotiated fee (profit) is fixed – consequently, the contractor has minimal responsibility for, or incentive to control, performance costs.

Types of firm fixed price (FFP) contracts might include:

◆ **Firm fixed price:** FFP sum contracts are used mainly for assignments in which the content and the duration of the services and the required output of the supplier are clearly defined. They are widely used for simple requirements. Payments are linked to outputs (deliverables). Lump sum contracts are easy to administer because payments are due on clearly specified outputs.

◆ **Fixed price incentive:** (in which final contract price and profit are calculated, based on a formula that relates final negotiated cost to target cost). These may be either firm targets or successive targets.

◆ **Fixed price with award fees:** used to 'motivate a contractor' when contractor performance cannot be measured objectively, making other incentives inappropriate

◆ **Fixed price with redetermination:** in this model the customer and supplier agree in advance to have two fixed price contracts – one negotiated now and one to be negotiated at a later stage

◆ **Fixed price with economic price adjustment:** FP contracts sometimes use agreed economic price adjustments to cope with economic uncertainties that threaten long-run, fixed price type contracts. There are many different indices that can be used to determine economic price adjustments for contracts. BEAMA (The British Electrotechnical and Allied Manufacturers Association) offers a range of standard clauses for the management of contract price adjustment. BEAMA also provides a labour cost index and there are also a range of raw and manufactured materials price indices that can be incorporated into contract price adjustment clauses.

One example of such a clause is the following supplementary clause for the use of home contracts electrical machinery, which reads as follows:

> If, by reason of any rise or fall in the rates of wages payable to labour or in the cost of material or transport or of conforming to such laws, orders, regulations and bye-laws as are applicable to the Works, above or below, such rates and costs ruling at the date of the tender, the cost to the Contractor of performing his or her obligations under this Contract shall be increased or reduced by the amount of such increase or reduction, which shall be added to or deducted from the contract price as the case may be, provided that no account shall be taken of any amount by which any cost incurred by the Contractor has been increased by the fault of negligence of the Contractor.

> For the purposes of this clause 'the cost of material' shall be construed as including any duty or tax by whomsoever payable which is payable, under or by virtue of any Act of Parliament on the import, purchase, sale, appropriation, processing or use of such material.

The operation of this Clause is without prejudice to the effect, if any, which the imposition of Value Added Tax, or any tax of a like nature will have upon the supply of goods and services under the contract.

Variations in the cost of labour and material shall be calculated in accordance with the following formulae:

a) Labour
The Contract Price shall be adjusted at the rate of 0.45% of the Contract Price per 1.0% difference between the BEAMA Labour Cost Index last published before the date of tender and the average of the Index figures published for the last two-thirds of the Contract Period, this difference being expressed as a percentage of the former Index figure.

b) Materials
The Contract Price shall be adjusted at the rate of 0.45% of the Contract Price per 1.0% of the difference between the Price index of materials used in the electrical Industry last published in the *Trade and Industry Journal* before the date of Tender and that Index figure last published before the end of the first three-fifths of the contract period, this difference being expressed as a percentage of the former Index figure.

Using such a clause might involve, for example, a contract period of 201 days starting on 10 January at a price of £10,000, ending on the 19 August.

Adjustments would take into account the following:

BEAMA Labour Index published before
date of tender = 156

Average of BEAMA Labour Index over last two
thirds of contract period = 170

Trade and Industry Journal Materials Index
published before date of tender = 220

Average of *Trade and Industry Journal*
Materials Index or last three-fifths of
contract period = 249

Labour adjustment:

This is the difference between the labour cost index published before the tender date and the average over the last two-thirds of the contract period.

170 - 156 = 14 – expressed as a percentage of the original figure = 8.97%

Adjustment agreed as 0.45% of the contract price for each 1% difference in index.

0.45% x £10,000 = £45.00

Labour adjustment = £45.00 x 8.97 = £404.

Materials adjustment:

Materials adjustment takes place in the same way Materials Index last published	= 220
Average of Index over last three-fifths of contract period	= 249
Difference	= 29
Difference as percentage of the original figure	= 13.18%
Materials adjustment (0.45% for each 1% index difference)	= £45 x 13.18 = £593

Total adjustment:

This means the overall payment for the contract will be:
£10,000 + £404 + £593 = £10,997.

As well as firm fixed price contracts, there are other contract types. These include:

♦ **Cost-reimbursement incentive contracts:** these are used when fixed-price contracts are inappropriate, due to uncertainty about probable costs. These may be either cost-plus-incentive-fee or cost-plus-award-fee. Three characteristics differentiate this contract from fixed price:

- there is no ceiling price
- total reimbursable costs are the final contract costs
- the maximum fee of the supplier is subject to limitations.

♦ **Cost fixed fee contracts:** these are self-explanatory. The supplier is reimbursed the costs expended on the contract plus a fixed fee (profit) for carrying out the contract

♦ **Cost contracts:** these may involve just the reimbursement of a supplier's costs with no fee paid. This type of contract is most often found in research contracts

- **Cost sharing contracts:** these may also be used for research contracts, where the supplier is reimbursed a proportion of the expenses incurred

- **Time and materials contract:** this type of contract is appropriate when it is difficult to define the scope and the length of services, either because the services are related to activities by others for which the completion period may vary, or because the input required to attain the objectives of the contract is difficult to assess. Payments are based on agreed hourly, daily, weekly, or monthly rates for staff (who are normally named in the contract) and on reimbursable items using actual expenses and/or agreed unit prices. The rates for staff include salary, social costs, overhead, fee (or profit), and, where appropriate, special allowances. This type of contract will often include a maximum amount of total payments to be made to the supplier. This 'ceiling' amount might include a contingency allowance for unforeseen work and duration, and provision for price adjustments, where appropriate. Time-based contracts need to be closely monitored and administered by the purchaser to ensure that the assignment is progressing satisfactorily, and payments claimed by the supplier are appropriate.

- **Retainer and/or contingency (success) fee contract:** these are widely used when consultants are preparing companies for sales or merger, notably in privatisation operations. The remuneration of the consultant includes a retainer and a success fee, the latter being normally expressed as a percentage of the sale price of the assets

- **Percentage contract:** these contracts are often used for services such as architectural services or procurement and inspection agents. Percentage contracts directly relate the fees paid to the consultant to the estimated or actual project construction cost, or the cost of the goods procured or inspected. The contract is negotiated on the basis of market norms for the services and/or estimated staff costs for the services, or competitively bid. It should be borne in mind that in the case of architectural or engineering services, percentage contracts implicitly lack incentive for economic design and are hence discouraged. Therefore, the use of such a contract for architectural services is recommended only if it is based on a fixed target cost and covers precisely defined services (for example, not works supervision)

- **Indefinite delivery contract (price agreement):** these contracts are used when 'borrowers' need to have 'on call' specialised services to provide advice on a particular activity, the extent and timing of which cannot be defined in advance. These are commonly used to retain 'advisers' for implementation of complex projects; expert adjudicators for dispute resolution panels, institutional reforms, procurement advice, technical troubleshooting and so forth, normally for a period of a year or more. An agreement is reached on the unit rates to be paid for the experts, and payments are made on the basis of the time actually used.

Summary

Making use of any of these types of contract rests upon a clear understanding of the nature of the task, the roles and relationships that underpin the contract and the nature of risk. Choosing the right form of contract to support the relevant relationship requires a broad understanding of the interaction between the contract and the relationship. Mismatch between the relationship and the contract can create problems in both areas.

In selecting contracts to support particular types of relationship, it is important to ensure that the way in which the contract is employed is perceived as equitable and appropriate for the relationship in question. The use of FFP contracts for long-term research or consulting projects may be beneficial in that it allows effective budgetary compliance. It may be less beneficial when the results of the contract are less than satisfactory.

Self-assessment question

SAQ 4.1

Identify three types of incentive or performance-based contract.

Relationship aspects of contracts

The syllabus learning outcomes for this subsection state that you will be able to:

◆ Propose alternatives to contracts where appropriate

◆ Determine appropriate approaches to the management of contracts, including payment methods

◆ Explain and demonstrate the use of clauses employed for incentivisation purposes

◆ Propose appropriate clauses employed for the purpose of accommodating changing costs.

This subsection will cover:

◆ **Introduction**

◆ **Performance-based contracts**

◆ **Escalation and savings**

◆ **Relational contracts**

◆ **Psychological contracts**

◆ **Alternatives to contracts**

◆ **Digital contracts**

◆ **Changing contracts.**

Introduction

When we consider contracts, it is important to remember that the role of contracts changes to meet changing business conditions and that, as well as different forms of contract, there are also different categories of contract.

For the purposes of this section we will consider four contracting categories:

1. Incentive.

2. Relational.

3. Psychological.

4. Digital.

In business, the basic building blocks of commerce are contracts between two parties. There are other types of obligation, such as promises, but these are by and large, not the core of business. Agreement is the basis of earning money.

However, contracts are, of themselves necessarily incomplete. Agreements are made in particular contexts, and those contexts can change in unexpected ways. Forecast demand can shift, machines can break down, people can misunderstand complex instructions, wars can break out etc. Maintaining an agreement in these circumstances can be difficult. There are two approaches to managing contracts in such circumstances. The first is to design incentive contracts that will motivate the parties to complete the agreement. The second is used where parties need flexibility in order to achieve their intended aims and objectives. This has led to the notion of relational contracts (also called, 'hybrid', 'symbiotic', or 'cooperative'), which are designed to allow parties to fulfil elements of an agreement that were not specified in the original contract.

Key elements of relational contracting are the:

◆ Identities and personal attributes of parties

◆ Norms of indeterminate duration

◆ Norms of behaviour, or shared codes of conduct, informing responses to new developments after the contract has been agreed

◆ Written documentation which is treated as a record of what has been agreed

◆ Norms of behaviour, or shared codes of conduct, overruling written documents in settling disputes.

Relational contracts provide the means to sustain ongoing relations in long and complex contracts by adjustment processes of a more thoroughly transaction-specific, ongoing administrative kind. This could include an original agreement, and, if it does, that may still not influence the relationships between the contracting parties.

These types of contract rely on a range of factors including the way in which the contract is perceived, the relationship between the parties, levels of trust and a wide range of other factors. Contracts of this type rely on effective relationships between the parties, but can also have drawbacks, as we shall see.

Underpinning relational contracts is the way in which contract perception impacts on contract performance. This involves considering how contracts are made, both between organisations and within organisations, and considers a concept borrowed from research into the employment contracts and looks at psychological contracts between parties.

In addition, we will also look at some of the issues arising from electronic trading and the way in which these contracts may impact on commercial relationships. Once an agreement is made, it rests upon good faith. This presumes that both contracting parties will complete their share of the agreement, but again circumstances change, as do the attitudes of the parties involved. One of the ways in which contracts can be used to deal with changing circumstances and changing motivations is through incentive- or performance-based contracts.

Performance-based contracts

As the scope of the goods or services contracted increases in size and complexity – whole sub-assemblies instead of bolts or facilities management instead of cleaning – organisations increasingly come to rely on incentive- or performance-based contracts. These contracts link part of the supplier's payment base to key performance areas and outcomes.

Although determining the type of contract to use is often the first type of incentive considered, it is important to understand that contract type is only part of the overall incentive approach and structure of a performance-based acquisition.

Setting objectives for performance

More complex contracts closely link performance and quality of service to profit and rewards to encourage good performance. When the buyer and supplier agree to the use of a performance-based contract, certain preconditions contribute to successful implementation.

Objective	Process
Alignment of purchaser/ supplier priorities	◆ Performance incentives that are aligned to the corporate strategy and direction of the organisation ◆ Clear identification of risk ◆ Flexibility to allow changes to incentives, key result areas, outputs and benchmarks during the term of the contract/agreement.
Incentives for improved performance	◆ Mechanisms that deliver mutual gain from achievement ('win-win') ◆ Incentives to achieve improved performance ◆ Incentives that add value to the purchaser's business and are based on performance ◆ Incentives that are easy to administer and can be operated in a cost-effective manner.
Measurement methods that support performance improvements	◆ Results that are measurable and not based on perception only ◆ Established and agreed minimum performance.

Ideally, if the purchaser is able to establish and agree with the supplier on the performance measures from the outset of the contract, the incentive scheme should then be negotiated during the tender/contract formulation period. A performance incentive scheme may apply after the first year or at the end of the original contract term in return for attaining high levels of service. A scheme may also commence in conjunction with granting an extension and/or continuance of the contract, thus providing a bonus in the form of continued service provision without the need to re-tender to obtain improved terms.

Incentive types

Alternatively, performance based contracts can include sanctions for non-performance, such as a percentage fee for late completion or flat rate for substandard levels of performance. It is important that contract managers pursue fair application of any sanctions in accordance with the contract and, where 'trade-offs' are used, they be appropriate to the objectives of the contracted goods or services.

Forms of incentive	Possible approaches
Extending the contract	◆ If the original contract was for three years, an extension could be granted for an additional one, two or three years.
For a project where time is critical, the supplier is given financial incentive for completing ahead of time (or alternatively penalised for late completion)	◆ Bonus payment amounts payable per day, week or month ahead of schedule (subject to quality checks).
Target costs established	◆ Appropriate in a relationship where the scope of services is broad and requires reimbursement at cost (established using an external benchmark). If the target is achieved, the ratio for shared savings may be on 50:50, 60:40 or an 80:20 basis.
Part (usually 50%) or all of the supplier's potential profit placed at risk against achievement of performance	◆ Appropriate when management fees are applied with 'transparent' pricing – alternatively, 100% of the supplier's potential profit may be placed at risk with an incentive of additional potential 'bonus' if performance targets are reached or exceeded.
A reward at the discretion of the purchaser	◆ Contract- and performance-based statement of work linked to the purchaser's strategic plan would be used to measure performance, but not necessarily to the formal incentive – the bonus is then based more on total customer satisfaction.

Escalation and savings

When using a performance-based contract, organisations need to consider escalation or savings provisions. Escalation addresses the need for pricing increases over the term of the contract. In single-year contracts, escalation is not normally necessary. In longer-term contracts, a facility for escalation is needed and a method of dealing with it adequately should be considered. Lengthy calculations or complicated formulae are not generally checked effectively, as time or other constraints and day-to-day pressures often apply.

Performance measurement systems (PMSs)

The contract manager is responsible for ensuring measurement and monitoring of the actual performance in relation to the planned or required performance as outlined in the performance-based contract. In order for the contract to be monitored, a performance management system (PMS) should be developed and applied for monitoring of service levels. The extent of the PMS, and the effort required to establish it, depends on the size and complexity of the contract and the number of contracts being managed by the contract manager. The PMS should recognise the dependencies between the performance of the supplier and purchaser.

There is some evidence showing that incentive contracts can have a negative effect on supplier flexibility, driving out the very flexibility that it seeks to achieve. This appears to be a downside of incorporating flexibility into a contract. Suppliers sometimes tend to treat it as another contract term, which reduces their autonomy, and therefore stick to the letter of the contract.

Relational contracts

As we have seen, transactional contracts define a single transaction. Most business operations rely on either a series of contracts or a single long-term contract. When we looked at partnership relationships earlier in the study guide, we saw that longer-term involvement timescales are seen as one of the key elements in establishing such a relationship. It is important to note that relational contracts do not necessarily need to be longer-term contracts and that, indeed, in some cases, relational contracts may be a series of shorter-term contracts or a long-term contract with clauses allowing significant variance.

Relational contracts involve a number of informal agreements and unwritten codes of conduct that powerfully affect behaviour, both within and between enterprises. Such relational contracts are often the 'lubrication' that keeps the enterprise moving. They may consist of informal quid pro quos between co-workers, as well as unwritten understandings between bosses and subordinates about task-assignment, promotion and termination decisions. Even ostensibly formal processes, such as compensation, transfer pricing, internal auditing and capital budgeting, often cannot be understood without consideration of their associated informal agreements.

Business-to-business dealings are also supported by relational contracts. Supply chains often involve long-term collaborative relationships through which the parties reach accommodations when unforeseen or uncontracted-for events occur. Similar relationships also exist horizontally, as in the networks of firms in the fashion industry or the diamond trade, and in strategic alliances, joint ventures and business groups.

Whether vertical or horizontal, these relational contracts influence the way enterprises deal with other enterprises. Both within and between enterprises, relational contracts help circumvent difficulties with formal contracting (i.e., contracting enforced by a third party, such as a court or an arbitrator). For example, a formal contract must be specified ex ante in terms that can be verified ex post by the third party, whereas a relational contract can be based on outcomes that are observed by only the contracting parties ex post, and also on outcomes that are prohibitively costly to specify ex ante.

A relational contract allows the contracting parties to make use of their detailed knowledge of their specific situation and to adapt to new information as it becomes available. For the same reasons, however, relational contracts cannot be enforced by a third party and therefore must be self-enforcing agreements.

The success of relational contracts depends upon a number of factors. When considering contracts, it is important to remember the effect of reputation, that is, the effect that failure or breach would have upon the party's future business activities. Each party's reputation must be sufficiently valuable that neither party wishes to renege on the contract.

This means that relational contracting rests on repeated interaction within a particular well-defined group together with a set of norms governing the behaviour of the group members.

In addition, two principles of behaviour are important:

1.   Solidarity.

2.   Reciprocity.

According to MacNeil, an authority on relational contracting:

> Getting something back for something given neatly releases, or at least reduces, the tension in an enterprise desiring to be both selfish and social at the same time; and solidarity, a belief in being able to depend on another, permits the projection of reciprocity through time.

For longer-term relational contracts, contract law faces the dilemma of, on the one hand, offering a means of commitment and, on the other, allowing for sufficient flexibility to adjust to changes in the environment. This tension between the need to fix responsibilities at the outset and the need to readjust them over time permeates the long-term contractual relationship.

Repeated contracting involves achieving cooperation through self-enforcing (possibly tacit) agreements. Repeated interaction may enable cooperation, because of the potential for a current deviation to be punished in the future. For this to work, four conditions must be met:

1. Any deviation must be observable.

2. Any deviation must be punishable.

3. This punishment must be credible so that it is clear that, when required, the punishment will be carried out.

4. The parties must be patient in the sense that the future matters to them.

One way of exploring some of the issues in relational contracting is through the use of game theory. Cooperation is usually analysed in game theory by means of a non-zero-sum game called the 'Prisoner's Dilemma'. The two players in the game can choose between two moves, either 'cooperate' or 'defect'. The idea is that each player gains when both cooperate, but if only one of them cooperates, the other one, who defects, will gain more. If both defect, both lose (or gain very little), but not as much as the 'cheated' cooperator whose cooperation is not returned. The whole game situation and its different outcomes can be summarised by the following table, where hypothetical points are given as an example of how the differences in result might be quantified.

Action of A	Action of B	
	Cooperate	**Defect**
Cooperate	Fairly good [+ 5]	Bad [- 10]
Defect	Good [+ 10]	Mediocre [0]

The table above shows outcomes for actor A (in words, and in hypothetical points) depending on the combination of A's action and B's action in the Prisoner's Dilemma game situation. A similar scheme applies to the outcomes for B.

The game got its name from a hypothetical situation involving two criminals who have been arrested under suspicion of having committed a crime together. However, the police have insufficient evidence to convict them.

The two prisoners are isolated from each other and the investigating detective visits each of them and offers a deal. The one who offers evidence against the other one will be freed. It is clear to both that if neither of them accepts the offer, they are in fact cooperating against the police, and both of them will receive only a small punishment because of lack of evidence. In these circumstances both gain.

However, if one of them defects by confessing to the police, the defector will gain more, because he is freed and the one who remained silent, on the other hand, will receive the full punishment, since he did not help the police, and there is now sufficient proof.

If both prisoners defect, both will be punished, but each one less severely than if they had refused to talk. The dilemma resides in the fact that each prisoner has a choice between only two options, but cannot make a good decision without knowing what the other one will do.

Such a distribution of losses and gains seems natural for many situations, as the cooperator whose action is not returned will lose resources to the defector, without either of them being able to collect the additional gain coming from the 'synergy' of their cooperation. For simplicity we might consider the prisoner's dilemma as zero-sum insofar as there is no mutual cooperation: either each gets 0 when both defect, or when one of them cooperates, the defector gets + 10, and the cooperator − 10, in total 0. On the other hand, if both cooperate, the resulting synergy creates an additional gain that makes the sum positive: each of them gets 5, in total 10. The gain for mutual cooperation (5) in the prisoner's dilemma is kept smaller than the gain for one-sided defection (10), so that there would always be a temptation to defect.

The problem with the prisoner's dilemma is that if both decision makers were purely rational, they would never cooperate. Indeed, rational decision making means that you make the decision which is best for you, whatever the other actor chooses.

The Prisoner's Dilemma has been used to study cooperative behaviour, and computer programmes have shown that the winning strategy over time is to open with a cooperative choice and thereafter mimic the strategy of the other player. These theoretical approaches do not, however, necessarily work in the real world and we will now consider why that might be.

Psychological contracts

Relational contracting is an attempt to obtain a change in the type of behaviour that purchasers require from suppliers. This is often discretionary, not directly or explicitly linked with contract terms, but which in aggregate, promotes the efficient and effective functioning of the relationship.

It means that the purchaser and supplier spontaneously go beyond the formally prescribed limits of the contract and create some type of partnership agreement. It should be noted, in passing, that alternatives to contracts may come about for unusual reasons. In certain cultures such as the Japanese and Vietnamese, low numbers of lawyers and an unwieldy or incoherent legal system make legal enforcement unfeasible.

What are psychological contracts?

The traditional focus of purchasing has been on the nature of the paper contract and ensuring the right sets of terms and conditions and the right clauses for variation and payment. All of these things are important. However, in an environment where purchasing is increasingly trying to incorporate better risk management and improved flexibility into contracts, they are much more than pieces of paper.

A contract needs to be underpinned by changes in the individuals and groups that are going to fulfil the contract. These changes may include loyalty, commitment, positive attitudes, responsiveness, participation, risk sharing, innovation, 'going the extra mile', 'putting the relationship first' and cooperation.

In order to obtain these changes, contracts need to be effective at behavioural, cognitive and affective levels. That is to say that contracts need to achieve changes in what the supplier does (building your rear axle assembly or delivering your financial package), shifts in the way in which they think (for example, 'We need to make sure this product or service is right first time'), and in the way in which they feel (for example, 'This relationship is important to us; let's make sure we don't mess it up').

The most effective contracts are made at all of these levels. Contracts are made over time or at one moment in time, but they do change over time, and these changes are rarely tracked. In addition, contracts may not be enforced across the whole of the organisation, which can lead to misunderstandings due to contracting parties receiving multiple and conflicting messages.

The stages of a psychological contract

Contracts shift markedly over time and a contract can consist of a number of stages. These stages may not always be clearly defined. Different approaches, such as social exchange theory or social economics, identify different stages but there seem to be a number of areas where these stages overlap:

◆   **Needs or problem definition:** when the contractor becomes aware of the problem or need which they face and becomes able to communicate that need

◆   **Prospecting:** where the contractor activity seeks other entities with whom it can seek to contract itself. The next stage in the process may be decision making to enter into the contract

◆   **Negotiation:** in this case, negotiation is the next stage of contract. Morley offers a useful view that negotiation is a tool which is designed to position a relationship

- ◆ **Entry:** this stage involves the fulfilment of the need or the resolution of the problem identified in stage one. This fulfilment may range from a single action at one point in time to a series of complex actions over an extended period. The entry stage and the negotiation stages of a contract are often blurred, particularly when need is not known or clearly communicated

- ◆ **Termination:** the final stage in the contract. Termination may come about for a variety of reasons and may be caused by one or both contracting parties. Just as the entry stage of a contract may be fraught with difficulty, so may the termination stage, as one party may seek to engage in harm-reducing or benefit-gaining behaviour. This has been called 'end game strategies'. Termination may also be difficult because either one of the contracting parties may still be involved in the contract at a behavioural, cognitive or affective level.

It should be noted that these stages are rarely clearly defined and one party may believe itself to be at one stage when the other party believes itself to be at a different stage. The stages often become confused in themselves with negotiation, termination and entry often blurring.

Who contracts?

It is very easy to perceive contracts as being between two contracting parties, despite the multiple constituencies within those parties. Where transactional or relational contracts might be between two or more enterprises, psychological contracts are more often between two people or one person and a number of others. Although TQM initiatives are designed to involve the whole of the organisation in a contract (as are other customer-focused initiatives), they may often fail to involve all staff. In such cases, supplier development initiatives, workforce communication programmes and comprehensive performance management systems can be used to affirm the contract.

As we have seen, one of the objects of contracting is to reduce harm to the parties involved. As a consequence, individuals and groups will seek to establish the credibility of a promise before entering into a contract. Promises which are made publicly (to a group) would seem to have more credibility than promises made to an individual.

There is a cultural aspect to contracting. Psychological contracts are also controlled, to a greater or lesser degree, by social norms as to the expectations contained in a particular social setting. Where traditional buyer supplier relationships have been adversarial, the organisation that wishes to change the nature of its contracts will find that social norms may work against the change.

Alternatives to contracts

A number of organisations, drawing on methods employed in Japanese management, do not employ contracts at all. Perhaps the more famous case of a non-contractual relationship is demonstrated in the case of William Baird, the clothing manufacturers, and Marks and Spencer. Baird and Marks and Spencer worked together over a considerable period of time without a formal contract. The fact that the eventual withdrawal of this contract led to legal action, and a finding that a relational contract was not, in fact, a contract, demonstrates some of the issues in this approach.

There are two main approaches to management without contracts.

1.   The first of these is governance through dependency.

2.   The second is governance through trust.

Both of these methods are subsumed into Sako's (1992) definition of 'obligational contractual relationships' (OCRs), although Sako herself does not differentiate between them. There are, however, clear differences both in the way in which they are achieved and in their effects.

Dependency management

It should perhaps come as no surprise that Sako names Japanese relational contracts as obligational. The concept of 'giri' or duty and social obligation is a strong one in Japanese culture. Obligation is, as we have seen, an element within a contract or a promise to perform. Combined with the idea of duty, obligation can shade into the fine line of dependency, where promises become a habit or a 'norm'. We have already looked at some of the spend/turnover proportions involved in these strategies. Here contracts have become so self-reinforcing that the removal of a contract is a threat of major proportions. The suppliers have moved through interdependence to dependence.

Management through trust

The more generally acceptable face of supply management is that of management by trust. We have looked at trust as being one of the factors that will impact upon commercial relationships. In addition, trust is created through interlocking directorates, shared investment and shared goals. It should be noted that there is little evidence of long-term relationships in themselves leading to trust except in the Far East where business ties in Japanese Keiretsu and the strong familial ties in Korean Chaebol seem to create trust. It seems possible to suggest that trust is embedded in a wider social fabric which may not exist in Western Europe and the United States.

Digital contracts

A contract is a contract is a contract. However, there is a growing body of concern with regard to electronic contracts and the way in which they are developed and enforced. The law in this field is changing rapidly, and at the time of writing (July 2002), EU directives were being considered with regard to digital or electronic contracts.

The objective of EU law (which aims to harmonise the differences between national laws) is to achieve the maximum opportunities for free trade. While national law and EU law are mutually dependent, EU law generally takes precedence over national law.

For the purposes of this study guide, directives are the most common form of European legislation. Directives are essentially instructions to the member states to introduce legislation. Directives indicate the goals to be achieved, but do not prescribe methods for achieving them. Generally, enforcement and remedies are left to the member states. On average, member states have two years from the date of publication of a directive to transform it into national law. Doing business in a particular member state requires awareness of the European regulation, and also of the national law.

The electronic commerce directive

The EU directive on eCommerce is designed to ensure that information society services, which include eBusiness (a legal definition of 'information society services' can be found in Directive 98/48/EC; laying down a procedure for the provision of information in the field of technical standards and regulations), benefit from the internal market principles of free movement and freedom of establishment. The directive states that, generally, information society services can be provided throughout the EU as long as they comply with the laws in their home member state.

According to the eCommerce directive, member states shall ensure that their legal system allows contracts to be concluded by electronic means. Exceptions to this are:

♦ Contracts that create or transfer rights in property (except rental)

♦ Contracts governed by family law or by the law of succession

♦ Contracts requiring the involvement of courts or public authorities

♦ Contracts requiring 'surety and collateral securities' supplied by persons acting for non-professional reasons.

The directive will not apply to services supplied by suppliers established in a non-European Union country. It aims to be consistent with relevant international rules and discussions within international organisations (UNCITRAL World Trade Organisation, Organisation for Economic and Commercial Development).

B2B contracts

National laws govern the main aspects of contract law. Laws governing the constitution of a contract and the point at which a contract is concluded currently vary from country to country. An offer may be binding in one country but not in another. In general, as we saw above, a contract is governed by the law chosen by the contracting parties.

The eCommerce directive provides that, except when otherwise agreed and except for contracts concluded exclusively by exchange of e-mail messages, the supplier should communicate comprehensibly and unambiguously prior to the placement of the order, the following minimum information:

◆ The technical steps needed to conclude the contract

◆ The language available for the conclusion of the contract

◆ The technical means for identifying and correcting input errors

◆ Whether and how the contract will be archived and the arrangements for access.

In the same ways as a normal contract is formed, the supplier must provide the buyer with the contract terms and general conditions in a way that allows him/her to store and reproduce them (for example, by e-mail). Finally, except if otherwise agreed, the supplier must indicate any relevant codes of conduct which are subscribed to and provide information on how such codes can be electronically consulted. In the case of electronic transactions, care should be taken that both buyer and seller understand where the contract is accepted. If the supplier is located in the United Kingdom and the buyer in Germany or the buyer is on the move, which law governs the contract?

According to the directive, the supplier should incorporate on his/her website an explicit clause of the applicable law. If the other contracting party accepts this clause, it will govern the contractual obligations of the parties based on the principle of party autonomy. The clause can be on the mandatory page (a page through which the purchaser must pass) and also in the general terms.

When the parties to the contract have not chosen the law applicable to a contract, the governing law is that of the country with which it is most closely connected. In almost all cases, a B2B contract is connected with the country of the establishment of the supplier of the product or service. A business establishment should be determined in accordance with the case law of the European Court of Justice. This recognises that the place of establishment of a company providing the products or services through an Internet website is not necessarily the place at which the technology supporting its website is located or where its website is accessed.

Usually, the place of establishment is the place where the business is legally registered. In the case of multiple establishments, the competent member state will be the one in which the supplier has the centre of his/her activities.

As noted, at the time of writing, consultation with regard to the directive is still underway in the United Kingdom. Applicable law in the United States and elsewhere is still changing rapidly.

Changing contracts

One issue is fundamental to the success of any longer-term commercial relationship: the ability to accommodate change successfully. We have seen that different levels of contracting may involve the need for small changes in the way in which a good or service is delivered.

Changes to requirements can involve small adjustments to existing specifications, planned step changes or major business change leading to a completely new contract, or anything in between.

Shorter lead times and faster product development cycles as well as service requirement changes involve the negotiation of contract change as an ongoing element of relationship management. The ability to manage change successfully is fundamental to any commercial relationship that is to succeed over time.

Processes

Change during the term of a contract can be categorised as follows:

◆ Routine change

◆ Initiated change programmes

◆ Unplanned change.

Changes may involve contract price adjustment, specification adjustment or changes in a range of performance measures.

Routine change

Routine change could include ongoing changes to user requirements, machine down-time, maintenance/enhancements to existing systems or planned technology upgrades. This type of change is most easily accommodated under, and is best suited to, formal change management processes. Well-constructed contractual agreements should contain express provisions detailing:

◆ The type of procedures to be used in initiating and delivering change through:
  - service user groups
  - change control boards
  - formal approval processes

- Procedures to be adopted for the escalation and resolution of disputes that may arise, such as:
    - pre-defined escalation routes and timescales
    - alternative dispute resolution procedures (neutral advisers, expert determination and arbitration)

- Procedures for amending contract documentation. These may include:
    - authorisation
    - audit trail.

Initiated change

Change can also be initiated to deliver efficiency improvements and associated cost savings. We looked at examples of this type of change in the section on performance contracts.

Unplanned change

Unplanned change is the most difficult type of change to manage and accommodate. It is also potentially the most damaging to the relationship. At worst it can serve to invalidate the contract for one or both parties, resulting in the termination of the contract or even the relationship.

Unplanned change often leads to conflict. The response to conflict is critical and must be structured. We looked at some tools that can be used to structure and analyse conflict earlier in the study guide. Joint processes might include:

- Assessing the impact of the change on the relationship – can this be dealt with under the existing change management clauses and procedures or does it require specialised procedures or resources?

- Escalation within both organisations as appropriate

- Reviewing the basis of the contract – is the original contract still viable?

- Assessing the nature and extent of the change required

- Negotiation of the necessary amendments.

It may be necessary for both parties to make real and significant concessions in the resulting negotiations in order to make the contract work for the future. A complete audit trail of developments is essential to ensure accountability.

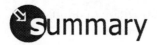

Summary

Contracting is complex and takes place at many levels and with many different motivations. In employing contracts, purchasing practitioners are faced with a range of choices, but they must often consider the wider issues involved in contracting. Broadly, we can identify transactional, relational, incentive and psychological contracts as having an impact on the commercial relationship we choose to develop. Each of these contract categories has strengths and weaknesses. Using a mixture of different categories is often the way to optimise contract effectiveness within the relationship.

It should also be recognised that contracts can change in both planned and unplanned ways. Effective contracting takes these issues into account and prepares for change. This change may be in contract price or the nature of the goods and services being delivered. Procedures for coping with change can assist in maintaining the strength of the relationship.

self-assessment question

SAQ 4.2

What are the main elements of relational contracting?

Relationships in the service context

The syllabus learning outcomes for this subsection state that you will be able to:

◆ **Access the relationship issues particularly relevant where relationships are concerned with service provision.**

This subsection will cover:

◆ **Introduction**

◆ **Classifying service contracts.**

Introduction

Developing relationship and contracting strategies for services requires an understanding of the differences between predominantly tangible and intangible goods. Services have a number of unique characteristics that impact on the design of appropriate relationship strategies.

Services are:

◆ **Intangible:** most service activity is intangible. Customers cannot perceive the service before it is bought. This means that they will assess the service provision differently to the way in which they assess products. The service provider, therefore, needs to find ways in which the service can be made more tangible, and risk in use can be minimised. This may range from improving the quality of supporting materials through to improving point-of-service staff motivation through shifts in reward policies, training and systems development

◆ **Perishable:** many services are literally consumed at the point of delivery. The service cannot be kept in a store. This means that managing supply and demand in service provision can be more difficult than managing production supply and demand. Managing supply and demand more effectively may involve improving staff flexibility through increased use of short-term contracts or through multi-skilling

◆ **Co-created:** services are not really something you do to the customer. They should always be something you do with the customer. Service production and service consumption are linked at the point of delivery. Again, because the service is co-created by the producer and consumer, it cannot be stored. Because the service is co-created it is also transparent at the delivery point – the customer can see it being made and failures are hard to hide. This again has an impact upon demand and staff availability. It also has an impact upon customer evaluation because delivery failures are obvious. Meeting these challenges may involve educating the customer in how to use the service more efficiently. Service co-creation, if handled properly, can offer real benefits in increasing customer retention

◆ **Variable:** because service delivery is co-created, it depends on the interaction between the customer and the staff member. Different levels of energy and different mindsets within both these groups can cause the quality of service to vary widely. Variability can be managed by ensuring that your staff recruitment, selection and motivation are excellent, and also by ensuring that the systems are in place to support consistent levels of quality. Long shifts, poor working conditions, lack of understanding how the job relates to employees' overall purpose, do not help maintain consistency

◆ **Hard to measure:** customer satisfaction is not an absolute, static quality that can be easily measured. It is dynamic and complicated. Levels of customer satisfaction potential can shift on a minute-to-minute basis. Customer satisfaction (delight, wow factor or whatever you call it) is linked to customer needs, expectations, experience, emotions and a whole range of other factors, many of which are beyond the control of the supplier. Satisfaction is also very difficult to measure accurately.

Classifying service contracts

When considering service contracts, it is often believed that the above factors create problems in both specification and evaluation of services.

The management of service contracts aims to achieve common understanding between the customer and supplier by negotiating and managing expectations and delivering and supporting desired results. In this sense, service contract relationships are similar to the service level agreements that we considered in section one of this study guide. Service contract management is therefore focused on three types of service process:

1. **Service specification development:** concentrates on the ways in which expectations are managed.

2. **Service management:** concentrates on the way in which services are delivered.

3. **Service quality monitoring:** demonstrates ongoing value for money and service improvement.

Commercial relationships in service contracts can require much more effort upfront, before the service is actually delivered. This focus is preventative, whereas a focus on goods can too often be remedial. In addition, because of the intangible nature of services, the purchasing and supply function will often have to take on an educational role which helps internal staff improve their skills as service users.

As well as intangibility, services should be expected to evolve in order to fulfil needs appropriately and to continue to offer value for money. This means that services may require a modular approach to implementation, as users become accustomed to new ways of working.

Effective service contract management

In order for service management to be effective, there are a number of elements which need to be put in place. These include:

◆ Defining the service profile. Balancing business goals and priorities with those of your customer(s) and supplier(s). Service profiles should, wherever possible:
  - co-develop the profiles using user-supplier workshops
  - rely on thorough market research
  - describe all work in terms of both what the required service output is and how it will be delivered
  - include measurable performance objectives and financial or other incentives
  - encourage contractors to develop and institute innovative and cost-effective methods of performing the work
  - include historic and projected demand data (to include surge and other requirements)

◆ Making an appropriate sourcing decision. This involves understanding the value of the service to your organisation both now and in the future

◆ Using appropriate payment mechanisms and performance measures to incentivise suppliers. Performance measures might include:
  - customer satisfaction
  - customer expectations
  - customer knowledge
  - service levels
  - adequate levels of service support
  - adequate levels of technical documentation and training
  - flexible, motivated staff within participating companies
  - improvements in participating company's understanding of customer systems and needs
  - increases in customer satisfaction
  - timeliness
  - accessibility
  - improvements in service back-up response and completion times
  - appropriate response times contingent upon the degree of service risk
  - improvements in communication between customers and participating suppliers
  - costs
  - corresponding reduction of participating company costs
  - customer satisfaction scores
  - participating company's knowledge of customer systems and needs

◆ Using an appropriate structure for service contract management. This may include role definition (where your responsibilities end and the suppliers begin

- Contracts with service suppliers must incorporate some degree of flexibility in defining obligations on both parties to allow for business requirements to change within a rapidly changing business environment

- Provision to monitor and modify the service as needed.

Developing a service management policy

In the event that an enterprise employs a wide range of service providers, it may be useful to generate a service management policy. If properly designed, this will enable the purchaser to take advantage of other contract experience to properly scope the service requirements and objectives to be achieved. Such a policy may also include a framework which sets out the approaches to take for risk assessment and management as well as monitoring and continuous improvement. A policy can also highlight the key roles and responsibilities required within the service management team, together with the use of third party consultants.

Service level agreements (SLAs)

We looked at service level agreements in section 1 of the study guide. A service level agreement can also be used across organisational boundaries. It is a formal contractual arrangement specifying the required service levels and the expected quality of service to be delivered. It must state the relevant responsibilities of the customer and supplier, ensuring that both parties are responsible for monitoring, revising and evaluating existing SLAs.

Service level management

Service contract management is the process which ensures that both parties to a contract fully meet their respective obligations as efficiently and effectively as possible, in order to deliver the business and operational objectives required from the contract and, in particular, to provide value for money. Typically, service contract managers require resources for contract management that are equivalent to 2% of the contract value. It is an integral part of the informed customer capability.

Service contract management may be carried out through SLAs, which can be used to monitor service levels, identify service improvements and ensure end-user satisfaction. SLAs may be regularly reviewed and also reviewed when significant changes to requirements take place.

Service blueprints can be used to capture the quality of service. This provides a basis for measuring service improvement and achievements using defined metrics for each service management process. The results of the programme may be monitored regularly, and appropriate action taken to correct any under-achievements. A cumulative record of service level targets and results can be maintained in an annual report.

Much service management also involves joint problem solving. Problem solving (also called root cause analysis) attempts to understand the root cause or reason for failures or successes. Having identified (either by benchmarking or other such measurement) current performance levels, the organisation will need to establish the reason behind any failures in order to rectify the situation and regain agreed service levels. Problem solving is a process by which cause-and-effect activities, and/or outputs, are systematically analysed until a root or source has been identified. Corrective action can then be taken to remedy the exact cause or problem identified sooner rather than later.

In order to effectively monitor the progress of the service contract, the purchaser needs to establish a reporting framework that matches the nature and complexity of the contract being managed. The purchaser should acknowledge the impact that the performance of the buying organisation has on the supplier and adjust information presented in performance reports to reflect this dependency.

To facilitate timely and accurate reporting on service delivery, the purchaser or contract manager should consider, in conjunction with the provider, the following issues in relation to the reporting mechanism:

◆ **The delivery method and format of reports:** with the variety of systems available, each being able to produce information in a variety of formats from hard copy through to various software types, it is important to ensure the transmittal medium is appropriate and effective. Will the types of computer model used today still be able to read your files in ten years' time or is there a cost for updating them and keeping up with the technology of the day?

◆ **The reporting time period:** the supplier may be asked to issue high level summary reports on a monthly basis for use by executive management, with weekly reports on the more detailed data. The decision on what to provide should be based on the needs of the parties receiving the reports. Suggested types of report have been provided in the list below. It is the responsibility of the contract manager to discuss reporting timings with those parties and then agree this with the provider

◆ **The analysis source:** reporting is not just about collecting data but is about providing information. For reports on the performance of the provider to be useful, they need to be presented in a way that allows easy comparison to the contract. They should include, where possible, simple and straightforward analysis of any relevant benchmarking information and performance over time

◆ **Quality assurance in reporting documents:** it is the contract manager's responsibility to monitor the quality of the information submitted by the supplier as well as the information to be presented to management, users and other stakeholders

- **Ongoing relevance:** it can be a temptation for both purchasers and suppliers to present too much rather than too little information. More is not always better. Too much information is a waste of resources in preparation time for the provider and checking time for the contract manager. Contract managers need to always be looking at the information provided and testing its relevance against the information they need in order to assess the performance of the contract. If the information needs of the provider or contract manager change, the reporting framework should be responsive enough to not only recognise the need for change, but also to adapt to providing the new information requirements.

Reporting documents may include:

- Performance management information, particularly instances of very good and very poor performance

- Achievement of milestones or progress against the time-frame for the contract

- Client feedback, particularly exceptions

- Action taken to address problem areas and whether successful

- Variations to the SLAs or contract

- Financial progress against the contract.

Within the context of service level management, it is also necessary to manage the service relationship.

Managing service relationships

Customer/supplier relationships may be highly formalised, strongly contractually based and closely performance/cost-conscious. Other relationships may be more flexible, based on shared objectives. The factors that help to establish the relationship and achieve the right benefits include:

- Better information exchange as the parties gain greater insight into each other's business processes and therefore pre-empting changed requirements

- The supplier having more confidence about investing for the longer term

- The customer identifying both its own and the supplier's strengths and weaknesses, and focusing effort into those areas where they will bring most return.

Service management approaches must be designed to accommodate change to improve the quality and/or efficiency of service delivery; and to accommodate working with partners in both the public and private sectors.

The skills used in managing commercial relationships are equally applicable to the management of service relationships. Commercial factors may include:

◆ Selecting appropriate service performance metrics

◆ Clearly providing for the need to alter service performance criteria – qualitatively or quantitatively

◆ Clear definition of responsibilities and methods of reporting and managing exceptions

◆ Providing for appropriate levels of service review

◆ Creating effective hand-off and transition arrangements

◆ Process visibility in service delivery

◆ Clear definitions for services that cross multiple service domains and/or contract boundaries.

Communications

Service management is all about achieving common understanding, managing expectations and delivering results. Good quality information underpins effective communications which can, in turn, develop the relationships and are critical to success. Good communication needs to take place across organisational interfaces at all levels and within the purchasing organisation as a whole. Continuous communication is key to keeping service delivery up to date and relevant to the customer's requirements.

Performance measurement

Service performance metrics should be consistent across different parts of the buying organisation. Consistency across both enterprise-level business objectives and detailed operational criteria helps to establish credibility. Credible measures are more effective as suppliers tend to take them more seriously. High-level objectives might include:

◆ Enterprise needs and requirements

◆ User needs and requirements

◆ Impact of measurement

◆ Links between measures and service process.

At a lower level, measures for a service contract may include:

Tangibles	The physical facilities, equipment, appearance of personnel and the presence of other participants.
Reliability	The ability to perform the promised service dependably and accurately.
Responsiveness	Willingness to help participants and to provide prompt service.
Assurance	Knowledge and courtesy of staff and their ability to convey trust and confidence.
Empathy	Caring, individualised attention to participants.

Other areas that need to be thought through before the contract is signed include:

◆ The contract management processes that will give the buyer the level of control required

◆ The level of knowledge required within the organisation to understand the technical direction in which the supplier is taking the organisation

◆ The level of service back-up

◆ Internal relationships of the supplier team within their own organisation. Do they have sufficient status to ensure that they will be able to get the resources required? Can they influence their own board?

◆ Contract continuity, making sure that the best teams are used to prepare the contract bid, but are substituted once the contract is awarded

◆ What does the supplier know about your current operations and how will it get up to speed? Has enough time been allowed for the supplier's learning curve in understanding the complexity of the business?

Summary

Developing and managing service contracts offers a number of challenges to the purchaser. These rest upon the nature of the service itself, which is intangible. All services share a number of characteristics which make tracking performance difficult. This means that the process of service contracting should be developed jointly wherever possible. The process of managing services can be structured by using a service contracting policy, which will set out roles and responsibilities, targets, metrics, reporting systems etc. These may be encoded in a service level agreement. Contracts and SLAs require both strategic and operational measures, which have the capacity to be varied in the face of changing circumstances.

self-assessment question

SAQ 4.3

Identify five low-level performance measures that could be used in managing a service contract.

Relationships in connection with hire or lease contracts

The syllabus learning outcomes for this subsection state that you will be able to:

◆ **Evaluate the use of leasing or hiring arrangements as an alternative to buying.**

This subsection will cover:

◆ **Introduction**

◆ **What is a lease?**

◆ **Types of leasing**

◆ **Types of lessor**

◆ **Advantages of leasing**

◆ **Elements in a lease structure**

Introduction

Financing new equipment (from computers to phone systems to capital equipment) is a major issue for many enterprises. Leasing, instead of purchasing, can offer a range of advantages for the buyer, as a method of financing assets. In other words, the user can look at leasing as a mode of financing, just as a loan, bond or other borrowing option.

Businesses may choose different lease types to achieve different objectives:

◆ **Tax reporting objectives:** minimise taxable income by maximising tax deductions

◆ **Financial accounting objectives:** maximise income and profitability.

This section will look at some of the issues faced in both leasing and hire purchase.

What is a lease?

A lease is an agreement, often long term, to rent equipment, land, buildings or any other asset. In return for most, but not all, of the benefits of ownership, the user (lessee) makes periodic payments to the owner of the asset (lessor). The lease payment covers the original cost of the equipment or other asset and provides the lessor a profit.

Types of leasing

There are several types of leasing which can be used for different purposes. For the purposes of this study guide we will look at three types:

◆ Financial leasing

◆ Operational leasing

◆ Sale and leaseback.

Financial leasing

Financial leases are the most common form of lease. A financial lease is usually written for a term not to exceed the economic life of the equipment. You will find that a financial lease usually provides that:

◆ Periodic payments be made

◆ Ownership of the equipment reverts to the lessor at the end of the lease term

◆ The lease is non-cancellable and the lessee has a legal obligation to continue payments to the end of the term

◆ The lessee agrees to maintain the equipment.

Operational leasing

The operating lease or maintenance lease can usually be cancelled under conditions spelled out in the lease agreement. Maintenance of the asset is usually the responsibility of the owner (lessor). Computer equipment is often leased under this kind of lease.

An operating lease is accounted for as a pure rental and the equipment is not shown as a liability nor an asset on the lessee's business balance sheet. An operating lease is one which is treated as a true lease (as opposed to a loan) for book accounting purposes. An operating lease must have all of the following characteristics:

◆ The lease term is less than 75% of estimated economic life of the equipment

◆ The present value of lease payments is less than 90% of the equipment's fair market value

◆ The lease cannot contain a bargain purchase option (less than the fair market value)

◆ Ownership is retained by the lessor during and after the lease term.

An operating lease is accounted for by the lessee without showing an asset (for the equipment) or a liability (for the lease payment obligations) on the lessee's balance sheet.

Sale and leaseback

The sale and leaseback is similar to the financial lease. The owner of an asset sells it to another party and simultaneously leases it back to use it for a specified term. This arrangement lets you free the money tied up in an asset for use elsewhere. Buildings are often leased this way, and can provide a major cash injection for an enterprise.

Other terms

You may also hear leases described as net leases or gross leases. Under a net lease the lessee is responsible for expenses such as those for maintenance, taxes, and insurance. The lessor pays these expenses under a gross lease. Financial leases are usually net leases.

Finally, you might run across the term 'full payout lease'. Under a full payout lease the lessor recovers the original cost of the asset during the term of the lease.

Financial leases and hire-purchase

In some countries, distinction is made between lease and hire-purchase transactions. A hire-purchase transaction is usually defined as one where the hirer (user) has, at the end of the fixed term of hire, an option to buy the asset at a token value. In other words, financial leases with a bargain buyout option at the end of the term can be called a hire-purchase transaction.

Hire-purchase is decisively a financial lease transaction, but in some cases, it is necessary to provide the cancellation option in hire-purchase transactions by statute. That is, the hirer has to be provided with the option of returning the asset and walking out from the deal. If such an option is embedded, hire-purchase becomes significantly different from a financial lease as the risk of obsolescence gets shifted to the supplier. If the asset were to become obsolete during the hire term, the hirer may off-hire the asset and close the contract, leaving the owner with less than a full payout.

Hire-purchase is of UK origin; the device originated much before leases became popular, and spread to countries which were then British dominions. The device is still popular in the United Kingdom, Australia, New Zealand, India and Pakistan. Most of these countries have enacted, in line with United Kingdom, specific laws dealing with hire-purchase transactions.

Contracting and relationships - Section 4d

Types of lessor

In the past, many lessors were financial intermediaries that specialised in leasing or other types of asset financing. As the use of leasing has increased as a method for businesses to acquire equipment and other assets, the number of companies in the leasing business has increased dramatically.

Commercial banks, insurance companies and finance companies do most of the leasing. Many of these organisations have formed subsidiaries primarily concerned with equipment leasing. These subsidiaries are usually capable of making lease arrangements for almost anything.

In addition to financial organisations, there are companies which specialise in leasing. Some are engaged in general leasing, while others specialise in particular equipment, such as trucks or computers. Equipment manufacturers are also occasionally in the leasing business. Of course, they usually lease only the equipment they manufacture.

Advantages of leasing

There are a number of advantages to leasing. These include the following:

◆ Leasing can offer 100% financing, which frees working capital for more productive uses. Often, though not necessarily, leasing is 100% funding – the lessor buys the equipment and leases to the lessee. In lending, it is most common for the lender to insist on the borrower contributing a percentage, therefore, it is common for the lessor to insist upon an upfront payment, either as a security deposit or as initial rentals

◆ Leasing can cost less than other methods of acquiring equipment. A lessor might affordably price a lease cheaper to other alternatives, particularly if its own costs are appreciably lower or if the lease offers it tax benefits

◆ Leasing is generally more flexible than other forms of financing. A leasing plan can always be customised to meet the particular needs of the lessee. Other forms of finance are not seen as having this advantage. It is, however, important to recognise that speed, flexibility or negotiability are features of the provider of the financial plan, and not those of the plan itself. Leasing can also be used more flexibly – for example if the nature of an industry demands the latest technology, a short-term operating lease can help enterprise upgrade or add equipment to meet changing needs

- ◆ Leasing increases the borrowing capacity of the lessee. This occurs in two ways:
  - – it contributes to maintaining a low debt/equity (D/E) ratio in the lessee so that this borrowing capacity is kept intact even after the lease-financing has been done. Depending on the accounting standards used, a lease is not recorded on the balance sheet of the lessee as a debt. As such, it does not affect the debt-equity (D/E) ratio of the lessee. This means that the lessee can borrow more, having a mix of financing methods rather than by relying on one source
  - – it represents an 'off-the-balance-sheet' method of financing. Where lease obligations do not appear as a liability on the balance sheet of the lessee, keeping debt-to-equity ratios low, this improves return on investment (ROI) ratios. This is a result of increases in operating incomes but debits in the balance sheet remain unchanged

- ◆ Leasing offers tax benefits in that it may permit a more rapid amortisation of the asset than would be permissible under the depreciation rules applicable in case of an owned assets. When the lessee owns the asset, the only method of writing off the cost is through depreciation, which would essentially depend upon the nature of the asset and the permitted depreciation rules. On the other hand, as lease rentals are tax-deductible, it is possible to write off the cost of the asset (represented by the principal repayment inherent in rentals) in the lessee's books over the lease period – say, 3 years. There are front-end loaded leases (that is, where rentals are high to begin with and reduce over time) which write off as much as 50% of the cost in the very first year

- ◆ Leases do not involve restrictive covenants. Loan agreements with banks usually contain coercive conditions such as restrictions on transfer of shares, issue of bonus shares, right to appoint nominee directors, convertibility clauses etc. Leasing companies do not generally impose such restrictions

- ◆ Leases offer a hedge against the risk of obsolescence. One of the most notable merits in case of operating leases is that the lessor bears the risks of obsolescence. Similarly, the lessee does not have to dispose of the asset at the end of its life. It is simply returned to the lessor

- ◆ Operating lessors can offer expert advice on selection of equipment.

Disadvantages of leasing

Although leasing is more flexible, it can be more expensive. Leasing can cost more because you lose certain tax advantages that go with ownership of an asset. Leasing may not, however, cost more if you couldn't take advantage of those benefits because you don't have enough tax liability for them to come into play.

Although disposal is easier, depending on the nature of the asset, an enterprise loses the economic value of the asset at the end of the lease term. Lessees have been known to grossly underestimate the salvage value of an asset. If they had known this value from the outset, they might have decided to buy instead of lease.

Furthermore, a lease is a long-term legal obligation. Usually you cannot cancel a financial lease agreement. So, if you were to end an operation that used leased equipment, you might find you would still have to pay as much as if you had used the equipment for the full term of the lease.

Elements in a lease structure

This is an explanation of the elements in a lease – the parties, asset, rentals and residual value, for example.

1. The nature of the transaction

The transaction of a lease is basically an asset-renting transaction. The difference between a lease and a loan is that in a loan money is lent, and in a lease an asset is lent.

Therefore, a lease could be generally defined as:

> A contract where a party, being the owner (lessor) of an asset (leased asset) provides the asset for use by the lessee at a consideration (rentals), either fixed or dependent on any variables, for a certain period (lease period), either fixed or flexible, with an understanding that at the end of such period, the asset, subject to the embedded options of the lease, will be either returned to the lessor or disposed of in accordance with the lessor's instructions.

2. Parties to a lease

As with any contract, there are two parties to a lease: the owner and the user, called the lessor and the lessee. The lessor is the person who owns the asset and gives it on lease. The lessee takes the asset on lease and uses it for the lease period. The status of a lessor and lessee are subject to the usual conditions as to competence to contract.

Technically, in order to be a lessor, it is not necessary to own the asset: the lessor merely has to have the right to use the asset. Thus, a lessee can be a lessor for a sub-lessee, unless the parent lessor has restricted the right to sub-lease.

3. The leased asset

The subject of a lease is the asset, article or property to be leased. Almost anything may be leased – an automobile, aircraft, machine, consumer durable, land, building or a factory. Only tangible assets can be leased – one cannot contemplate the leasing of intangible assets since one of the essential elements of a lease is handing over of possession, along with the right to use. Hence, intangible assets are assigned, whereas tangible assets may be leased.

The concept of leasing will have the following limitations:

♦ What cannot be owned cannot be leased. Thus, human resources cannot be leased

♦ Although the lease of movable properties can be effected by mere delivery, immovable property is incapable of deliveries in a physical sense. Most countries have specific laws relating to transactions in immovable properties: if such a law provides a particular procedure for a lease of immovable or real estate, such procedure should be complied with. For example, in Anglo-Saxon legal systems (such as UK, Australia, India and Pakistan), transactions in real estate are not valid unless they are effected by registered conveyance. This applies to both the lease of land and buildings and permanent attachments to land

♦ A lease is structurally a rental for the lease period, with the understanding that the asset will be returned to the lessor after the period. Thus, the asset must be capable of re-delivery: it must be durable (at least during the lease period), identifiable and severable.

The existence of the leased asset is an essential element of a lease transaction, which means the asset must exist at the beginning of the lease, during the lease and at the end of the lease term. Non-existence of the asset, for whatever reason, will be fatal to the lease.

4. The lease period

The term of lease is the time period for which the agreement of lease is in operation. Because the recovery of the asset by the lessee at the end of the lease period is necessary to the lease being a lease, the lease period must be defined. During this period, the lessee may have a right of cancellation, and beyond this period, the lessee may be given a right of renewal, but a lease should not equate to a sale, that is, the asset being given permanently to the lessee.

In financial leases, it is common to differentiate between a primary lease period and a secondary lease period. The primary lease period would be the time during which the lessor would recover their investment. The secondary lease period allows the lessee to exhaust a substantial part of the remaining asset value. The primary period is normally non-cancellable and the secondary period is often cancellable.

5. Lease rentals

The lease rentals represent the consideration of the lease. In the case of a financial lease transaction, lease rental will generally consist of the recovery of the lessor's principal, and a rate of return on outstanding principal. Lease rentals consist of a bundled principle repayment and interest spread out over the period of the lease. If it is an operating lease transaction, the rentals might include a range of other charges depending upon the costs and risks borne by the lessor. These might include:

◆   Interest on the lessor's investment

◆   Lessor's maintenance repairs, operation or insurance costs

◆   Depreciation on the asset

◆   Service charges.

6. Residual value

Residual value is the value of the leased equipment at the end of the lease term. If the lease contains a buy-out option, then residual value would generally mean the value at which a lessee will be allowed to buy the equipment. If there is no embedded purchase option, within the agreement, residual value might mean fair market value as the value that the lessee, or an agreed valuation, represents as the minimum value of the equipment at the end of the lease term.

This is typical in case of financial leases where the lessor cannot grant a buy-out option to the lessee. In order that the lessor can be protected against asset-based risks, they could take an assured residual value commitment either from the lessee or from a third party, typically an insurance company.

7. End-of-term options

The options allowed to the lessee at the end of the primary lease period are called end-of-term options. These might include:

◆   Option to buy (buy-out option) at a bargain price or nominal value (typical in a hire-purchase transaction), called a bargain buy-out option

◆   Option to buy at a fair market value or fixed, but substantial value

◆   Option to renew the lease at nominal rentals, called a bargain renewal option

◆   Option to renew the lease at fair market rentals or substantial rentals

◆   Option to return the equipment.

The decision as to which option will be suitable is based on the nature and objectives of the lease transaction, and also the applicable law.

8. Upfront payments

Lessors may require one or more upfront payments from a lessee. These may include:

◆ Initial lease rental or initial hire or down payment

◆ Advance lease rental

◆ Security deposit

◆ Initial fees.

The initial lease rent or initial hire (the word 'hire' is more common in cases of hire-purchase transactions) is a surrogate for a margin or borrower contribution in cases of loan transactions. Note that, given the nature of a lease or hire-purchase (an asset-renting transaction), it is not possible to expect a lessee's contribution to asset cost as such. Hence, the down payment or first lease rent serves the purpose of a margin.

The security deposit is a proper deposit to secure against the lessee's commitments under the contract – it is generally intended to be refunded at the end of the lease contract.

Summary

Leasing is a complex alternative to purchasing which offers a number of benefits and a number of drawbacks. Leases generally fall into three types which are:

◆ Financial

◆ Operating

◆ Sale and leaseback.

Each of these offers opportunities for the enterprise to achieve both financial and tax advantages. Leasing is a growing area, and consequently offers a more flexible form of asset finance. Nonetheless, care should be taken when considering leasing, as it represents a long-term commitment for the enterprise.

Self-assessment question

SAQ 4.4

Identify three types of lease.

Contracting and relationships - Section 4d

examination questions

Exam 4.1

Discuss the view that relationships with suppliers are of greater importance and significance where contracts are for services rather than goods, and explain how service contracts might be managed.

Exam 4.2

1. Discuss the pros and cons of leasing or hiring as an alternative to buying.

2. Explain the implications of leasing or hiring, rather than buying, on the client's relationship with the provider.

Exam 4.3

Explain the principle of incentive contracting, illustrating your answer by means of a simple incentive clause. Include in your answer a note on the idea of 'penalty' clauses.

saq responses

SAQ 4.1

◆ **Fixed price incentive contracts** (in which final contract price and profit are calculated based on a formula that relates final negotiated cost to target cost): these may be either firm targets or successive targets

◆ **Fixed price contracts with award fees** (used to 'motivate a contractor' when contractor performance cannot be measured objectively, making other incentives inappropriate)

◆ **Cost-reimbursement incentive contracts** (used when fixed price contracts are inappropriate, due to uncertainty about probable costs): these may be either cost-plus-incentive-fee or cost-plus-award-fee

SAQ 4.2

Key elements of relational contracting are:

◆ The identities and personal attributes of parties

◆ Norms of indeterminate duration

◆ Norms of behaviour, or shared codes of conduct, inform responses to new developments as they unfold

◆ Written documentation is treated as a record of what has been agreed

◆ Norms of behaviour, or shared codes of conduct, overrule written documents in settling disputes

SAQ 4.3

Some low-level performance measures that could be used in managing a service contract are:
◆ Customer satisfaction
◆ Customer expectations
◆ Customer knowledge
◆ Service levels
◆ Adequate levels of service support
◆ Adequate levels of technical documentation and training
◆ Flexible, motivated staff within participating companies
◆ Improvements in participating company's understanding of customer systems and needs
◆ Increases in customer satisfaction
◆ Timeliness
◆ Accessibility
◆ Improvements in service back-up response and completion times
◆ Appropriate response times contingent upon the degree of service risk
◆ Improvements in communication between customers and participating suppliers
◆ Costs
◆ Corresponding reduction of participating company costs
◆ Customer satisfaction scores
◆ Participating company's knowledge of customer systems and needs.

SAQ 4.4

Three types of lease are:
◆ Financial leasing
◆ Operational leasing
◆ Sale and leaseback.

Contracting and relationships - Section 4

examination responses

Exam 1.1

The candidate may choose from the following list:

- **Purchasing policy:** stores knowledge but can become outdated quickly

- **Computer-supported collaborative working:** helps in the case of geographically separated teams, but often faces problems with different perspectives and knowing what information is important

- **Cross-functional teams:** also faces problems with different perspectives and knowing what information is important

- **Communities of practice**

- **Service level agreements.**

Exam 1.2

The primary purpose of such legislation is often to foster economy and efficiency in the use of public funds – to give value for money. The state and its subsidiary organs are normally obliged, under domestic law and various international agreements, to transact procurement in a fair, transparent and non-discriminatory manner. Public procurement legislation for this purpose normally:

- Makes open tendering the default procedure

- Describes, in detail, the steps involved in open tendering (preparation of invitations to tender and tender documents, advertisements, submission and opening of tenders, examination and evaluation of tenders and award and conclusion of contract)

- Defines the circumstances under which methods, other than open tendering, may be used (for example, restricted tendering and request for quotations)

- Describes those other procedures

- Lays down rules concerning essential elements in the process (for example, qualification of tenderers, technical specifications, records of proceedings and evaluation of tender).

Exam 1.3

Transactional dependence:

ACR

◆ Buyer seeks to maintain low dependence by trading with a large number of competing suppliers within the limits permitted by the need to keep down transaction costs

◆ Supplier seeks to maintain low dependence by trading with a large number of customers within limits set by scale economics and transaction costs.

OCR

◆ For a buyer, avoidance of dependence is not a high priority; it prefers to give security to few suppliers, though may still dual- or triple-source (some from a fringe group of suppliers with whom it has ACR relations) for flexibility

◆ For a supplier, avoidance of dependence is not a high priority, but it may well have several OCR customers (plus, perhaps, a fringe group of ACR customers).

Contractual trust:

ACR

Supplier never starts production until written orders are received.

OCR

Supplier often starts production on the basis of oral communication, before written orders are received.

Goodwill trust

ACR

Multiple sourcing by buyer, combined with supplier's low transactional dependence.

OCR

Sole sourcing by buyer, combined with supplier's transactional dependence.

Competence trust

ACR

Thorough inspection on delivery; the principle of *caveat emptor* predominates.

OCR

Little or no inspection on delivery for most parts (customer may be involved in establishing supplier's quality control system).

Exam 1.4

The transactional relationship exists where cash or some other form of payment is exchanged for goods or services, without there being a long-term involvement of the parties with each other.

The characteristics of such relationships include the following:

- Product easy to specify
- Competing suppliers
- Competing customers
- Both sides seek value
- Cost allocation rather than cost sharing motivation
- Both parties will offer standard terms and conditions of contract.
- Barriers to entering or leaving the relationship will be low or non-existent.

It should not be suggested that the transactions relationship is inferior in any way to closer forms. Such relationships are entirely appropriate for routine supplies, where supplies of low commercial or strategic impact are acquired.

Exam 1.5

There is a great difference between cost transparency and open book costing. The core of the difference is the distinction between collaboration and competition. Much of the open book costing traditionally practised in the United Kingdom was a one-way process where the customer used its relative power over an established or prospective supplier to 'open their books'. The suspicion remains that this had more to do with the customer securing a short-term negotiating advantage than with long-term, sustainable competitive advantage for the supply chain. Indeed, open book costing often arose because customers felt it unwise to accept the word of suppliers at face value. Anecdotal evidence exists that suppliers sometimes resorted to keeping two sets of books, one for normal purposes and the other to be opened to customers.

On the other hand, cost transparency is a *two-way* exchange of information intended to enhance the long-term competitive advantage of both parties. It is certainly not intended to be used as leverage within the negotiation process, nor should cost transparency be seen as an admission of weakness by either party. Supply chain costs are made 'transparent' so that the entire supply chain may benefit by optimising its effectiveness and efficiency as wasteful practices are identified and eliminated. This does, however, call for a mature relationship between customers and suppliers based on mutual advantage over an extended time period.

Exam 2.1

The candidate here should consider the different approaches that might be taken to manage cross-functionally. Such approaches might include:

- Policy deployment
- Cross-functional teams
- Collaborative working tools
- Communities of practice
- Service level agreements
- Training and the intelligent customer
- Internal services marketing.

The candidate may then wish to consider the advantages and disadvantages of the chosen approaches. The candidate may wish to place the approaches in context, perhaps arguing for the use of cross-functional teams in large product development projects, and pointing to the drawbacks of using such an approach in smaller organisations, where roles are less fixed. Marks would also be awarded for an overview of implementation within an organisation.

Exam 2.2

This answer might begin with a description of the changing nature of risk within organisations and the benefits and risks that can be part of a volatile, customer-driven environment. Here the candidate may also wish to consider the need to balance performance and risk when managing commercial relationships. The candidate may wish to offer an overview of risk management methods, considering examples such as supplier assessment and effective contract monitoring using properly designed key performance indicators. Marks would be awarded for showing a coherent understanding of the nature of risk in commercial relationship, and also for demonstrating an understanding of the relationship between risk and performance. The candidate may also wish to highlight some of the working methods that can be used in the management of risk, including risk classification and risk analysis.

Exam 2.3

The candidate should demonstrate a good understanding of the fact that relationships are dynamic entities and that there are many factors that impact upon those relationships, engendering change. The candidate may commence their answer by looking at some of the drivers for change. These might include

- **Cost pressures**: better information is replacing inventory. The capabilities of supply chain software applications are growing to manage inventory that enterprises can't see and don't own, but which represent costs within the chain. Other costs and wastes can be identified and driven out. Good information management allows enterprises to identify costs, lower inventory and better utilise existing assets

- **Time pressures:** the need for faster and more customised deliveries has disrupted traditional production management policies and transportation choices. The lead times provided to customers has a knock-on effect, directly affecting their subsequent lead times, and thereby the velocity and flexibility of the entire value chain. By decreasing the lead time, businesses can gain competitive advantage

- **Reliability pressures:** when promising delivery dates or product quality to customers, enterprises need to ensure that they are capable of delivering on that date and to quality. Customers are becoming less tolerant

- **Response pressures:** customers are increasingly demanding real-time information into capabilities, products, configurations, and availability, as a way of managing risk. The ability to provide that information automatically is increasingly necessary

- **Transparency pressures:** the ability of a supplier to provide visibility into their order status is critical. Turning the supply chain into a 'glass-pipeline' will allow customers to identify current states, anticipate future states and proactively manage their inbound supply chain

- **Globalisation pressures:** the increasing complexity and globalisation of the interactions among suppliers, manufacturers, distributors, retailers, and consumers requires sophisticated coordination of multiple distribution channels.

The candidate may then wish to discuss levels at which these drivers might act. These include both intra and inter-organisational issues, team and personal elements. The candidate may complete his or her answer by considering how these different elements can create a relationship that is difficult to work within or predict, and highlight the need for effective cross-functional organisation to make such a relationship work.

Exam 2.4

One model of an integrated supplier development programme might include six elements:

1. Sourcing strategy.
2. Analysis strategy.
3. Communication strategy.
4. Infrastructure strategy.
5. Motivation strategy.
6. Standards strategy.
7. Development strategy.

Integrating these elements into an integrated supplier development programme is much more than an emphasis on quality of production, and the sharing of information. It involves a wide ranger of activities that need to be integrated into a cohesive whole to ensure robustness and effectiveness. Examples such as supply base reduction have benefits in that they reduce the cost of management and sourcing. They have a downside in that they can leave buyers at the mercy of first-tier suppliers.

Activities should support each other, as the overall effect will be much greater than if single activities were used in isolation. Different combinations of strategies will work in different industries and for different enterprises. Choosing the right combination of strategies is the critical challenge faced by the purchasing and supply function.

Exam 2.5

The candidate may wish to define these terms, and explain how they are used. Purchasing consortia, for instance, are groups of companies or organisations that come together to purchase goods and services so as to obtain a range of benefits. Once the candidate has defined the examples chosen, he or she may wish to describe their deployment in more detail. Again, in the case of consortia, these can range from the rudimentary form of organisation where two or more companies come together to buy MRO goods through to the complex where companies are involved in a research and development joint venture.

The candidate should clearly set out the benefits of the examples chosen. For consortia these may include price-related benefits or may involve extending knowledge, reducing administrative cost or improving the positioning of the purchasing function within the organisation, by increasing leverage.

As well as offering benefits, consortia can also involve drawbacks and costs. Consortia also involve costs in terms of management and organisation. Consortia and joint venture performance should be measured and monitored accurately. Many failures within joint ventures and consortia arise because of unclear objectives and poor monitoring mechanisms

Exam 2.6

Here the candidate may wish to comment on the fact that relationships often can and do survive problems with individual contracts. He or she may wish to illustrate this with examples from a familiar sector and consider situations where organisations have failed to carry out a contract, but been awarded similar contracts by the same buyer within a relatively short space of time.

The answer may then go on to consider some of the issues in managing contract failure. These include the need to ensure that the termination has the following characteristics:

- Be well structured with proper procedures
- Have valid, well-articulated reasons
- Be clearly communicated
- Involve accurate, balanced feedback
- Be prepared for by both parties
- Involve acknowledgement of the work within the existing contract
- Frame the contract/relationship in terms of long-term objectives
- Leave the door open for renewal or replacement of the old contract with a new one.

Contracting and relationships - Section 4

Processes that might support this could include:

- ◆ Giving the violating party an opportunity to explain the violation
- ◆ Being open to this explanation
- ◆ Looking for evidence
- ◆ Offering an opportunity to remedy the violation
- ◆ Ensuring that the remedy is fair
- ◆ Building stages into the process to slow down escalation.

Exam 2.7

The first stage in answering this question might include a definition of terms. These terms are often used interchangeably, and so are prone to misinterpretation. The candidate might also point out that the relationships between organisations are constantly evolving and continually renegotiated or forced to change by external trends, changes in the constraints and opportunities of the environment in which the organisations operate, or changes in role.

In considering the differences between traditional, relational and long-term contracts it can be can be useful to consider a number of factors. The first of these is focus. Traditional contracts are narrow in focus, usually of short and specific duration, and generally economic or extrinsic in the nature of the exchange.

However, other relationships can be of this type as well. Temporary employment is a good example. Even in long-term buyer-supplier relationships, parties can frame the relationship in traditional terms. In such relationships, contracts will focus very narrowly on specifications, and payment will focus very narrowly on salary and benefits.

In contrast, relational contracts are broader in scope, longer and more open-ended in duration, more dynamic, and have more socio-emotional elements (for example, loyalty, identity and shared destiny) in the exchange. Such exchanges are often supported by mutual trust and can benefit from parties providing assets not narrowly defined by contract terms.

Networks function more effectively when suppliers and buyers go beyond the narrowly defined elements of the contract in doing their work. Such behaviours, sometimes referred to as extra-role behaviours and sometimes as citizenship behaviours, include such things as supplier development, variation of payment terms at request, etc. These extra-role behaviours are essential to organisational effectiveness and are most likely to occur when the relationship is seen as relational as opposed to traditional/transactional.

Exam 2.8

There are wide-ranging individual factors that might impact upon commercial relationships. The candidate might wish to place his or her discussion of these factors in the context of different approaches to the study of relationships. He or she may choose to consider process or functional approaches to the question of relationships and consider how historical factors in the wider economy impact upon these factors.

The candidate may then choose to identify categories such as:

- The nature of the goods and services being supplied
- The geographical location of the parties
- The information and communication systems and processes used
- The business processes used
- Relative power between the parties
- The nature of interpersonal relationships involved
- Transactional issues.

He or she may then illustrate these using examples from the literature or from personal experience.

Exam 2.9

Candidates should point out here the effect of context on appraisal and decision making. This means that no single strategy applies to all purchases. Differing strategies based on value and risk factors yield differing results.

The candidate may wish to consider the changing nature of supplier appraisal, and consider some of the ways of choosing metrics. These may be more than the traditional 'three bids and financial checks on suppliers' as the main focus of pre-contract scrutiny.

The candidate may identify some of the changes taking place as end customers become more educated, and fault intolerant. This means that as production tolerances tighten and quality control challenges waste, the supplier's ability to assure product or service quality is more important than ever.

The candidate may also identify the issue of costs, and the growing trend towards contracting out more activity, meaning that organisations are becoming increasingly dependent on a high-quality supplier base to support their business goals. And as some businesses may spend up to 70 - 80 percent of their sales revenue on purchasing materials and services, effective supplier assessment has become critical to overall success.

In maximising effectiveness of such systems the candidate may consider factors such as:

- Cost-effectiveness
- Timeliness
- Accuracy of information
- Completeness of information
- Validity of collection methods.

The candidate may wish to place these in the context of fast-changing, volatile environments and the need for effective monitoring and verification to assess risk.

Exam 2.10

Service contracts have often been difficult to manage, because of factors common to services. These include the fact that services are:

♦ **Intangible:** most service activity is intangible. Customers cannot perceive the service before it is bought. This means that they will assess the service provision differently to the way in which they assess products. The service provider therefore needs to find ways in which the service can be made more tangible, and risk in use can be minimised. This may range from improving the quality of supporting materials, through to improving point-of-service staff motivation through shifts in reward policies, training and systems development

♦ **Perishable:** much service is literally 'consumed' at the point of delivery. Service cannot be kept in a store. This means that managing supply and demand in service provision can be more difficult than managing production supply and demand. Managing supply and demand more effectively may involve improving staff flexibility through increased use of short-term contracts or through multi-skilling

♦ **Co-created:** services are not really something you do 'to' the customer. They should always be something you do 'with' the customer. Service production and service consumption are linked at the point of delivery. Again, because the service is co-created by the producer and consumer, it cannot be stored. Because the service is co-created, it is also transparent at the delivery point – the customer can see it being 'made' and failures are hard to hide. This again has an impact upon demand, and staff availability. It also has an impact upon customer evaluation because delivery failures are obvious. Meeting these challenges may involve educating the customer in how to use the service more efficiently. Service co-creation, if handled properly, can offer real benefits in increasing customer retention

♦ **Variable:** because service delivery is co-created, it depends on the interaction between the customer and the staff member. Different levels of energy and different mindsets within both these groups can cause the quality of service to vary widely. Variability can be managed by ensuring that your staff recruitment, selection and motivation are excellent, and also by ensuring that the systems are in place to support consistent levels of quality. Long shifts, poor working conditions, lack of understanding how the job relates to employees' overall purpose do not help maintain consistency

♦ **Hard to measure:** customer satisfaction is not an absolute, static quality that can be easily measured. It is dynamic and complicated. Levels of customer satisfaction potential can shift on a minute-to-minute basis. Customer satisfaction (delight, wow factor or whatever you call it) is linked to customer needs, expectations, experience, emotions, and a whole range of other factors, many of which are beyond control of the supplier. Satisfaction is also very difficult to measure accurately.

Some steps that might be used to minimise the problems that arise from these characteristics include:

- Defining the service profile. Balancing business goals and priorities with those of your customer(s) and supplier(s). Buyers should, where possible:
  - co-develop the profiles using user-supplier workshops
  - rely on thorough market research
- Describing all work in terms of both 'what' the required service output is and 'how' it will be delivered
- Measurable performance objectives and financial or other incentives
- Encouraging contractors to develop and institute innovative and cost-effective methods of performing the work
- Including historic and projected demand data (to include surge and other requirements)
- Making an appropriate, and well-supported sourcing decision
- Being prepared for contract variation, and having procedures in place to deal with this.

Exam 2.11

The concepts of lean supply and total quality management can be portrayed as being very similar indeed, the difference, perhaps, being that lean supply is, by definition, concerned with just one aspect of business, whereas TQM is much more pervasive in its application. Both see perfection as the goal, and both are rather broad philosophies rather than specific techniques. Students will be expected to relate to ideas, such as smoothing, flow and value, in their exploration of lean supply, and to the idea that TQM is a company-wide philosophy focused on meeting the wishes and needs of customers, be they internal or external. This customer-centredness might, justifiably, encourage students to explore TQM as a philosophy concerned with relationships, as well as quality.

Exam 2.12

Kraljic's matrix has become an important tool of analysis in supply management. Probably influenced by the Boston Grid (arguably the marketing counterpart of this matrix), Kraljic developed a two-by-two grid that enables the classification of goods and services as falling into one of the following categories:

- **Routine:** easy to buy, plenty of competing suppliers and non-critical
- **Bottleneck:** difficult to buy, few (if any) competing suppliers and may be critical
- **Leverage:** easy to buy, orders attractive to vendors, high spend implying small percentage savings lead to large sums of money. May be critical but attractiveness of contracts leads to willing suppliers
- **Strategic:** high degree of interdependence between buyer and seller, each party of strategic importance to the other.

Exam 2.13

This is a developing area, and some students will undoubtedly be actively involved in the development of eCommerce solutions to supply problems, and will be able to contribute original thinking.

Possible themes for development include:
- The use of eCatalogues by users, making the user-seller relationship more direct
- Electronic auctions might lead towards the reversion to more transactional approaches in some circumstances
- The web facilitates reverse marketing. This changes the commercial relationship in that the buyer becomes more active and the seller more passive
- Information is freely available on a global basis. This may lead to firms dealing with more geographically widespread suppliers, and hence different relationships.

A new and different culture seems to be developing around eCommerce.

Exam 3.1

Outsourcing is not simply another word for buying. It is the process of taking a whole section or function of a company, such as catering, cleaning or purchasing, and giving the responsibility for the relevant activities to an outside contractor. The question as to what, if anything, to outsource is based around consideration as to what is, and what is not, a concern's core business.

The following list gives examples of the considerations that candidates might appropriately discuss.

Reasons for outsourcing:
- Cost reduction
- Lower labour costs
- Greater flexibility
- Better information systems
- Economies of scale
- Benefits arising from specialisation
- Resources released to enable attention to core business.

Exam 3.2

The following observations are some of those that would be expected in a good answer to this question:

A first-tier supplier:
- Is a direct supplier
- Is empowered to relay the original equipment makers' (OEMs) standards and working practices to second-tier or indirect suppliers
- Takes on a share of the management of the overall vendor base

- ◆ Usually involves long-term relationships
- ◆ Usually supplies complex or high cost assemblies, or undertakes a 'kitting' or major coordination role
- ◆ May invest in assets specifically designed to meet the needs of the OEM
- ◆ Is part of a small group
- ◆ Needs to have management as well as technical capabilities
- ◆ Is responsible for larger numbers of second-tier suppliers
- ◆ Is part of a supplier hierarchy.

Exam 3.3

Total quality management (TQM) has provided purchasing and other managers with a philosophy that has almost universal applicability and offers major benefits to the company and its suppliers. The following are common themes contained in the philosophy of TQM:
- ◆ A foundation for continuous improvement
- ◆ A philosophy for running a business
- ◆ The only way to manage
- ◆ Total people empowerment
- ◆ A focus on the needs of the customer
- ◆ A commitment to quality
- ◆ An investment in knowledge
- ◆ Just simple business sense.

TQM is, therefore, a change in attitude and behaviour that adopts the highest quality approach to anything that the individual becomes involved with, and for many companies TQM is simply a 'way of life'. TQM is a universal tool that is not simply restricted to the function of quality management. Rather, it is a general management tool and one that has tremendous benefits for the process of purchasing management.

Historically the activities of purchasing professionals have been based on a stereotypical view of suppliers, for example:

- ◆ Suppliers dislike work; they work for monetary reward and their own gain at the expense of the purchaser

- ◆ Suppliers are not capable of managing themselves and should be directed.

Professional purchasing has changed in emphasis away from traditional adversarial assumptions, towards the development of TQM techniques with the suppliers. At this point it should be noted that TQM does not necessarily equate to collaborative purchasing strategies, but rather TQM has been a vehicle with which such strategies have been developed. The following characteristics have been used to describe the TQM approach to supplier and relationship management:

- ◆ All relationships are based on the belief that the customer comes first

- ◆ All energies must be directed towards the continuous improvement of the business relations between customers and suppliers

◆ Waste in the product or relationship needs to be identified and eliminated to create customer satisfaction and to jointly benefit

◆ Suppliers are capable and do want to take part in decision making; purchasing agents must find ways of allowing this to happen

◆ Creativity must become part of the customer-supplier relationship

◆ The ideal working environment is one where both companies can participate and contribute to continuous improvement, no matter how small that contribution may be

◆ Mutual goals are defined and the benefits of TQM create a competitive supply chain.

Exam 4.1

A good answer to this question will emphasise the major differences between the acquisition of goods and the receipt of services, mentioning the difficulties connected with services such as:
◆ Services cannot be stored
◆ Services difficult to inspect
◆ Services difficult to specify
◆ Service provider often present
◆ Service provision often needs to be scheduled.

An important aspect is that services, for example cleaning, consultancy, security and data processing, are often provided over a period of time, with the end date not necessarily predetermined. Service contracts, therefore, commonly exist in the context of an ongoing relationship, and the management of the contract is, essentially, relationship management.

Exam 4.2

Leasing or hiring decisions will take the following, and other, considerations into account.

Benefits:
◆ Cash flow preserved
◆ Less risk
◆ Supplier may provide maintenance
◆ Latest technology likely to be available
◆ No disposal problems when asset no longer needed.

Disadvantages:
◆ Greater overall cost
◆ Restrictions on use
◆ Duty of care for assets of supplier
◆ Possibly adverse balance sheet implications (equipment not reflected as asset in accounts).

Relationships are likely to be continuous and of great importance with organisation from which equipment is rented or leased. Such matters as regular payments, maintenance, access, difference between fair wear and tear and damage and replacement policy, imply a continuous dialogue between contractor and client.

Exam 4.3

The idea behind the incentivisation of a contract is simple: to reward the contractor for better performance. Contractor and client need to establish and agree with the supplier on the performance required, and the methods by which this performance will be measured at the outset of the contract. The incentive scheme should then be negotiated during the tender/contract formulation period. A performance incentive scheme may apply after the first year or at the end of the original contract term in return for attaining high levels of service. A scheme may also commence in conjunction with granting an extension and/or continuance of the contract, thus providing a bonus in the form of continued service provision without the need to re-tender to obtain improved terms.

Any contract variable, including price, quality, delivery or service can be incentivised, provided that it can be measured. It essential that the incentive clause can be objectively applied.

Alternatively, performance-based contracts can include sanctions for non-performance, such as a percentage fee for late completion or flat rate for substandard levels of performance. It is important that contract managers pursue fair application of any sanctions in accordance with the contract and, where 'trade-offs' are used, they be appropriate to the objectives of the contracted goods or services. The idea of penalty clauses is encountered in connection with sanctions of this kind, but such terminology should be employed with caution. In the UK, at least, the courts will not support the imposition of penalties or punishments by contracting parties – the idea of liquidated damages, which are a genuine pre-estimate of loss suffered through non-performance or conformance, expressed in liquid/cash terms.

An example of a simple incentive clause for a 'cost plus' follows:

> The target contract cost is £100,000, and the contractor will receive a payment of £10,000 if this target is achieved. Any amount by which the cost under- or over-runs will be shared by the client and contractor in the ratio 60:40.

The effect of this clause is to reward the contractor by paying 40% of any saving that might be made, and discouraging cost overruns by requiring that 40% of any additional cost above target is borne by the contractor.

Contracting and relationships - Section 4